THE INTERNATIONAL INSTITUTE FOR APPLIED SYSTEMS ANALYSIS

is an interdisciplinary, nongovernmental research institution founded in 1972 by leading scientific organizations in 12 countries. Situated near Vienna, in the center of Europe, IIASA has been for more than two decades producing valuable scientific research on economic, technological, and environmental issues.

IIASA was one of the first international institutes to systematically study global issues of environment, technology, and development. IIASA's Governing Council states that the Institute's goal is: *to conduct international and interdisciplinary scientific studies to provide timely and relevant information and options, addressing critical issues of global environmental, economic, and social change, for the benefit of the public, the scientific community, and national and international institutions.* Research is organized around three central themes:

- Global Environmental Change
- Global Economic and Technological Change
- Systems Methods for the Analysis of Global Issues

The Institute now has national member organizations in the following countries:

Austria
The Austrian Academy of Sciences

Bulgaria
The National Committee for Applied Systems Analysis and Management

Canada
The Canadian Committee for IIASA

Czech and Slovak Republics
The Committee for IIASA of the Czech and Slovak Republics

Finland
The Finnish Committee for IIASA

Germany
The Association for the Advancement of IIASA

Hungary
The Hungarian Committee for Applied Systems Analysis, Hungarian Academy of Sciences

Italy
The National Research Council (CNR) and the National Commission for Nuclear and Alternative Energy Sources (ENEA)

Japan
The Japan Committee for IIASA

Netherlands
The Netherlands Organization for Scientific Research (NWO)

Poland
The Polish Academy of Sciences

Russia
The Russian Academy of Sciences

Sweden
The Swedish Council for Planning and Coordination of Research (FRN)

United States of America
The American Academy of Arts and Sciences

INTERNATIONAL
MULTILATERAL
NEGOTIATION

I. William Zartman
Editor

EDITORIAL COMMITTEE

Guy-Olivier Faure
Victor A. Kremenyuk
Winfried Lang
Jeffrey Z. Rubin
Gunnar Sjöstedt
I. William Zartman

PROJECT LEADER

Bertram I. Spector

INTERNATIONAL
MULTILATERAL
NEGOTIATION

Approaches to the
Management of Complexity

A publication of the
Processes of International Negotiation (PIN) Project
of the
International Institute for Applied Systems Analysis

Jossey-Bass Publishers · San Francisco

Substantial discounts on bulk quantities of Jossey-Bass books are available to corporations, professional associations, and other organizations. For details and discount information, contact the special sales department at Jossey-Bass Inc., Publishers. (415) 433-1740; Fax (415) 433-0499.

For sales outside the United States, contact Maxwell Macmillan International Publishing Group, 866 Third Avenue, New York, New York 10022.

Manufactured in the United States of America. Nearly all Jossey-Bass books and jackets are printed on recycled paper that contains at least 50 percent recycled waste, including 10 percent postconsumer waste. Many of our materials are also printed with vegetable-based ink; during the printing process these inks emit fewer volatile organic compounds (VOCs) than petroleum-based inks. VOCs contribute to the formation of smog.

Library of Congress Cataloging-in-Publication Data

Zartman, I. William.
    International multilateral negotiation : approaches to the management of complexity / I. William Zartman and associates.
        p.   cm. — (The Jossey-Bass conflict resolution series)
    Includes bibliographical references and index.
    ISBN 1-55542-642-5
    1. Negotiation in business. 2. Conflict management.
  3. International business enterprises—Management. 4. Intercultural communication. 5. Communication in international relations.
    I. Title. II. Series.
    HD58.6.Z37   1994
    302.3—dc20   93-48660
                                             CIP

FIRST EDITION
HB Printing   10 9 8 7 6 5 4 3 2 1   *Code 9440*

Contents

**Part Three:
Evaluating the Analyses**

Preface

International Multilateral Negotiation is a response to a growing awareness of a great hole in the expanding field of negotiation analysis. Currently, no conceptual work addresses the vast area of multilateral negotiation. Although a few studies of negotiation concepts include a section on multilateral processes and many insightful empirical studies have been made of multilateral cases, an explicit conceptual treatment of the subject is lacking. Implicitly or explicitly, all negotiation theory addresses bilateral negotiation, but the complexity of multilateral negotiations remains untreated.

This situation poses a major challenge. It means that practitioners ride—often very skillfully—on the seat of their pants. It means that analysts explain—often very insightfully—by induction and context. Operating on intuition and reflexes learned through on-the-job training is what diplomats do, and their actions are what analysts study. However, unless the process generated by those actions and interactions, when performed well, is studied for regularities, generalizations, and conceptualizations, it can never escape the prison of uniqueness and can never be evaluated, improved on, taught, or learned from.

Yet at the same time, there are a number of theoretical approaches that are potentially useful for providing generalizations and explanatory concepts. It is impossible to test all of them, so some preliminary selection must be made. Political science, economics, social psychology, sociology, and mathematics all analyze aspects of multilateral negotiation. The problem with a disciplinary approach is that these fields also address many other related phenomena, and many of them address the same concepts, sometimes differently but often quite similarly. Thus, all the disciplines mentioned discuss coalition, many discuss power, several discuss decision, others discuss leadership, and so on.

In this book, we use conceptual approaches as the basis for the analysis of multilateral negotiation, gaining richness through interdisciplinary means whenever possible. In addition, to add spice to richness, proponents of these approaches were asked to compete in an academic contest to provide the best explanatory conceptualization for the multilateral process. The result is the first broad attempt to provide tools of analysis designed specifically for the characteristics of multilateral negotiation; this attempt is useful both to those involved in multilateral negotiation and to those who analyze the subject.

In the process, behind this competitive diversity and overarching its analytical pluralism, a paradigmatic unity has appeared. The competition brought

out the fact that no approach was trumps because each was an attempt to provide a segmentary answer to a single question that lies at the heart of the multilateral negotiation process: how to manage the inherent complexity of multilateral agreement. Using the management of complexity as an organizing paradigm allows a general understanding of the nature of the problem and permits an examination of its many forms. The complexity inherent when many parties in many roles need to reach agreement on many issues has to be managed for analysis and decision, and each analytical approach presents a different way of managing that complexity.

Thus, this work provides both a general understanding of and specific analytical approaches to the problem of multilateral negotiation. Although it is an analytical work, its findings and insights should be useful to practitioners as well as to analysts. Both face a similar task in seeking to manage complexity: the one to explain results and the other to produce results. By making the individual efforts of practitioners generalizable and transmittable, analysis repays its debt to practice for work well done. Thus, the authors present this work as a contribution both to the analysis of the multilateral problem and to the training of good negotiators and the improvement of multilateral negotiations.

About the Project

This study is the fifth to be produced by the Project on the Processes of International Negotiation (PIN) at the International Institute for Applied Systems Analysis (IIASA) in Laxenburg, Austria. The PIN Project came into being in 1986 through the recommendation of a steering committee of IIASA's Council in 1981 and a decision by the council in 1984. It owes much to IIASA's first director, Howard Raiffa of Harvard University, whose career centered in many ways on the field of negotiation analysis (and practice) and to whom this work is dedicated. Its first product was *Processes of International Negotiations* (Mautner-Markhof, 1989). The Project was initiated by Frances Mautner-Markhof in 1986 and fully constituted in 1988 by Robert Pry, then IIASA director, and Bertram I. Spector was engaged as its leader.

The work of the project has been organized by an international steering committee of six scholars working with Spector: Guy-Olivier Faure, a French anthropologist from the University of Sorbonne; Victor A. Kremenyuk, a Russian political scientist from the Russian Academy of Sciences; Winfried Lang, an Austrian diplomat and jurist from the University of Vienna; Jeffrey Z. Rubin, an American social psychologist from Tufts University; Gunnar Sjöstedt, a Swedish political economist from the Swedish Foreign Policy Institute; and I. William Zartman, an American political scientist from the Johns Hopkins University. Three times a year for up to a week each time, this international committee has met to work on the study of international negotiations in its many forms; the gatherings were in themselves an exciting, collegial exercise in international negotiation.

The keystone work of the project was *International Negotiation: Analysis,*

Approaches, Issues (Kremenyuk, 1991). It was followed by *International Environ-mental Negotiations* (Sjöstedt, 1993) and by *Culture and International Negotiation* (Faure and Rubin, 1993). Other works are in progress, including *Negotiating International Regimes: Lessons Learned from UNCED* (Spector, 1994), *Power and Asymmetry in Negotiation* (Rubin and Zartman, forthcoming), and *International Economic Negotiations* (Kremenyuk and Sjöstedt, forthcoming). Each of these works has been the product of collaboration among a large group of international scholars and is the result of a workshop supported by IIASA for authors and others to discuss the draft contributions.

Acknowledgments

In this effort, I am grateful for the collective participation of the steering committee members and the project leader, all of whom provided a constructive atmosphere and helpful comments at many stages of the project. I also appreciate the flexible and responsive participation of the chapter authors, some of whom are also steering committee members and others of whom joined the project from a number of countries. Particularly helpful were Juliet Lodge and Gunnar Sjöstedt, authors of the two case studies, whose subjects were moving targets and who had to tell their own story while at the same time providing material that could be useful for analysis from six different approaches. I am also grateful for the ongoing support for the project by IIASA's director, Peter deJanosi, who made PIN's productivity possible. Basic help for all our activities and careful and pleasant attention to all the details of our work has been provided by Ulrike Neudeck, project administrative assistant, aided by Anna Korula of the IIASA staff. Somehow, the whole is larger than the sum even of these fine parts and is magnified by the magic quality of Laxenburg, Vienna, and the Austrian connection. Enlightened by Metternich and Mozart, the land of the Concert of Europe evokes power and harmony and gives inspiration to the study of negotiations in the summer palace of Maria Theresa.

Washington, D.C.,   I. William Zartman
and Laxenburg, Austria
January 1994

To Howard Raiffa,
who launched IIASA and inspired PIN,
a scholar of vision

Contributors

STEVEN J. BRAMS is professor of politics at New York University. His primary interest is application of game theory and social choice theory to political science and international relations. He is the author or coauthor of eleven books, the most recent being *Negotiation Games: Applying Game Theory to Bargaining and Arbitration* (1990) and *Theory of Moves* (1994).

ANN E. DOHERTY received her M.A. degree (1992) in international politics from New York University. She worked as a policy researcher and lobbyist in connection with the United Nations Conference on Environment and Development (UNCED) and with the Student Environmental Action Coalition (SEAC) in New York City. She was a IIASA Young Scientist in 1992.

CHRISTOPHE DUPONT is director of the "Negotiation Laboratory" at the Business School of Lille, France; he is also consultant at CRC Conseils Associes, Jouy-en-Josas, France, and a member of the advisory board of the *Negotiation Journal*. He is the author of *La Négociation: Conduite, Théorie, Applications* (forthcoming 1994), and coauthor of several books and articles on negotiation, international relations, finance, and management.

GUY-OLIVIER FAURE is associate professor of sociology at the Sorbonne University, Paris, where he teaches international negotiation. His major research interests are in business negotiations, especially with China and other Asian countries, focusing on strategies and cultural issues. He is also concerned with developing interdisciplinary approaches. Among his latest publications are the following coauthored books: *International Negotiation: Analysis, Approaches, Issues* (with V. Kremenyuk, 1991), *Processes of International Negotiations* (with F. Mautner-Markhof, 1991), *Evolutionary Systems Design: Policy Making Under Complexity* (with M. Shakun, 1993), *International Environmental Negotiations* (with G. Sjöstedt, 1993), and *Culture and Negotiation* (with J. Z. Rubin, 1993).

DEBORAH M. KOLB is professor of management at the Simmons College Graduate School of Management and executive director of the Program on Negotiation at Harvard Law School. She received her B.A. degree (1965) from Vassar College, her M.B.A. degree (1973) from the University of Colorado, and her Ph.D. degree (1988) from M.I.T.'s Sloan School of Management. She is currently

carrying out field research on gender issues in negotiations, dispute resolution, and diversity and on work/family practices and gender equity in corporations. She is the author of *The Mediators* (1983), coeditor of *Hidden Conflict in Organizations: Uncovering Behind-the-Scenes Disputes* (1992), and the editor of *Making Talk Work: Profiles of Mediators* (forthcoming).

WINFRIED LANG is an Austrian career diplomat and professor of international law and international relations at the University of Vienna and Austria's Ambassador to International Organizations in Geneva. He chaired the OECD Transfrontier Pollution Group (1977 to 1982) and presided over UN conferences on the protection of the ozone layer (1985), on biological and bacteriological weapons (1986), and on substances that deplete the ozone layer (1987). He has published several books and articles on integration policy, protection of the environment, international negotiations, neutrality, and the law of treaties.

JULIET LODGE is professor of European politics, Jean Monnet Professor of European Integration, and co-director of the European Community Research Unit, University of Hull, U.K. She is also visiting professor at the Institut des Etudes Européennes at the Université Libre de Bruxelles, and at the Vrije Universiteit Brussel, Belgium; she is also a NATO research fellow. Her current research is on European Union and European Community security policies. Her latest books are *The European Community and the Challenge of the Future* (1993) and *European Union: A Crisis of Political Authority* (forthcoming).

JEFFREY Z. RUBIN is professor of psychology at Tufts University, senior fellow in the Program on Negotiation at Harvard Law School, and adjunct professor of diplomacy, Fletcher School of Law and Diplomacy, Tufts University. He is the author, coauthor, or editor of more than a dozen books and numerous articles on interpersonal and international conflict and negotiation, as well as on the role of third-party intervention in the dispute settlement process. His recent books include *Social Conflict: Escalation, Stalemate, and Settlement* (with D. Pruitt and S. H. Kim, 1993), *Leadership and Negotiation in the Middle East* (with B. Kellerman, 1989), *When Families Fight* (with C. Rubin, 1990), *Negotiation Theory and Practice* (with J. W. Breslin, 1991), and *Culture and Negotiation* (with G.-O. Faure, 1993).

GUNNAR SJÖSTEDT is senior research fellow at the Swedish Institute of International Affairs and associate professor of political science at the University of Stockholm. His research work is concerned with processes of international cooperation and consultations in which negotiations represent an important element. He has studied the OECD as a communication system and the external role of the European Community and is currently working on a project dealing with the transformation of the international trade regime incorporated in GATT and its external relations. Among his latest publications are *International Environmen-*

tal Negotiation (1993) and *International Environment on Process, Issues and Contexts* (1993).

B ERTRAM I. SPECTOR is director of the Center for Negotiation Analysis and senior fellow at the Foreign Policy Institute of the Johns Hopkins University School of Advanced International Studies. He was formerly leader of the Processes of International Negotiation Project at IIASA. He has directed research in the field of international negotiation and decision support techniques for foreign policy analysts and policymakers at two research organizations in Washington, D.C. He is currently studying the prenegotiation processes of the UN Conference on Environment and Development and is investigating the use of creativity heuristics as mechanisms to resolve negotiation impasses. He is editor of a special issue of *Theory and Decision* on decision support systems for negotiation.

W ALTER C. SWAP is professor of psychology and dean of undergraduate education at Tufts University. For six years he chaired the Department of Psychology at Tufts. Prior to coming to Tufts he was a study director at the Research Center for Group Dynamics at the University of Michigan. He received his B.A. degree (1965) magna cum laude from Harvard University and his Ph.D. degree (1970) in social psychology from the University of Michigan. He has published in the areas of decision making, personality theory, attitude change, altruism, aggression, and environmental psychology. He was editor of *Group Decision Making* (1984).

A RILD UNDERDAL is professor of political science/international politics at the University of Oslo, Norway. From 1993 he was vice rector of the university. His main research interests are the study of negotiations, international cooperation (with particular reference to environmental management), and foreign policy decision making. His latest books are *Rationality and Institutions* (with R. Malnes, 1992), and *Overordnet styringsinstans og sideordnet part* (*Government and Negotiating Party*, with R. Sørensen, 1992).

M ATTHEW L. WEIDNER received his B.A. degree (1992) in political science (international relations) from Yale University. He is currently pursuing a public service career in Washington, D.C.

I. WILLIAM ZARTMAN is Jacob Blaustein Professor of Conflict Resolution and International Organization at the Nitze School of Advanced International Studies (SAIS) of the Johns Hopkins University. He is author of *The Practical Negotiator* (with M. Berman, 1982) and *Ripe for Resolution* (1989) and editor and coauthor of *The 50% Solution* (1983), *The Negotiation Process* (1978), and *Positive Sum* (1987), among other books. He is organizer of the Washington Interest in Negotiations (WIN) Group and has been a distinguished fellow of the United States Institute for Peace.

INTERNATIONAL
MULTILATERAL
NEGOTIATION

Introduction

Two's Company and More's a Crowd
The Complexities of Multilateral Negotiation

I. William Zartman (USA)

As the incisive common wisdom on social interaction reveals, the chemistry changes when more than two are working out a relationship. The dyad has its own dynamic, but the complexity introduced by a larger number of parties defies straightforward analysis. Negotiation theory, such as it is, has focused exclusively on bilateral bargaining, based on assumptions strictly dependent on the existence of two parties. Therefore, its answers to the basic analytical question—How are negotiated outcomes achieved/explained?—are at least suspect because of inapplicable assumptions and may be entirely invalid for multilateral interactions. A new and specific answer has to be sought for the same question in a multilateral setting.

Negotiators in a multilateral encounter enter with such questions as, What is going on here? How can we find our way through this scene? How can we give some direction to these proceedings? How can we make something happen? Negotiators need to orient themselves both to the other parties and to the issues, and at the same time to an array of roles, particularly of competing leaders and contributing followers. This is a very different array of roles from that found in bilateral negotiations, where the two parties are immediately cast as adversaries and where analysis seeks to capture the inherent adversarial dynamics—as players in a two-party game of strategic choice, as convergers through concessions, as Indian wrestlers, or as inventors of an overarching collaborative formula to overcome their differences. In multilateral negotiation, the initial perception is not adversarial because participants do not know who is the adversary and because structuring the dynamics on the basis of confrontation would turn all parties into

1

a coalition of opponents. In bilateral negotiation, the situation is already structured by definition; in a multilateral situation, it must be structured, according to the parties and issues, through a use of roles.

The one discipline that has provided answers to its own form of the basic analytic question comes up with a tantalizing result. Instead of seeing bilateral decision making as a straightforward problem and multilateral decision making as a complex problem, economics presents a reversed picture. "The theory of bilateral monopoly is indeterminate with a vengeance," write two economics authorities. "When either pure competition or pure monopoly prevails, there are clearcut solutions to the firm's price and output decision problems" (Scherer and Ross, 1990, p. 519). Why go any further? Why not hand over the multilateral bargaining problem to the economists and declare victory? Unfortunately, multilateral negotiation is not pure competition but rather oligopoly, a very different problem. "Oligopoly pricing is interesting and important . . . because it poses such difficult problems for the economic theorist" (Scherer and Ross, 1990, p. 199). In multilateral negotiation, numbers are large but not infinite, generally between 10 and 150. Size matters, and parties are not equal (as they generally are assumed to be in bilateral negotiation). Interests differ, and so roles differ as well. As a result, economists can provide insights, but the basic problem cannot be left in their hands for a solution.

Similarly, political scientists studying regimes have also focused on a form of multilateral negotiation, but they explain the outcome of the process in terms of its preconditions. As Touval and Rubin (1987, p. 1; compare Touval, 1989) point out, explaining how "is not the same as asking *why* agreements are concluded." To show "that cooperation and agreement take place because the parties give priority to common interests over conflicting ones" not only assumes away the problem by focusing on the common interests already achieved but avoids the problem by explaining the outcome through preconditions rather than process. Nor do the preconditions explain the process. They only open the way to an analysis of negotiation, which cooperation studies generally do not pursue. Analysis is left at the doorstep of the basic issue, an explanation of the way in which many parties with mixed motives achieve an agreement.

The regimes branch of political science draws its roots originally from game theory, where there is also a well-developed analytical approach to multilateral decision making. Starting with parties' shares, which are imputed variously from security points, or from innovative or integrative strategies (Iklé, 1964; Walton and McKersie, 1965), the theory determines outcomes that can be obtained by players acting according to both collective rationality and individual rationality using formulas based on impartial, equitable, or stable justice (Davis, 1970; Rapoport, 1970a, 1970b). It also shows the conditions under which a partial coalition will be preferable for some or all parties to a great coalition—that is, a unanimous joint decision. But its emphasis is on explaining nonagreement more than on explaining agreement, and its cases of agreement are coincidences of the initial imputations. It does not tell how to move to larger positive-sum

outcomes or how to obtain a consensual agreement when smaller coalitions are preferred by some players.

As a result, the challenge is open. The stage can be set for meeting it by setting out the characteristics of multilateral negotiation that define it and distinguish it from bilateral negotiation and then turning to the several theoretical approaches proposed to provide explanations from the phenomenon as identified.

Distinctions

The overarching characteristic of multilateral negotiation is its complexity along all conceivable dimensions. Although most studies of the subject say little about multilaterality as its essential characteristic, those that do tend to agree with this emphasis on complexity, beginning with two seminal works in 1977. Midgaard and Underdal (1977, pp. 334, 339–341) emphasize that in negotiations the more the messier, to the point where negotiation itself is inversely successful in relation to size; they focus on ways of organizing that complexity by reducing the size to make it manageable for negotiation—through mediation, coalition, and even increased roles for chance. Winham (1977a) also points to the characteristic complexity of multilateral negotiations, with oversimplified cognitive structures, fading appreciation of concessions, and increased end-game pressures as its major effects. His in-depth case study a decade later (Winham, 1986) brings out both the messiness and the concessional inconclusiveness of multilateral negotiations in the General Agreement on Tariffs and Trade (GATT). Raiffa (1982, pp. 252–254) devotes an entire section to negotiations of "many parties, many issues," insisting that they are conceptually different but not specifying the nature of those differences; he does, however, mention complexity and concentrates on two ways of handling its issue and actor components—the single negotiating text and the coalition.

The silence of most studies on the difference between multilateral and bilateral negotiations, however, might be taken as evidence that the difference is only one of degree, not of essence. Both Winham (1982; 1986, Chap. 9) and Raiffa (1982, p. 251) reject this view, but there is still little discussion in the literature of why bilateral analysis cannot be merely extended to multilateral negotiation. Instead, some authors (Lipson, 1985, p. 220; Snidal, 1985, p. 53) contend the reverse, that multilateral negotiations need to be reduced to their bilateral dimension to be susceptible to analysis. The argument can be made that this is what happens in reality because ostensibly multiple sides often congregate into two camps, either institutionally (as in the Cold War) or issue by issue. Yet, also in reality, practitioners and analysts alike have often decried the constraining aspect of bilateralism, with the nonaligned nations coming into being to break down the bilateralism of the Cold War and crosscutting coalitions being proposed to overcome the North-South stalemate (Mortimer, 1984; Zartman, 1987, Chap. 10).

Winham (1986) make the important theoretical point that conflicts tend to bilateralize, but he modifies its practical import by emphasizing the lower level of conflict in nonmilitary encounters. Thus, even if there is enough conflict over

a negotiated issue to polarize the sides, there is usually at least a third side that sees its interests best served by neutrality and mediation. Furthermore, if polarization is the principal effect of one issue, the multi-issued nature of multilateral negotiations means that there will at worst be many crosscutting, two- or three-sided face-offs, none of which is overriding enough to line up parties into a bipolar conflict or a bilateral negotiation. This idea has been carried to the point of characterizing multilateral negotiations as merely the negotiations of many dyads (Preeg, 1970, pp. 89-90, 133-134, 184-194), but this characterization has not been used to analyze results. If analysis were to be based on dyads, either the picture would be incomplete or the result would be chaos. The very purpose of multilateral negotiation is to give difficult but necessary coherence to the complexity created by a congeries of dyads (Sebenius, 1984, pp. 99, 108; Rummel, 1982). Analysis must meet the same test.

Characteristics

To understand the phenomenon under consideration, it is important to identify the minimal and basic characteristics that define multilateral negotiation and distinguish it from bilateral agreement. Within the standard definition of negotiation as the process by which conflicting positions are combined to form a common decision (Zartman and Berman, 1982, p. 1), six characteristics with their relevant implications define the multilateral version of the process.[1]

First, and most obviously, multilateral means *multiparty* negotiations. Although any party may agree with any other party, and eventually all parties presumably reach agreement, the multiparty assumption implies autonomous entities each with interests and interest groups of its own to underpin its separate position. Many sides do not just constitute a numbers game but rather a challenge to the reconciliation of multifaceted interests.

A second characteristic is the *multi-issue* nature of multilateral negotiations. This attribute is based in reality but is not inherent; negotiations with many sides could be on only one issue, but in fact the large forums under consideration always do involve many issues, not all of them even related to the broad topic. Conversely, bilateral negotiations may also deal with multiple issues; the difference between the two types of negotiations on this dimension is one of degree rather than of nature. Multiple issues provide the means as well as the subject of agreement because they allow for trade-offs that provide the network for a single outcome. They also create texture in the negotiations because not all of the many parties have the same intensity of interest on any issue, any more than they have the same substantive interest. This texture allows Homans's maxim—"The more items at stake can be divided into goods valued more by one party [or parties] than they cost to the other[s] and goods valued more to the other party [or parties] than they cost to the first, the greater the chances of successful outcome" (Homans, 1961, p. 62)—to be played out to the fullest, and Homans's maxim is the key to any negotiation. How it works in multilateral negotiations is the subject of analysis in Chapters Three and Four.

The third defining characteristic is the *multirole* nature of the negotiations. Just as texture is present on the issue dimension, combining intensity and interest, so is it present on the party dimension, adding role differential to numbers and interest groups. But role presents its own dimension beyond the simple matter of intensity. In the process of being more or less active in multilateral negotiations, parties select from a limited list of roles that differ in nature. They can drive, conduct, defend, brake, or cruise (Sjöstedt, 1993; Yukl, 1989). Drivers are leaders who try to organize the participants to produce an agreement that is consonant with the leaders' interests. Conductors, also called managers, also seek to produce an agreement but from a neutral position, with no interest ax of their own to grind. Defenders are single-issue participants, concerned more with promoting their issue than with the overall success of the negotiations. Brakers seek to block an agreement and protect their freedom of action, often with reference to a limited number of issues. Cruisers are filler, with no strong interests of their own, and so are available to act as followers. Without such role diversity, the issue and party complexities could not be combined into an agreeable outcome. Although the list may appear ad hoc, it actually encompasses the main roles available to parties. Additional research could usefully check cases for other roles. It could also pursue detailed role analysis, including such questions as the relation between role and power or the effects of different role interactions. Some of these questions are addressed in Chapter Seven.

Bilateral negotiations are characterized by variable values, as opposed to fixed choices that must be voted for or against. Negotiated decisions are possible because the parties can reformulate the proposed outcomes and because one party can influence the value that the other party attaches to those outcomes (Zartman, 1978, p. 70). However, the number of parties is fixed, by definition, in bilateral negotiations, and so the roles the parties play are fixed or are at least highly limited. Multilateral negotiations, in contrast, are composed of *variable values, parties,* and *roles*—that is, participants can, and therefore must, play at all three levels of interaction, working to shape not only the values attached to various outcomes and the outcomes themselves but also the parties and their roles in order to come to an agreement. They must do so because if they choose to ignore these possibilities, others will make use of them, forcing the other parties to play at the three levels in response. Again, the immense complexity of having to deal with many parties, issues, and roles makes doing so the price of winning an agreement, thus further increasing the characteristic complexity.

The fifth and sixth characteristics of multilateral negotiations concern the outcomes. Agreement has been used thus far to characterize the outcome, but in fact—again because of the complexity-induced difficulty of reaching unanimous agreement—a looser term is needed for multilateral negotiations. Multilateral agreement is frequently by *consensus,* a decision rule in which, essentially, abstention is an affirmative rather than a negative vote. Multilateral agreements are arrived at by consensus when a significant but unspecified number of parties are in favor and the rest do not oppose. Even where voting is provided for in the rules, multilateral decision making tends to save it for exceptional cases—cases of vital

national interest, in the terminology of the European Communities—and focuses instead on the mechanisms of building consensus.

The implications of this condition are significant. In bilateral negotiations, each party has a veto, and therefore there is a basic element of equality. Veto is a looser notion in multilateral negotiations if it exists at all. Parties not agreeing can abstain without blocking the outcome, and parties opposing can be left out as long as their number does not become significant. Strategies of incremental participation and agreement then become possible (Zartman, 1987, Chap. 10). At the same time, the significant-number requirement means that lowest-common-denominator agreements without teeth are a residual possibility but also that such agreements can form the basis of an incremental process that creates international sociopolitical pressures rather than legal obligations to conform (Zartman, 1993). Thus the implications of consensus rather than agreement are significant and invite further research, as indicated in Chapters Four and Six.

Fifth, the outcomes of multilateral negotiations are mainly matters of *rule making* rather than the redistribution of tangible goods. Neither of the basic characteristics of division and exchange is often present in multilateral negotiations; instead, the main goal is to harmonize national legislation or to establish rules that can be applied by and to states (Winham and Kizer, 1993). Having this goal does not mean that tangible goods are not thereby affected, but it does mean that the effect is uncertain, long-range, and universal, rather than simply being contingent on the other party's actions. It does mean that the importance of the formula is even greater in multilateral negotiations than in bilateral negotiations because the adoption of a rule depends more on a convincing justification or a notion of justice than on exchanged concessions in detail. Trade-offs between rules, however, are often a major part of the structure of multilateral agreements, although the framework for the analysis of such trade-offs needs further research; this framework is addressed in Chapter Five.

Finally, and obviously, multilateral negotiations are characterized by *coalition* (Rapoport, 1970b; Lax and Sebenius, 1991). Through the formation of coalitions, "the [multilateral] negotiatory situation becomes less complicated" (Stenelo, 1972, p. 58). Although coalition has been proposed as a major approach to analyzing multilateral negotiations, particularly through game theory, it should be considered one—even if a salient one—of many ways in which parties in many-partied negotiations handle their own large number by bringing that number down to a manageable size. But coalition is a mechanism not only available to the many parties but also applicable to the many issues. Because the goal of negotiations is to arrive at decisions on issues, it is necessary to reduce their complexity and make them, as well as the number of parties, manageable. Packaging, linkages, and trade-offs—the basic devices of the negotiation process—are all ways of making coalitions among issues, interests, and positions. Although there is much disparate work on coalition formation, further research is needed both on its operation and on the framework for analysis, as discussed in Chapter Seven.

The defining elements of the multilateral negotiation process form the

framework for an appropriate analytical approach to the subject. Roles are used to produce party and issue coalitions so that the complexity of the multilateral situation becomes sufficiently manageable for a consensus decision to emerge. Analysis focusing on the use of different roles to produce consensus among parties on issues responds to the needs of both observers and practitioners to understand and deal with the management of complexity.

Approaches

This basic approach may be pursued from a number of different angles provided by different disciplines or schools of analysis. No single approach can claim a monopoly on explanation, for any natural or social phenomenon can be explained by a variety of insights and from a variety of angles. But some angles can provide a better view of the phenomenon by using parameters and techniques that explain more than other approaches do. Both the innate appropriateness of the approach and the skill with which it is used are involved. In each case, the use of an approach for analyzing multilateral negotiations has to rise above some inherent limitations associated with its use for bilateral analysis. Although other approaches could be added to the following group, these are prominent vantage points in social disciplines for the study of multilateral decision making.

1. *Decision analysis* is based on seriatim consideration of each player's outcome values, followed by comparison among them. In order to deal with the many parties in multilateral negotiations, they are grouped into a small number of coalitions based on similar preferences (Barclay and Peterson, 1976). The many issues are handled one at a time, with attention focused on salient concerns. By moving back and forth between major coalitions and major issues, analysts and practitioners can come up with some notion of trade-offs. Decision analysis does not purport to be predictive or explanatory but merely serves as a simplified guide to decision making—a simple, straightforward, practical way of managing complexity. It can, however, portray a distribution of positions on an issue in such a way that results and the need for change become apparent; it can then multiply these "snapshots" to produce a moving record of evolving positions and allow inductive generalizations to be made about the patterns of movement (Friedheim, 1987, 1993). This analysis can then be played back in a "what if" mode to explain why the parties acted as they did, assuming best-interest rationality.

2. *Strategic analysis* using game theory is also based on the structure of values the parties assign to different outcomes. It pluralizes decision analysis because it considers outcomes to be the product of social interaction. The multilateral form of strategic analysis, n-person game theory, is based on coalitions, not as an insight or an outcome as in other approaches but as the characteristic starting point. Beginning with the parties' security points or with innovative or integrative outcomes from which the parties' shares can be imputed (Davis, 1970; Rapoport, 1970a), the theory determines outcomes that can be achieved by players acting rationally, either collectively or individually, according to formulas for

agreement that embody various notions of justice (Rapoport, 1970b). It also determines the level and conditions under which a great coalition (or joint decision with unanimous agreement) can be formed or will be rejected by some parties as inferior to partial coalitions.

Because strategic analysis is based on coalitions, however, it is limited to three or four collective players; "n-player games are usually too complex for classical game theory to provide clear answers" (Fraser and Hipel, 1984, p. 324; Davis, 1970). Like two-person game theory, it tells where rational outcomes lie, but it does not tell much about shaping them. Using fixed values, it does not tell how to move to large positive-sum outcomes or how to devise consensual outcomes to overcome preferred partial coalitions. It is not surprising, therefore, that this approach has shown more usefulness in the analysis of voting, which is a different process than negotiation (Riker, 1962; Midgaard and Underdal, 1977, p. 341; Zartman, 1978, pp. 69–71). Yet it does provide powerful insights into the comparative chances of choices, which is the promise of its approach.

3. *Organizational analysis* is based on the institutional setting of multilateral negotiation; it explains outcomes through parties' behavior as deduced from their position within an organization or from their need to find their way through the constraints of the organization—that is, as they operate with or against the organizational imperatives. These imperatives can be either the specific rules of a given organization or the broader constraints of collective institutionalized behavior inherent in all organizations. Use of the specific rules, typical of public administration approaches, is captive to the idiosyncratic details of the case, and use of the broader constraints is captive to the assumption that all multilateral negotiation is dominated by its institutional context. But both approaches provide a powerful insight into limiting and channeling factors that can work to produce outcomes, and the more generalized notions of organization theory add a dimension of external logic that is not apparent in a simple study of actors' choices.

Thus, multilateral negotiation can be analyzed using the theorem that the organization moves its members to an agreed outcome, whenever possible, through its rules, culture, and institutions. "Whenever possible" is determined by the characteristics of the organization and its members, which may constitute barriers to the type of agreement being sought. The result is an interesting type of cybernetic interaction whereby members, specifically defined, set up their own rules, which then guide their subsequent actions, which then impinge on and inform further modifications of the rules, which then guide subsequent actions, and so on in a forward-moving series of communication loops. Rules, characteristics, and behaviors are all inputs and outputs of the recycling system.

4. *Small group analysis* is also a contextual approach, explaining outcomes of a peculiar interaction that occurs in a restricted pluralist setting. An innovative use of small group analysis, which is usually applied as an explanation of conformity pressures, can reveal the dynamics of agreement in multilateral bargaining. Like other approaches, small group analysis handles complexity by assuming a reduced number of players and focusing on both within-group and

among-group interactions, both seen as small group behavior. Decision making is analyzed as an aggregative process in which the group moves through the large uncoalesced mass of many parties to form one or several core groups and then moves to a single consensus. Small group analysis comes from social psychology and thus focuses on the interpersonal and intergroup pressures rather than simply on the organizational structures that operate on the actors. The actors' behavior then becomes a function of the nexus created by their own interaction.

5. *Power-coalition analysis* could be seen as "all of the above," but it also has a specific angle of its own to explain multilaterally negotiated outcomes. Whereas other approaches to coalition see it as either the starting point or the by-product of analysis, coalition analysis can be employed as a specific focus to explain outcomes. It does so by analyzing the use of power to create coalitions; the purposive actions of the parties are its parameter. Whereas game theory tells which coalitions will be optimal under conditions of full information and rationality, power-coalition analysis concentrates on the way in which parties form coalitions by manipulating information and overcoming conflicts of rationality. Both outcomes and side payments are used as inducements and dissuasions to move parties into coalition on given issues.

Coalitions can be identified as various types, depending on their size, stability, "hardness," and cohesion, and then correlated with the tactics of power appropriate for each type. Strategies in the decision-making process, such as Sjöstedt's (1993) driving, braking, and modifying, also vary with different types of coalitions. Thus, the particular constellation of parties and interests determines the type of coalition, which in turn determines the available and appropriate power needed to further the parties' interests.

6. *Leadership analysis* focuses even more sharply than coalition analysis on the negotiating agent, analyzing tactics and strategies used to reduce the complexity of both parties and issues to the point where a consensual decision emerges. It identifies a major role and treats other roles in relation to it, thus handling the three components of multilateral complexity. Leadership itself has its own modes. In a historical-descriptive or personality mode, it has frequently been used as the basis for the "great man" school of history, giving examples of unilateral actions toward other parties. Another mode, "coercive" leadership, is related to coalition analysis as already presented. And, in a mode analyzed in this book, instrumental or entrepreneurial leaders contribute to the design of "good" solutions or procedures through cooperative arrangements and tie together the tactics of orchestrating complexity with the creation of positive-sum outcomes.

Spokespeople for these six schools of analysis were invited to present their approach and to focus its explanatory power on a few selected multilateral negotiation cases; in the process they were asked also to refine the approach beyond its current state of development into new levels for multilateral analysis. The invitation was for a competition, in which the submissions vie to provide the best explanation of outcomes, using the cases as illustrations. Earlier a similar competition was held for the definition and analysis of the basic bilateral process

(Zartman, 1978). The result brought out the comparative strengths of different disciplinary approaches as well as the basic unity of views on the subject of negotiation itself. In that instance, the different approaches were then illustrated by case studies that employed the modes of analysis to explain various bilateral encounters. Some years later, a different competition was set up using a single case—the Henry Kissinger disengagement negotiations in the Middle East in 1974–1975—as the subject of competing analyses and evaluations (Rubin, 1981). There the purpose was not merely to analyze and explain outcomes but also to make judgments about the conduct of diplomacy and the appropriateness of the methods employed.

In this study, two cases have been chosen for analysis by the competing schools. Although many cases could have been studied, space limitations imposed a choice of two; they were selected because of their innate importance, their numerical and institutional variation, their complex process, and the fact that they are in general typical of multilateral negotiations. One is the negotiated decision of the twelve members of the European Communities in 1985 to adopt goals and procedures to consolidate their integration by 1993; the result is known as the Single European Act. The other is the negotiated indecision of the 108 signatories of GATT facing their eighth round of tariff reductions between 1986 and 1993, a process fraught with multiple breakdowns. The cases are presented as significant events in themselves, worthy of analysis, but also as examples of two types of many-party negotiations separated by an order of magnitude—one with about ten parties, termed plurilateral, operating within an institutionalized context; and the other with over a hundred parties, termed multilateral, operating within a much looser institutional framework. Thus, the secondary purpose of the analysis to see whether this span in size makes any difference to the process, outcome, or analysis. Prima facie evidence would suggest that larger numbers make agreement more difficult, but finer analysis is needed. It is to the presentation of cases and the subsequent analyses that this study now turns.

Note

1. This list is necessarily similar to but importantly different from that of Young (1989c, pp. 359–366). His "multiple actors" category is of course the same. "Consensus" replaces "unanimity" as being more accurate; "coalition" and "variable values, parties and roles" replace "transnational alliances" and "shifting involvements" as being more specific. Young's "integrative bargaining" seems to mistake an optimal search for a basic characteristic. Both "uncertainty" and "[selective] problems and approaches" are interesting features but do not appear to be defining characteristics.

PART ONE

EXEMPLARY
CASES

Chapter 1

Negotiating the
Single European Act
in the European Community

Juliet Lodge (UK)

The Single European Act (SEA) is a document that covers amendments to the 1957 treaties establishing the European Communities (EC). It does not have the status of a new treaty, although it was subject to the unanimous approval of the twelve EC member governments—France, Germany, Italy, and the Benelux countries (the original six) plus the United Kingdom, Denmark, Ireland, Portugal, Spain, and Greece—and ratification by their usual constitutional processes. In practice, this procedure gave a final role to national parliaments (normally irrelevant to EC decision-making processes). In the event, only one parliament—Ireland—challenged the SEA's legality, on the grounds that its Title III on political cooperation compromised Ireland's neutrality. This chapter on the plurilateral negotiations over the SEA is divided into six parts, as outlined in the earlier study by the International Institute for Applied Systems Analysis Processes of International Negotiation Project (Kremenyuk, 1991): background and aims, actors, structure, strategy, process, and outcomes.

Background

The SEA Inter-Governmental Conference (IGC) negotiations were the product of earlier *démarches* by key actors, and their experience of success and failure conditioned the whole process. Stagflation; ossified decision-making procedures; a declining capacity to act decisively, responsively, and accountably; persistent rows over the budget and the United Kingdom's contributions to it; the prospect of further enlargement of the EC to the poorer Mediterranean periphery; and

slippage in the EC's position in the international political economy in the late 1970s and early 1980s led the Commission of the European Communities and the European Parliament (EP) to consider a strategy for injecting a new dynamism into the EC and into the process of European integration. For several years, the Commission's annual reports on the progress of the internal market had identified problems and the additional, avoidable costs incurred because of physical, technical, and fiscal barriers to freedom of movement of goods, services, capital, and persons within the EC.

Not until 1985, however, was the Commission's white paper on the completion of the internal market (subsequently known as the Single Market) published. It catalyzed wide public debate and governmental response. By then, it had become part of conventional wisdom among Euro-official and business elites, some of whom had played a role in provoking discussion and in lobbying the Commission and EP for appropriate initiatives. Business elites wanted official Commission intervention to remove internal borders to help them attain their corporate goals and increase their profit margins. In the early 1980s, the EP's Albert-Ball report on the causes of and remedies for economic decline in the EC was published. It coincided with political initiatives being taken within the EP to advance the idea of a European Union.

In short the political-economic costs of "non-Europe" and the imperatives for cutting them were given priority and placed on the EC's agenda for urgent action, with a specific deadline and strong pressure to meet it. It was unusual for the EC to build in deadlines for the attainment of policy goals. That it did in this case underlined the sense of urgency and the consensus-based commitment to the general goal of completing the Single Market. The peaks and troughs of such pressure can be charted, with peaks coinciding with the most visible, high-level political negotiations at the European Council meetings (notably in Milan and Luxembourg in June and December 1985). In addition, further pressure came from the principal EC actors (the Commission and the EP) with their proposals to reform the EC's traditional system of decision making to ensure fast action. Such reform was a sine qua non for meeting the January 1993 target but was one of the most controversial and sensitive issues.

The SEA was neither unexpected nor completely novel. It was part of a long process of constitutional adjustment within the EC that had its origins in the mid-1970s, within the overall context of advancing European union (a nebulous, ill-defined term). Its roots can be traced to the Tindemans Report on European Union in 1975 and the 1980 Genscher-Colombo initiative for a Draft European Act (which eventually surfaced in attenuated form in the Solemn Declaration of European Union in 1983) and more importantly to the EP's 1984 draft treaty establishing the European Union, which had a decisive influence on the SEA's content.

These predecessors to the SEA were important, as they encapsulated both the minimalist (no or minor change) and maximalist (fundamental constitutional change, new treaty) positions of the various governments, national and supranational political parties, and EC institutions. Regarding the key issue of

constitutional reform of EC decision-making practices, the actors were broadly aware of the main parameters and the arguments for and against reform because these had already been rehearsed in the immediate past. Even though governments in some of the member states changed in the interim, a broad inference could be drawn as to what reforms each was likely to entertain realistically.

Thus, opening positions bore some resemblance to past known positions. It also meant that governments could play a high-profile pro- or anti-European Union role with impunity as part of their opening negotiating gambit, as EC rules (both written and unwritten) prescribe concession making to achieve consensus, usually around the midpoint positions of all players. Compromise is the name of the game. This is known from the outset and is reflected in bargaining tactics. Governments can switch from tough to soft to moderate positions according to the issue under discussion to achieve an overall package that corresponds neither to their lowest acceptable deal nor to their optimal goal on every issue.

Cooperative behavior is the norm in the EC. But on individual issues, usually for tactical reasons, a state may adopt an initially antagonistic position in the expectation that others will engage in behavior that is more accommodating to its own interests than it might expect through usual negotiations. Although such extreme behavior is relatively rare, it may be the product of the personality of a particular leader (Margaret Thatcher of the United Kingdom is the example in this case study). It may also occur on issue-specific occasions (for example, the U.K. budget dispute) when compromise seems undesirable or when vital national interests seem endangered. It might even occur, although even more rarely, when the majority lines up against one state that is blocking progress wanted by the others (this too happened in the SEA case). But, normally, the expectation is that initially antagonistic behavior will turn sufficiently cooperative to permit bargains to be struck. The two may coexist simultaneously across different issue areas, giving the EC a propensity to go for package deals as part of an overall bargain, as typified by the SEA negotiations.

So why was a new type of initiative needed in the shape of the SEA? The answer lies in the perceived urgency of the problems confronting the EC and the apparent incapacity of existing mechanisms to handle them adequately and speedily. Small amendments to the founding treaties of the Communities had been undertaken on a piecemeal basis in the past in selected areas, but this time a more radical approach was wanted by both key EC institutional actors and most governments. The original goal of some governments was to secure the adoption of a new treaty to supersede the Rome Treaty. This proved impossible. That the treaty revisions could be grouped together in a single document was something of a triumph. But the SEA was initially neither understood as nor intended to be a major constitutional document in the way that the European Union Treaty (EUT) was.

Some governments, notably the Italian, held the high European ground, and not simply for strategic or tactical reasons. Some, such as Germany, could play the rhetorical European role in the expectation that the antagonistic position of another (notably the United Kingdom) would lead to compromise that

approximated their real interests (less enthusiastically pro–European Union than Italy or their own rhetoric). All could rely on the fact that the EC works by problem solving: the Commission and the various government working parties are intent on preparing options that will be acceptable to all parties. In the normal course of events, the Commission does not even formally table proposals that it knows, through preliminary soundings, will antagonize most of the member states. And major political initiatives can be underpinned by high-level political intervention through the European Council. But, in the SEA process, the Commission did not perform its initiating role because the decision-making process was not supranational but intergovernmental. This process gave governments the key role.

The Milan European Council had in fact approved four different institutional initiatives: the revision of the treaties in accordance with the Article 236 procedure for an intergovernmental conference (IGC); the drafting of a treaty on political cooperation; a request to the Council of Ministers to "study the institutional conditions in which the completion of the internal market could be achieved within the desired time limits"; and the launching of the Eureka scientific cooperation project outside the EC framework. It also agreed that the first and second initiatives might be taken together or separately.

Slightly earlier, political *démarches* had been initiated within the new, directly elected EP for wholesale constitutional reform and the EC's transformation into a genuine European Union. The EUT was devised as the constitutional basis for the Union. It has many of the hallmarks of a written constitution and also corresponded to the maximalist position for the SEA process. It stood as a concrete alternative to the SEA but did not have a realistic chance of being adopted because it was too federal in its prescriptions. Thus it provided a modest threat position because governments' slow moves toward further integration could be compared with the EUT and shown as failing to provide the institutional reforms necessary to ensure the completion of the Single Market. This threat was a potent factor in motivating governments to agree to institutional reform and was also necessary after years of prevarication. Furthermore, it was implicit that given the EUT's unacceptability, almost any agreement from the SEA process would be better than none at all. Those sympathetic to the EUT, however, had an interest in ensuring that the outcome of the negotiations approximated as far as possible the EUT recommendations. Thus, the EUT was an essential reference point for the SEA negotiators both in its actual content and in the strategy and tactics used for its development and adoption by the EP.

Inspired by Euro-federalist Altiero Spinelli, the all-party deliberations of the parliamentarians' unionist "crocodile club" and later the EP's special ad hoc Institutional Affairs Committee (IAC) created broad-based, cross-party, cross-national support for the EUT in the EP and in member countries. The strategy adopted was based on past experience of failure. Transformation had always been thwarted by national governments anxious lest treaty reform clip their autonomy and erode national sovereignty, goals that had priority over effective, efficient, responsive, and democratic decision making. The IAC sought to overcome this

anxiety by creating wide support for the EUT inside the EP and outside it, including within national parliaments that it lobbied. Both the strategy and the content of the EUT were designed to inform governments and influence the content of the SEA. Without the EUT, it is doubtful that the SEA would have seen the light of day. The EUT remains, moreover, the benchmark for subsequent constitutional deliberations in the EP (such as the Martin and Colombo reports of 1990) and indirectly, therefore, for the intergovernmental conference (IGC) on political union in 1990–1991.

The SEA's aims were to realize the internal market (later the Single Market); to introduce measures that would enable the attainment of that goal, such as institutional reform and amendment of key articles of the Rome Treaty; to limit the formal requirement for unanimity; to encourage majority voting in the Council; to expand the jurisdiction of the EC; and to advance the European Union.

Actors

The EC is a unique supranational organization. It has many of the features of a federal state but is not a state. Its decision-making system is geared to the emission of binding legislation. This is a distinguishing feature of the EC which makes it unlike other international organizations. It is not in the business of making agreements with which compliance is voluntary. Legislation taking the form of regulations and directives is binding on the member states, directly applicable and superior to national, domestic legislation that may conflict with it. Member states cannot opt out. They can be arraigned before the EC Court of Justice for inadequate compliance with EC law that they have approved as a group. Under majority voting (more common since the SEA), states in a minority are obliged to comply with legislation.

The methods involved in this legislative process both include and go beyond those of intergovernmental cooperation and bargaining. Thus, the EC Commission, which alone initiates legislation, does so only when it has taken informal soundings in the member states. Once it tables a piece of draft legislation, the aim is to see it adopted (in amended form if necessary) by the Council of Ministers. Under the old single-reading decision-making procedure, the adoption process could be exceptionally protracted, in the more notorious instances— for example, the architects' directive—taking over a decade, but it normally runs from two to five years. Under this system, the Council could reject legislation only unanimously but could adopt by unanimity (where prescribed by the treaty), by effective unanimity (whereby discussions and concession making continue until there is a majority consensus in favor of the legislative proposal), or by a qualified majority (when prescribed by the treaty and where votes are weighted according to the size of the member state and to ensure the support of a mixture of large and small states). The unanimity requirement so that member governments could not easily throw out draft legislation underscores commitment to

problem solving on a joint basis. Consequently, building majority consensus on issues is the norm.

At the political level, such consensus may be built through formal channels or through a series of bilateral tête-à-têtes between the Council president and his or her counterparts in key member states before critical meetings of the Council. It may occur within the Council of Ministers, in the "fireside" chats of foreign ministers, or in meetings in the corridors. At the level of officials, similar meetings take place. When actual legislative proposals are on the table, however, the Commission assumes its critical role as honest broker and arbitrator. In such instances, it alone is formally able to draft amendments to the original proposals.

Although the treaty prescribes weighted majority voting in some instances, the practice has been for states to continue bargaining—with the help of the intermediary of the Committee of Permanent Representatives (COREPER) and the Commission—until a consensus is discerned. Relatively rarely have issues been formally put to a vote. States may veto draft legislation only if a vital national interest is at stake; the veto is applied only rarely and tactically. Indeed, one of the issues during the IGC process was whether rules should be introduced to compel the Council president to call a vote or whether several states could themselves demand a vote. Since the SEA, voting has increased because of the increased number of instances in which majority voting is prescribed and because the EC has been preoccupied with Single Market legislation, which falls mainly under the majority voting rules (for details, see Lodge, 1989).

Controversial and exceptional as the IGC process was, all the participants expected it to lead to some outcome in the short term—either to a new treaty (maximalist position) or to an amendment to the existing treaties (midpoint position) rather than simply to confirmation of the status quo (minimalist position). The convening of an IGC was itself a mark of commitment. It also indicated how high the stakes were, not least since the decision to convene followed an extremely acrimonious Council meeting at which the Council president had acted extraordinarily in calling for a decision based on a majority vote. Time pressure meant that prevarication pending consensus was not an option; the majority was not prepared to cede the initiative to minimalist states wanting to preserve the status quo. There was a further commitment because the process had been initiated by the heads of state government at the Milan European Council. The public profile of the European Council meetings as part of the IGC process was higher than usual, as were the political stakes of key players.

In the normal course of events, the dominant actors are the Commission, which alone is responsible for initiating and amending draft legislation; the Council of Ministers, which is responsible for adopting it as the EC's "legislature"; and, to a lesser extent at the time of the SEA, the EP, whose formal opinion on draft legislation has been required in many cases. Individuals and personalities matter. Member states' interests are represented in EC institutions through the Council of Ministers, which comprises the member states' functional ministers; the European Council, which groups together the member states' heads of

state or government but which does not have a legislative role, was not part of the institutional system set up by the treaties, and until the SEA was not mentioned in the Rome Treaty; and COREPER, consisting of member governments' official representatives (often drawn from their foreign offices) acting as gatekeepers between the member states and the Commission. COREPER is charged with preparing compromises and consensus on draft legislation initiated by the independent Commission and submitted to the Council, but it cannot amend legislation. Only the Commission can do that at any stage of the legislative process. All along the line, the stakes are relatively high, but all know that ultimately inaction will merely delay a decision, not abrogate it.

The member states are not the only or even the most important actors in the EC. Of central importance is the uniquely independent Commission, which is a hybrid of an international secretariat and an independent political executive. As a result, its internal organization; learning processes; policy-making styles; processes of brokerage, mediation, and decision making; and bureaucratic politics reflect identifiable "bureaucratic" features. However, because it has been given the task of initiating legislation, mediating among divergent interests (notably through a process known as *engrenage* via links with national bureaucracies—a process that itself induces learning and European socialization of national administrators), devising package deals, ensuring that legislation is implemented and that member states honor their commitments, and developing policy over the short, medium, and long term for the agreement of the member states, it plays a distinctive executive and political role.

Negotiations take place across departmental and national boundaries. Bureaucratic interpenetration, mediated and fostered by COREPER, encourages negotiation by civil servants on Commission proposals. The aim is to ensure that their content is acceptable to all member states. The name of the game is consensus. Consensus-seeking behavior normally typifies Council meetings and did even before the SEA came into effect irrespective of whether the treaty prescribed unanimity for the adoption of a proposal. Avoidance of divisive behavior led to Council presidents' avoiding putting proposals to the vote. The effect was nondecision and procrastination. Insofar as this behavior was seen as an obstacle to realizing the Single Market, voting practices in the Council needed to be reformed, which was very controversial per se. It also meant that the Council could not be entrusted with evolving reforms for the IGC given its past failures to reform decision making and its continuing interest in the status quo.

The composition of the Council and voting practices vary according to the subject matter of the draft legislation on the table. To a greater or lesser extent in the early and mid-1980s the emphasis was still on securing compromises that had unanimous support. Because the process might take years, member states' ministers and even the ideological leaning of a government might change between the first submission of a proposal and its eventual adoption, requiring a different type of compromise. One of the aims of the SEA negotiations, therefore, was to overcome what was seen as a major flaw in the EC's legislative process.

This was another reason why a permanent body to prepare the IGC had to be convened (Keatinge and Murphy, 1990).

The EP is a supranational parliament; before the SEA, it had only limited authority and few legislative powers. It is directly elected every five years. Its members (MEPs) are autonomous and have an individual mandate. They sit in transnational party groups. National contingents within them often vote across ideological lines and often against the known position of their governments and home parties. The EP devises its own agenda (a potent political tool) and its own rules of procedure and interprets them tactically and strategically (Jacobs and Corbett, 1991). Its opinion is necessary under the founding treaty for some but not all areas of legislation, and the Council must await the opinion before adopting its decision. Before the SEA, the EP did not have a right to amend draft legislation or to be consulted on either Commission amendments or the eventual draft voted by the Council.

Getting a genuine legislative role was an important EP objective because the EP's role in the legislative process was marginal and incompatible with notions of democratic legitimacy and practice. The emphasis on promoting efficient, effective, responsive, and accountable decision making was closely tied to increasing the EP's legislative power (Cardozo and Corbett, 1986). It is all the more striking, therefore, that the SEA process arose out of an initiative of the EP. It is wholly misleading to suppose that plurilateral diplomacy alone applied, during this time, to coalition-building behavior among the member states. Without the EP's initiative for the EUT, the SEA process would not have been launched or been run in the way that it was.

The member states' views on a formal reform of the EC were by no means uniform at the start of the process. Their likely position on the sensitive issues raised by the idea of convening an IGC to reform the EC could be inferred fairly accurately from their MEPs' votes on the EUT, adopted on February 14, 1984. Those member states traditionally anxious about preserving national sovereignty—the United Kingdom, Greece, and Denmark—exhibited the usual reticence and inhibitions when faced with a treaty having federal overtones. Spain and Portugal were associated with the process even though they had yet to accede to the EC. Their position throughout tended to be positive.

The advancing European Union needed a national champion, preferably one of the big four. The French, not known for supranational enthusiasm, were nevertheless well placed to assume the role. Had France opposed further integration, it is unlikely that the IGC would have materialized. The succession of member states to the Council presidency was crucial at this stage. France held the presidency at a critical juncture and could be sure that a major initiative on the European Union would not fade the moment it passed on the leadership position to the next state. In Ireland the member states had a pro-EC honest broker. Italy was a state with Euro-ambitions but one that would not steal Ireland's and France's thunder. France could continue to assume the mantle of the realist champion while Italy played the idealist.

Structure

The EUT was a major catalyst for action on the institutional front. In May 1984, President François Mitterrand in his speech to the EP called for preparatory consultations about a new treaty arrangement based on the EUT and the Solemn Declaration of 1983. In June 1984, the Fontainebleau meeting of the European Council decided to set up two committees on the European Union. One, instructed to advance proposals for a "people's union," was known by its chairman's name: the Adonnino Committee. The other was known by several names: the Ad Hoc Committee on Institutional Affairs, the Spaak II Committee (after the 1955–1956 committee that prepared the original Treaty of Rome), or the Dooge Committee (after its Irish chair). The three names revealed the multiplicity of tasks facing the committee and highlighted the concurrent pursuit of different types of diplomacy throughout this period. These ranged from the normal bilateral encounters, as between the presidency and individual member states or among key states themselves (for instance, Anglo-German, Franco-German, and Benelux talks); to plurilateralism, notably in the Spaak II guise, where a sense of mission (promoting the European Union) prevailed, and in interactions between the twelve nations and the Commission; to a mixture of both, "Dooge."

The Dooge Committee's affinity with the original Spaak I Committee, source of the 1957 Rome Treaty that created the EC, arose from the fact that it too had been composed of personal representatives rather than government delegates. The distinction is subtle but important. Spaak II consisted of personal representatives from the European Council's members. Because they were directly accountable to the European Council, it was assumed that the new committee would operate outside the usual administrative frameworks (Keatinge and Murphy, 1990). But the idea of a new enterprise like that which launched the Spaak committee at Messina was belied by the fact that the European Council's conclusions refer, a good deal, to "cooperation" but never to "union."

During the first phase of the Dooge Committee (up to the Dublin European Council of December 1984), enlargement dominated the agenda. The Council took note of the Dooge Committee's interim report and requested a final report for its Brussels meeting in March 1985 (phase two). The issue was to be given full consideration, however, only at the Milan meeting of the European Council in June 1985 (phase three).

The first phase reflected the anxiety and ambiguities over the nature of the committee just set up. Ireland claimed the chair because it held the presidency and put forward as its "personal representative" the Council president, James Dooge. This move immediately undermined any pretensions to the committee's being a Spaak II Committee because the chair was not independent and Dooge did not see himself as a Spaak-type motor. His role became, instead, that of manager, the more traditional honest-broker role of a small state holding the Council presidency. He was not proactive in advancing change but rather sought compromise to facilitate the process. Belgium felt it had a claim to the chair

(recalling Tindemans and the Spaak tradition) as did Germany (which wanted former President Carsten in that role). However, once the pattern was set, inertia crept in, and no change in the nature of the chair resulted from a change in the states holding the presidency. The other members of the Dooge Committee had different degrees of domestic political shrewdness and influence (Lodge, 1986d).

In phase two, the Dooge Committee's task was to explore the ground for agreement. Because the member governments had not been overly enthusiastic about the EUT, the Dooge Committee could not base its recommendations entirely on it. The Italian representative, Mauro Ferri, could however be seen as an EUT advocate in view of his close association with it and the EP's IAC chair, Spinelli. French representative Edgar Faure likewise enjoyed a good deal of autonomy and good personal relations with his patron and kept France to the fore. The Committee met eleven times and worked on topic-specific briefing papers. It did not try to secure unanimity. France presented the general overview report. Close informal working links were kept with the IAC. Spinelli attended three meetings, and the EP president, Pierre Pflimlin of France, met with the Dooge Committee twice. Spain and Portugal were kept informed toward the end.

As Dooge proceeded on the basis of majority views in phase three, the final report was littered with footnotes that reflected national reservations, but a broad consensus over the body of the report had been attained. The task of securing governmental approval then fell to the Italian presidency, which was keen to use the report as the basis for action at Milan. To this end, Italy engaged in a good deal of bilateral diplomacy, and foreign ministers met in Stresa in June before the European Council. Italy's commitment to the European Union was critical at this stage because by now the other big states were jockeying for position. The United Kingdom alone seemed out to wreck the endeavor, presenting counterproposals at Stresa that were later upstaged by the Franco-German plan on the eve of the Milan summit. From the skirmishing in and around the Dooge Committee, it is clear that Italy, France, and, to a lesser extent, Germany were determined to preserve the idea of a goal that was a qualitative leap forward in European union. A number of smaller states, notably Belgium, supported them in this. Denmark and Greece expressed reservations.

The Dooge report was divided into three main sections: priority objectives (substantive policies); the means (decision making); the method (procedure to implement the report). On substantive matters, economic convergence and solidarity proved highly contentious, with Greece taking a strong line backed by Ireland. Germany, Belgium, and the Netherlands called instead for convergence of economic policies. External identity issues and particularly the extension of the European Political Community (EPC) to security issues elicited predictable Danish and Greek reservations, supported by Ireland on the security side. The United Kingdom, however, broadly concurred with the original six.

On the means, the EUT had advocated a transformation of EC decision making along clear federal principles and had proposed a full-blown bicameral legislature based on the EP and the Council. Denmark, Greece, and the United Kingdom objected even to Dooge's much diluted proposals. Germany sided with

the United Kingdom in objecting to proposals regarding the Commission; the United Kingdom objected to the Commission president-designate being given a chance to influence the choice of other Commissioners; and the Germans objected to a proposed cut in the Commission's size. Consolidating the role of the Court of Justice evoked consensus. Changing Council voting practice elicited sharp disagreement and a good deal of trading between the interim and final reports. The interim report was peppered with footnotes containing formal reservations from all but France, Italy, and Ireland. Ireland left the Franco-Italian maximalist camp at the end of phase two. The majority agreed on omitting references to the "vital national interest" wanted by the status quo minimalists: Denmark, Greece, and the United Kingdom. Ireland and Luxembourg indicated ambiguous positions among the majority.

On the method, an intergovernmental conference was to negotiate a draft treaty based on the *acquis communautaire* of the Solemn Declaration and the Dooge report and guided by the spirit and method of the EUT. Calling an intergovernmental conference would be the initial act of the European Union. Britain, Greece, and Denmark opposed this suggestion, which was extremely controversial. The United Kingdom consistently disputed the need for one. When the Italian Council presidency, nevertheless, decided to set aside the usual consensus-seeking practice at the European Council in favor of an unprecedented vote on convening the conference, there was an uproar in the U.K. camp. Although the president could be certain of winning the vote, it is interesting that several governments, particularly the French, subsequently stressed that a precedent had not been set and that usual practices would continue (Lodge, 1986d).

The Italian presidency's tactic had been inspired by the EUT formula (which foresaw progress if a majority of two-thirds of the Union's population concurred) and by the fact that unanimity was not prescribed for European Council decisions. The EUT provision, as well as the attendant strategy, has subsequently become a key feature of plurilateral bargaining within the EC. It provided the rationale and the legitimacy for arguing that the majority of member states should not be prevented from advancing integration by the least communitarian state or states. The EUT formula was adapted for SEA provisions on the cooperation procedure. At this point, however, it served to remind the British that although they might not condone further integration, the majority of states was prepared to go ahead without British involvement. Thus, a carefully managed strategy evolved of allowing states to isolate themselves from the wishes of the majority only at their peril.

Equally important, given the consensus prevailing among the procommunitarian original six members of the EC, the minority was in a weak position numerically and politically. Internal splits within the minority left the six room for maneuvering. However, uniformity did not prevail among them either, leaving the door open for sabotage or bargaining. Moreover, the Milan mandate did not call for a single draft treaty on the European Union à la Dooge but instead implied piecemeal amendment of the existing treaties under Article 236, which could undermine the coherence of the endeavor. The U.K. and Franco-German

drafts on political cooperation were even more limited in scope. The task of pulling all this together fell to the smallest state, Luxembourg.

Luxembourg immediately submitted a proposal to amend the treaty. Before the IGC could be convened, the Commission, Council, and EP had to give their opinions as required by Article 236. Favorable opinions were all put before the Council of Ministers by July 22, 1985. The Council then called the initial meeting for September 9 and set the scheduled December 1985 meeting of the European Council as the deadline for decisions to be made.

Strategy

It was known at this stage both generally and through the specific opinions of the Commission and EP that these two bodies were in favor of the IGC and that the member states were divided. Several member states still objected to the calling of the IGC and expressed reservations over the Council's opinion, which was, nevertheless, passed unanimously. Their objections can be explained by the fact that the Milan European Council's highly controversial and unprecedented majority vote decision to proceed with an IGC reflected known divisions and that the field for dispute, and ultimately for cooperative behavior and compromise, had been delineated before Milan. The fact that the Milan vote was taken by majority reflected the high degree of political commitment to advancing the European Union in principle, irrespective of disagreement over its details.

It is axiomatic that no major initiative can proceed in the EC without the consent of France and Germany, even though qualified-majority voting in the Council does allow for other coalitions. The "rule" does not give the same power to Italy or the United Kingdom. Moreover, the "rule" does not always have to be translated into a strategy that rests on joint Franco-German initiatives. Indeed, in the case of the SEA, all that was necessary was that the Germans not try to thwart or compete with France's lead. Had both lost interest in the European Union, however (as their faint-hearted political cooperation proposals seemed to suggest), the whole venture might have been eclipsed. That it did not owes something to the countervailing multinational, cross-party, and elite pressures, expectations, and awareness generated by the EP.

In many respects, the SEA process was atypical of normal plurilateral bargaining in the EC in that it was indirectly driven by one of the EC's juridically weakest institutions, the EP. As in the EUT process, the EP relied on the work of its IAC.[1] The IAC consulted as appropriate with other EP committees, notably those on political and legal affairs. The IAC divided responsibility for subject areas covered by the IGC among eight of its members. Their comments and a synthesis by Vice Chair Herman Croux provided the basis for a set of conclusions adopted by the whole IAC for the use of Pflimlin in his talks with IGC players. The EP's delegation to the IGC comprised Pflimlin and Spinelli plus, on one occasion, Chair Roberto Formigoni of the Political Affairs Committee (Louis, 1985).

The EP's initial strategy was to get in on the act. It hoped to ensure that,

in the absence of a direct role in the negotiations, it would have a role that was one stage removed. It wanted the adoption of reforms to be conditional upon its assent, preferably on an item basis or, failing that, collectively. When it was denied anything but a loose consultative role, it modified its strategy accordingly. Based on its EUT strategy, it concentrated on identifying and lobbying appropriate governments, parliaments, and political, intellectual, trade, labor, and business elites as well as opinion leaders. The EP used the support it had generated among national parliaments for the EUT in a tactical way to bolster its demands for changes in institutional provisions. The Italian and Belgian parliaments, in particular, adopted positions that reinforced the EP's claims to be consulted about the outcome of the SEA negotiations and about the actual reform of its powers.

Although the critical action took place among supranational-level actors, influence was exerted at the national level by bodies that were normally irrelevant to the content and outcome of the EC's legislative process but that, by dint of national constitutional provisions regarding the ratification of treaties, were in a position either to prevent the SEA's adoption or to prevent or protract the SEA's implementation. Used tactically and sparingly, this power gave national parliaments, if they wished, the opportunity for shaping expectations in certain directions. None definitively influenced the SEA's content. Negotiators, however, needed to ensure that the SEA would be broadly acceptable to a majority of the members of national parliaments, many of whom remained ill-informed about both the EC and the SEA.

Moreover, throughout the process rumor played a part in creating the facilitative conditions that made the players receptive to dialogue. It is often said that the EC thrives and works on rumor (Budd, 1987; Butler, 1987), and although the impact of informal communication cannot be quantified, there can be little doubt that it does lead states to explore more alternative options than they might otherwise do. It must be remembered that whenever a majority has to be maintained for a given position, there are opportunities for all kinds of deals, side payments, and cross-bargaining. Similarly, the EP was in a position to influence an important Euro-event, the second elections to the EP in summer 1984 (Lodge, 1986a). The EUT and the general issues of the Single Market and European Union surfaced to a greater or lesser degree in the campaigns in the member states. This gave *Europe* a high public profile, and the EP worked to maintain it.

From the outset, the EP's strategy was one of cooperation. Indeed, only by adopting such a strategy did it stand any chance of gaining a clear insight into the process and of having some opportunity for influencing the IGC deliberations. Commission President Jacques Delors reported to the IAC the day after his return from Milan. Before breaking for its summer recess the EP passed a resolution representing the EP's formal opinion as required under Article 236.[2] It endorsed the convening of the IGC, called for the EP to be treated as an equal partner in the IGC, and reaffirmed the EP's view that the European Union should be allowed to proceed if a majority of states favored it. EP President Pflimlin then, by letter, stated that this resolution could be considered a favorable opin-

ion.[3] This endorsement was important because the Luxembourg presidency had formally proposed the revision of the treaties and anything less than the EP's endorsement would have meant that the IGC would be delayed; it met on July 22, 1985. Greece, Denmark, and the United Kingdom said they would participate in the procedure but reserved their position on the outcome.

Nonetheless, the EP sharply distrusted intergovernmental conferences because most of their work was influenced by officials who, MEPs felt, lacked a sense of overarching Euro-political vision and who consequently tailored their proposals to the lowest common denominator and bureaucratic inertia (Corbett and Lodge, 1986). For this reason, during the EUT process, the EP had involved itself directly with political forces and national parliaments throughout the EC. Its majoritarian Spinelli formula for avoiding national vetoes also highlighted its belief that although an intergovernmental conference was necessary, its conduct according to Article 236 was not. Having repeatedly called for an intergovernmental conference, the EP argued that a Euro-input to balance national bureaucratic stances was imperative, and it advocated making the conclusions of such a conference subject to the combined approval of the EP and the IGC. It recommended repeatedly and unsuccessfully a conciliation procedure in the event of differences between the two. Formal combined approval would have given the EP a veto, which it justified on the grounds that a major constitutional issue was at stake. Subsequently, the EP was given the right to approve major international treaties in the reforms of Articles 237 and 238 introduced by the SEA. To some extent, the EP's requests for a role, and specifically the kind of procedural innovations and amendments that it sought, were akin to those that it wanted to see introduced as part of the IGC's reform of the EC's decision-making process.

Governments were divided over the nature of the EP's association with the IGC. As a result, Pflimlin sent a letter setting forth equal participation as the EP's first goal. This goal was rebuffed when it was referred to during the initial ministerial meeting on September 9 but with assurances that the IGC would take into account the EUT and any further proposals the EP wished to submit. The ministers proposed to meet with MEPs during the course of the IGC deliberations and agreed "to submit" the results of their work to the IGC. This proposal implied more than an intention to inform the EP about the IGC deliberations but also a good deal less than EP participation as an equal partner. The term *submit* led to wrangling between the EP and the IGC until, in the end, it was specified that submit meant that the EP would be informed and given the chance to express an opinion, a lesser arrangement than a second reading or a right of amendment, veto, or conciliation.

The EP's strategy then turned to strengthening its rights of submission, capitalizing on the Article 236 procedure of getting one member state to indicate that it would thwart the attainment of unanimity as required. It persuaded Italy to declare that it would ratify a new treaty only with the EP's approval. Only when the EP had debated the IGC outcome and referred its view to the IGC would the EC-level process (assuming EP approval) be concluded. Thus, the strategy was refined to make a blocking coalition between an EC-level institution (respon-

sible for the initial political momentum behind treaty reform but formally excluded from the IGC process) and at least one of the governments central to the IGC process, the one that had already broken with tradition by holding the majority vote on the issue in the first place. As part of the system of associating past, present, and future presidents in a leadership troika, Italy still played an important executive role as immediate past president. This move proved vital in ensuring that the IGC negotiators were kept in a dialogue with the EP.

The EP also hoped, as its second goal, that the EUT would serve as a basis for the IGC's work because it defined how institutional relationships might be refined in the EC's transformation into a European union. Its representations to this effect failed. Commission President Delors assured the EP that the Commission's proposals were based on the EUT and that relevant extracts were included in the briefs on sections of the treaties likely to be amended.[4] However, it would not have been expedient politically for the IGC to say that the starting point was a neo-federal treaty drafted by an institution that lacked genuine legislative powers and whose authority remained contested both among the EC institutions and member governments and among the EC's electorate. Still, the failure was only partial, for there can be little doubt that Dooge and IGC deliberations were informed by the EUT.

The EP's third goal was close scrutiny of the IGC. The EP received tabled documents either officially or via the back door. It had a three-pronged tactic based on close monitoring of the IGC proceedings and papers, on reaffirmation of the EP's position at all stages both through formal resolutions and by constantly shadowing the IGC and lobbying recalcitrant parliaments and potential government alliance partners, and on delegation of tasks to the IAC to act on its behalf.

Dissatisfied with the apparent reluctance of the Commission and the governments to table proposals in line with the Dooge Committee and Adonnino Committee reports, the EP adopted an emergency (Herman) resolution on October 10, 1985.[5] MEPs used their right to question the Commission and Council president at the October 25 session. The EP delegation had several meetings with the IGC. The results from initial talks were unsatisfactory from the EP's viewpoint and were dominated by the Luxembourg presidency of the Council. The EP had greater success a little later when it managed to expose divisions among the member states, notably over reforms of the EP's powers. The EP's plurilateral diplomacy and alliance with Italy yielded important results at this stage, not least because further plurilateral interaction had led Belgium, the Netherlands, and France to appreciate the Italian position.

The continuity of the alliance was vital to the December Luxembourg Council. The EP adopted a resolution condemning several areas of the IGC package (especially those relating to EP powers) as "unsatisfactory." On the eve of the summit, the EP's enlarged bureau issued a statement contesting the content of the IGC's preparatory work submitted to the European Council.[6] It was particularly anxious lest reform be sacrificed in favor of quick agreement. In the event, Italy entered a formal reserve against the reform package agreed on by the

European Council pending the position of the EP and Italian parliament. There were signs that Belgium might back this line. Denmark entered a general reservation against the whole package lest it be too radical for the Danish parliament. The Danish reservation weakened Italian resolve and meant that an Italian veto on behalf of the EP was likely to be sacrificed for compromises that had been left to the foreign ministers to complete. This development did not deter the EP from keeping up the pressure, notably on the explosive issue of institutional reform, over which the member states were seriously divided.

As a result of this pressure, a strategy was needed to ensure that the European Union proceeded according to the wishes of the member states rather than as a response to a treaty drafted by an institution often vilified as talking shop. This criticism came from opponents of further European integration and from governments anxious lest further EC reforms denude them individually and collectively (in the Council of Ministers) of authority. The way for the members to keep overall control of the situation was to insist on reforms and an IGC based on the Article 236 procedure. However, this insistence was coupled with constant reference to the need for the majority will to prevail à la Spinelli.

The strategy had to be implemented in such a way as to combine commitment to the European Union with governments' interest in retaining as much autonomy as possible for themselves. Although governments could be relatively open to steps to advance the Single Market (such as the replacement of unanimity by majority voting in the Council on selected policy sectors), they had to be more careful about reforms that would alter the interinstitutional balance. It was imperative to maintain a balance between distancing themselves from the EP and appearing to listen to EP suggestions. For this reason the ten agreed that account would be taken of the EUT and other EP proposals, that the IGC would meet an EP delegation, and that the EP would have a chance to express its views before the IGC text was signed. Commission President Delors was instrumental in getting this concession and was backed by foreign ministers Dietrich Genscher, Giuglio Andreotti, and Leo Tindemans.

Rather than playing merely a secretarial or bureaucratic role, the Commission acted politically, tactically, and strategical at critical moments (Freil, 1991). Trade-offs were made as normal EC bargaining processes would lead one to expect. But the dominant coalition was not always uniform across all the issues raised by the SEA. The Franco-Italian axis was critical in sustaining the general public political momentum for the European Union, but the Commission was the driving force throughout. Even before the IGC opened, it proposed that agreement should be encapsulated in one document. This was a highly political and sensitive issue because political cooperation, strictly speaking, fell outside the domain of supranational decision making. Contentious as this proposal was, support for it grew during the negotiating process. It was probably realized from the start that this issue was one over which, ultimately, a majority could appear to make a major compromise to appease those who contested the desirability of the IGC in the first place. However, the proposal was not just a tactical move by the Commission, a "bargaining chip" for purposes of trade-offs. It was one

of the Commission's many initiatives on policy issues that helped to maintain momentum and spur member states into action.

Domestic politics affected the momentum behind the process. Mitterrand, in particular, and Chancellor Helmut Kohl maintained the pace as chief protagonists. Domestic elections in both cases quelled Euro-enthusiasm. In Germany's case, their first-ever use of the veto (on cereal prices), two weeks before the Milan European Council, seriously undermined their Euro-credibility. Domestic politics in Italy had a positive effect in reinforcing Italy's assumption of the leadership role. At the political level, personalities came into the equation: Spinelli, as a father of European integration, was bolstered by Delors and flanked by Mitterrand and Kohl. Thatcher epitomized an inward-looking and sometimes arrogant British isolationism, and her personality tended to jar her colleagues.

The timing of the enterprise was itself tactical. The task of conducting the IGC fell to Luxembourg as it assumed the rotating Council presidency. This development was more than fortuitous: Luxembourg was considered pro-European. It had few major vested national interests in critical issue areas. By itself, and even with the support of small states, it could not block or advance anything unless it had the support of at least one big state. Moreover, there is an expectation in the EC that the smaller states will make the most of any opportunity they have to play a major statesmanlike diplomatic role when occupying the EC presidency: a high-profile, political role on the European, and even the international, stage at times. In short, they have a role to play and try to play it better than the big states. This gave Luxembourg an incentive for acting accordingly and also for encouraging its partners to focus on the broad issues addressed by the European Union rather than on the minutiae. This too is a typical Euro-tactic when major decisions have to be taken: details are left for future discussion when the broad parameters have been agreed on. This tactic is certainly conducive to action and compromise. Thus, Luxembourg set out its version of the agenda in a document known as a treaty framework *(charpente d'un traité)*, and the IGC deliberations proceeded on the understanding that delegations should make their submissions in the form of treaty texts by October 15, 1985.

The member states adapted many of their usual tactics to the IGC process and the higher public and political profile surrounding the European Union. These included posturing, coalition formation—involving trade-offs and the Spinelli formula (in effect a threat) to remind recalcitrant states of the consequences to them of isolation—and, ultimately, agenda adjustment (dropping and hiding irreconcilable issues).

The big four engaged in posturing to a greater or lesser degree. Germany played its traditional "rhetorical European" role (publicly proclaiming itself in favor of greater union while concealing its reservations under Britain's uncommunitarian cloak). France assumed the mantle of leader. Italy took up the most progressive—that is, most federal—position. Denmark and Greece fell to the other extreme. The United Kingdom unsuccessfully touted the vision of an alternative Europe based on intergovernmental cooperation. Indeed, the United Kingdom's position became an easy public target for Benelux, French, German,

and even Spanish rhetoric. The reality of governments' positions was sometimes not that far removed from the rhetoric. However, apart from Italy, none could match the pro-Union high ground occupied by the EP.

Coalition formation worked in the positive sense of building and maintaining commitment to advancing the European Union and the Single Market. Although a negative coalition of Denmark, Greece, and the United Kingdom was theoretically possible, it did not evolve into a solid, blocking minority. Internal divisions meant that the Spinelli formula could be deployed on an issue-by-issue basis if trade-offs failed. Moreover, for tactical reasons, states could adopt uncharacteristic positions either to regain ground at the EC level by showing a communitarian face or to divide domestic opposition parties. For example, Denmark tabled proposals on energy and local voting rights that were more advanced than even the most procommunitarian states were able to accept, in the expectation that they would fail. In the event, they were dropped.

Agenda adjustment and time pressure constituted another tactic. The Commission set the agenda, producing and submitting formal treaty texts on the internal market, the environment, and research and technological development, and later on cohesion, monetary policy, and cultural policy. The imperative of realizing the Single Market by January 1, 1993, meant that the IGC had to come to a reasonable conclusion by the end of 1985. The time scale for reform was dictated by this deadline and by the attendant need to allow time for the signing and ratification of any agreement. The agenda had to be adjusted (cut) accordingly. Moreover, impending elections in member states (notably France, Germany, and Greece) favored an expedient rather than optimal outcome.

Particular member states were associated with particular issues. The Germans, for example, advocated major reforms of the EP's powers, but these would have fallen on deaf ears but for Italy's insistence on the EUT line and persistent EP lobbying. Equally important, although there was little general enthusiasm for increasing the EP's legislative powers, it was recognized that some institutional change would have to be accepted if the Single Market were to become a reality. The report on the institutional costs of non-Europe had hit home. Given the constant refrain in favor of democratizing EC decision making, as well as rendering it more efficient, a small concession to the EP needed to be made. The result was a process introduced to speed up decision making on vital internal market issues, termed the cooperation procedure—another example of compromise and fine-tuning of the agenda.

The Dooge Committee's tactic of keeping up the momentum for the European Union by advancing issues having majority support carried over into the subsequent IGC deliberations. Issues without wide support were dropped from the agenda. These included Dutch, Italian, and Commission proposals on cultural Europe (an issue also relevant to the Adonnino Committee), Dutch and Danish proposals on a common development aid policy, French proposals on differentiation, and Danish proposals on a common development aid policy, French proposals on differentiation, and Danish proposals on energy and voting rights in local elections. The willingness of states to see certain areas removed

from the immediate agenda can be interpreted in tactical terms as either a willingness to trade off one interest against another or an outflanking damage limitation ploy to redress anticommunitarian images. In short, states were not necessarily equally committed to initial positions across the Dooge/IGC agenda.

Agenda adjustment of this nature was essential to ensuring that the member states did not lose sight of the need to have in place the requisite treaty changes relating to decision-making practices. Without them, the 1992 deadline would not be met. All states recognized the need to afford priority to increasing the EC's decision-making capacity. Agenda adjustment also avoided member states' becoming involved in protracted negotiations (implying various levels of disagreement) likely to obscure the overall objective and encourage procrastination as governments faced domestic elections and coped with the implications of other major changes in the international environment, including the reactivation of the Western Europe Union (WEU). The agenda adjustment was subtle in that items were not so much dropped as either slipped into the SEA's preamble, as in the case of human rights, or put aside to a future date. It is, for example, significant that the Commission's opinion of October 1990 on proposals for the political-union intergovernmental commission specifically allude to provisions strengthening the objectives and the instruments of cooperation and development aid to make it effective.[7]

Process

Throughout the deliberations a steady campaign was kept up, often via the media, to advance the European Union and to warn the United Kingdom that it could not stop the others from moving forward. On November 19, 1985, Benelux prime, foreign, and European ministers issued a declaration listing five priority goals: completion of the internal market by the end of 1992, generalized Council majority voting, more powers for the EP, more power for the European Monetary Union (EMU), and more EC technological development.[8] The French European minister had already indicated commitment to majority voting and to giving the EP the powers that an elected parliament should have (which was not the same thing as endorsing the EP's quest for greater legislative authority), and the German president argued that the EC could not be less democratic than its member states.

The United Kingdom's view was that the EC already was a European union, as it was in the process of deepening and broadening the scope of its European activities, and that change should be minimal and pragmatic. The United Kingdom called only for agreement on an EPC treaty. Italy warned that it would not accept anything lacking teeth. Denmark's starting position was ambiguous and geared toward domestic public opinion, but it hinted that it might accept limited amendments. Reactions to the United Kingdom were colored by annoyance over the ongoing budget dispute, and the United Kingdom was less than diplomatic in the handling of the two issues at high political levels. Italy assumed the role of honest broker and coalition cementer when it was clear

in November 1985 that splits among the Eleven threatened the whole venture. The United Kingdom was effectively seen as irrelevant because there was general acceptance that if the United Kingdom chose not to go along, the other members would proceed anyway. This was considered enough of a threat to encourage the United Kingdom to put aside its rhetoric and recognize the importance of being part of the new venture.

Italy and France were keen to maintain the wide pro-Union coalition. The consensus was reinforced by the favorable positions taken on the European Union by many national parliaments (including the Italian, Belgian, German, Dutch, Irish, and French), some of which mirrored their favorable treatment of the EUT proposals. Consensus emerged over increasing the EP's powers and majority voting in the Council. The Italian parliament took the lead in arguing for the EUT to remain center stage and for a significant increase in EP powers. Shortly before the December IGC, it condemned the proposals as unacceptable in terms akin to those of the EP.

Political parties, notably the transnational federations—the European People's Party (EPP), the Confederation of Socialist Parties (CSP), and the Federation of European Liberals and Democrats (ELD)—adopted positions designed to influence the outcome of the deliberations. These views mirrored known governmental and national positions to a fairly high degree. The CSP's Madrid congress adopted a policy document on the European Union that (unusually) did not bind all parties, thereby permitting the Danes and British to maintain their opposition and reservations. All three basically approved measures advocated by the EUT. The U.K. members of the European Democratic Group gave a press conference on November 26 indicating wide disagreement with their government and accord with the majority of MEPs.

Although priorities on the issues diverged, there was broad agreement on extending the scope of EC activity. Denmark, Greece, and the United Kingdom generally opposed intensifying the level of integration. Others could accept deeper integration only with specific qualifications, especially in regard to inter-institutional relations. For that reason this issue, above all, required sustained pressure from the EP and its allies. Because the institutional question was divisive, it made political and tactical sense to focus on internal market matters. This focus rendered the IGC process less threatening to the more wary and skeptical participants and infinitely more pragmatic (and hence less repugnant) to U.K. Prime Minister Thatcher. Moreover, institutional reforms could be slipped into substantive policy-sector amendments: majority voting in the Council and increased power for the EP and for the Commission were introduced by small changes to existing provisions.

The Commission's initial proposal of September 18 broadly defined the internal market as an area "without frontiers in which persons, goods, services and capital shall move freely under conditions identical to those obtaining within a member state." These are the "four freedoms," and they are to be attained by removing physical, technical, and fiscal boundaries. The Commission also suggested the following: replacing unanimous voting with qualified majority voting

in the Council for all but freedom of movement of persons; adoption of implementing measures by the Commission save where the Council unanimously reserved that right to itself; and automatic mutual recognition by the member states of each other's rules if provisions had not been adopted by the end of 1992. Italy and the Benelux countries broadly endorsed the Commission's proposal.

The member states split over various issues: the definition of the internal market (too broad for the United Kingdom, France, and Germany); majority voting and delegation of powers to the Commission (opposed by Denmark and Greece); fiscal and taxation matters (qualified objections from the United Kingdom, Ireland, Germany, and the Netherlands); banking and insurance (Ireland); and social security for migrants and the organization of professions (Germany). The poorer states (Greece, Ireland, and Portugal) were worried about the effect of the internal market on their economies and the potential for an increased rich/poor, center/periphery divide (encapsulated by the phrase *economic and social cohesion*); they made their agreement contingent on the outcome of the negotiations on cohesion. The richer states, notably those with higher standards in key areas (Denmark and Germany), feared that harmonization provisions could lead to social dumping and lower EC standards. Germany suggested a quasi-veto formula to ensure that decisions in this field were made only if the higher-standard states were part of the majority (Corbett, 1986).

Political momentum was injected into the negotiations by France and the Commission, which tabled revised proposals for a political declaration on the harmonization of indirect taxes by 1990 and the internal market by 1993, and on altering the Rome Treaty to provide for majority voting in the Council when the EP had approved a Commission proposal. These moves subsequently proved critical. The Luxembourg presidency advanced revised proposals that were based on diluted versions of those of the Commission.

After long and sometimes acrimonious negotiations over Irish and U.K. health regulations, a lengthy set of articles and declarations was agreed on. The Commission's definition of the internal market as an "area" was eventually endorsed by France, Germany, and finally the United Kingdom, but its scope was cut and the reference to identical conditions deleted. Several articles were amended to permit majority voting in specified areas or to meet specific reservations. A new Article 100a providing for majority voting was inserted in place of Article 100 except for fiscal policy, free movement of persons, and employee rights. This change eliminated the need for recourse to the unanimity required by Article 235 (which in the past was fraught with difficulties). The momentum was maintained by obliging the Council to act before 1992 and to consult the EP, and by requiring progress reports from the Commission in 1988 and 1990. By using the tactic of agenda adjustment, final decisions were postponed until after the December IGC. Similarly, declarations in the Acts of the Conference spelled out other divisive issues such as crime, terrorism, and others where member states nevertheless agreed to cooperate. Greece, Portugal, and Ireland entered unilateral declarations on economic issues, and Denmark on safeguard measures under Article 100a.

Although the budget was largely neglected by the IGC (and while it remained an explosive Eleven-versus-the–United Kingdom issue), monetary capacity and the EMU were covered. There was one additional player in this field: the Council of Finance Ministers, the only sectoral council to be involved. An informal meeting on September 21 indicated their concern that they might be denied an input. Delors promised to discuss draft amendments with them prior to sending them to the IGC. The Commission's proposals centered on amendments to Article 107i designed to codify existing procedures and open the door for further development. These amendments were discussed by the finance ministers on October 28 and November 18. The United Kingdom, Germany, and the Netherlands objected in principle to monetary policy being part of the general treaty revision. The British dismissed EMU as pointless, whereas the Dutch and Germans had specific reservations not least concerning the role and autonomy of central banks. Italy, France, Belgium, and Ireland dismissed the Commission proposal as too weak. The Commission's revised proposal had to accommodate diametrically opposed views and fared no better.

The big four states were split down the middle. To avoid impasse, one had to be persuaded to change sides. Kohl obliged. He isolated Thatcher shortly after a bilateral meeting with her on November 27, which Thatcher mistakenly thought had drawn him into her camp. To secure Kohl's "defection," Italy and France took on board German reservations and announced measures to liberalize their exchange controls. This left the United Kingdom in splendid isolation again on a major issue as late as the first night of the European Council.

Monetary capacity and, in the longer term, EMU were seen as vital to the effective operation of the Single Market, an issue too important to be dropped from the agenda. Consequently, further compromise proposals were considered at the summit from the Commission, the Dutch, and the Germans. Although it was agreed to add a new chapter hedged about with restrictive Article 236-type qualifications, the real battle was postponed. The intractable problem of EMU led to the adoption of a tactic used for controversial items that were dropped: namely, amendments to the preamble indicating commitment to the overall goal—in this case, EMU. A further tactic was used to confirm that the EC's monetary capacity could be further developed (except where institutional matters were concerned) without recourse to the Article 236 procedure. This tactic was revealed using the device of a declaration by the presidency and the Commission added to the Acts of the Conference. In short, the commitment to monetary matters seriously divided the states. To avoid adding yet another empty statement on EMU to the list that had grown since 1972, the issue was slipped in wherever possible.[9]

Ireland, Italy, Greece, and France (to a lesser extent perhaps) feared that EC enlargement would divert structural funds from traditional beneficiaries to Spain and Portugal. This fear was shared by the United Kingdom though it did not make much of it given its wider concern to halt the European Union and its opposition to an increase in the EC budget. The Commission proposal of September 27 on reducing economic divergence between the regions and related

structural-fund matters divided the member states along the lines of the likely beneficiaries and fund contributors. Germany opposed some measures (notably the idea of new EC loans), while the Dutch quite blatantly said that periphery states' support for the Single Market would have to come as part of a quid pro quo on cohesion. France objected to any reform smacking of merger of the structural funds and tabled amendments to Commission proposals designed to maintain their integrity. Greece's proposal called for additional resources, as did Ireland's on the Regional Fund. Ireland also opposed a revision of the Social Fund (Articles 123–127, advocated by the Commission) and submitted amendments to the Commission's revised proposal of October 15.

The Commission elaborated a compromise that focused on the key issue dividing the states—center/periphery economic discrepancies. German, French, and Irish objections were accommodated. The new EC loan was dropped along with the Commission's original plans to improve working and social conditions, and the Regional Fund was specially mentioned. Given the United Kingdom's concern over EC resources and unwillingness to set figures down, no limits were specified. Reference was made instead to the Brussels 1984 European Council agreement to increase structural funds' resources significantly. In this area, the Commission played a crucial honest-broker role.

The potential for dispute was particularly large on the environmental front. This potential owed as much to the usual disagreement over whether the Council should go over to majority voting in such matters as to the fact that EC intervention in this field remained contested. Once again, however, the overarching demands of the Single Market's realization impelled action. The question of expanding the EC's scope to environmental matters provoked little comment.

The Commission took the lead in proposing four new articles laying down aims, principles, and specific measures, with majority voting for implementing measures but unanimity for defining aims and principles. Denmark had a specific interest in environmental action and was keen to ensure that it should not be forced to lower its standards to accommodate any new EC norm. It put forward a six-article proposal akin to that of the Commission. Against Denmark were the "dirty" states: the United Kingdom, Ireland, and Greece; these states considered stringent legislation costly. Ireland (backed by Greece) put forward an amendment on the need to balance environmental and economic considerations. Greece and the Netherlands objected to the extensiveness of the specific measures. Greece and Denmark objected, for different reasons, to majority voting. Only Germany suggested expanding the proposal's ambit (à la EUT) to include animal protection.

Bilateral trade-offs and diplomacy were clearly important in this sector. It was relatively easy and cheap for the "greener" states to put forward proposals unlikely to win the support of the less-clean states. They could appear advanced and communitarian in the expectation that not much would happen. The Commission's proposal was diluted to accommodate the requests from the "dirty states" that it take into account scientific evidence, costs to industry, regional differences, and the need for economic development. The subsidiarity principle was confirmed. The agenda adjustment tactic was used to postpone the decision-

making battle. The side-stepping tactic was used to include reference to the controversial matter of the European Court of Justice's competence and to subordinate EC environmental action to national energy policies. In brief, the idea of an environmental attachment to all EC policies as a matter of course was neatly qualified to assuage certain states' objections.

The research-and-development (R&D) issue ran parallel to the Eureka initiative. Fearful that France's lead on Eureka would denude the EC of an effective R&D role, the Commission (supported by several states) quickly submitted a proposal on September 16 for seven new treaty articles. The timing of the submission indicates the degree of concern the issue raised in principle. The Commission's revisions took into account member states' suggestions. Belgium formally sought an amendment, while Denmark tabled an alternative but in some ways complementary proposal. The Luxembourg presidency assumed the role of honest broker and submitted a redraft of the Commission's proposal to the member states, which accepted the various forms of EC action envisaged. However, Germany, suspecting that it would be asked for additional resources to fund the actions, sought a veto over the budgetary issues by insisting on unanimity. In the event, a complex compromise was agreed on that partly met German objections and limited the EP's budgetary powers in the R&D sector.

Denmark and the Commission made proposals in the social-policy sector. The Danish proposal was fairly detailed and was designed to overcome domestic opposition to the idea of revising the treaties. The Commission proposed introducing a "social space" to the EC's social goals and a two-part revision of Article 118 on social areas of collaboration. Article 118b was accepted, and a compromise based mainly on the Danish proposal was agreed on for a new Article 118a. The United Kingdom was fairly isolated in its objections both to the content of the proposals and to the decision-making procedures, which, it suspected, would lead to its being outvoted and to an expansion in EC competence. Accordingly, it pushed for the retention of unanimity until the last moment, when it was persuaded to accept the agenda adjustment and side-stepping tactics: its reservations were accommodated in an extra paragraph and declaration appended to the Acts of the Conference; they recognized that small businesses should be protected from "unjustified burdens." This amendment did not obscure the fact that the United Kingdom objected in principle to expanding the EC's competence into industrial relations areas (as its refusal to sign the Social Charter the following year confirmed) and to majority voting in this sector. Contentious as further EC action in this sector proved, the Commission believed it imperative that the IGC bring the issue into the general treaty revision, not least because action on this front was seen as necessary to shield the EC from the charge of creating a Single Market for the benefit of business only.

The question of political cooperation exposed Britain's reservations for what they were: deep-seated opposition to European integration. Paradoxically, however, this was the arena in which the United Kingdom could happily engage in Euro-rhetoric. It was the one area in which it submitted proposals and in which it hoped to remain a leader. The term *cooperation* particularly appealed

to Britain because it avoided supranational connotations and implied intergovernmentalism, which suited Britain perfectly. Therefore, the United Kingdom advocated increased cooperation in a host of matters, including security, even though Euro-wisdom had it that security cooperation and integration were where autonomous nation-states ended and a federal European union began.

In some respects, it was odd that political cooperation should be part of an agenda otherwise dominated by Single Market issues. However, the Genscher-Colombo initiative of 1980 for a Draft European Act to formalize EPC had been diluted into the 1983 Solemn Declaration on European Union, and the EUT had clearly expected "political cooperation" (that is, foreign policy cooperation) and the European Council to be integrated into the Community's structure and competencies. Political cooperation was separated from the rest of the IGC proposals in terms of expectations and process. There was no consensus that any agreement on entrenching EPC would form part of a treaty revision under the IGC. Nor were EPC proposals tabled in parallel to those on the Single Market issues. Rather, initial EPC proposals had been tabled before the Milan summit by Britain, France, and Germany.

The British proposal was tactical inasmuch as Britain hoped it would recoup some of its Euro-credentials amidst its hostility toward the convening of the IGC at all. It was also very much in line with the United Kingdom's pro-Atlantic foreign policy and advocated increased cooperation among the EC, the North Atlantic Treaty Organization (NATO), and the WEU. The Franco-German proposal emasculated the British tactic and robbed it of its impact. It also closely approximated the British proposal in several respects, but differences in nuance highlighted subtle differences in substance. The British and the Dutch proposals, for example, advocated increased cooperation within the WEU for EC states so inclined and hinted at the possibilities of enlarging the WEU. The Italians proposed increased cooperation between EPC and WEU presidencies and combined EP and WEU assembly meetings. Italy specified the very security issues that were omitted from the SEA but that were slipped onto the agenda of the 1990 IGC on political union: peace, arms control, external threats, and Euro-security. The Dutch proposal purported to be a compromise between the first two. Like the Italian proposal, it owed a good deal to the U.K. proposal and supported the British suggestion (contained in the annex to rather than the body of the text) that EPC be supported by a small secretariat with backup provided by the Council secretariat. Italian and Dutch fears that anything grander would eclipse the Commission, would evolve into an intergovernmental secretariat along the lines of the Fouchet model of the 1960s, and would be dominated by France and Germany were shared by many small member states.

In the case of political cooperation, big-state/small-state anxieties and divisions resulted in tacit alliances across pro- and anti-integration lines. The Netherlands appeared interested in maintaining amicable links with the United Kingdom. Belgium also supported the idea of links with the WEU, which suggested a more flexible approach than its traditional role of wanting to keep discussions within the framework of the Rome Treaty. Luxembourg was gener-

ally pro-Union apart from its reserve on majority voting (which might be explained in terms of a lack of precise instructions). Ireland's sensitivity over the security issue and neutrality prompted it to enter a reserve, but on the whole it maintained a positive approach. Denmark's position on political cooperation was in line with its general position of sticking to the letter of the treaties. Greece adopted a generally negative line and stressed the need for action on center/periphery disparities at every opportunity.

Institutional and decision-making capacity was the biggest arena for division among the member states and also the most important one to the whole European Union debate. Argument centered on the respective powers of the EP and the Council of Ministers. States divided roughly into those ready to concede that the EP should be given some additional legislative powers and those that wanted to maintain the status quo. The EPC arguments over whether the EP should be "informed" (status quo, United Kingdom) about EPC matters or be "associated" (Franco-German proposal) or be given an "essential role" vis-à-vis EPC (Italy) were in line with the general positions taken up on institutional reform.

The draft mandate for the IGC drawn up by the Italian presidency in May 1985 recognized that the aims of creating a homogeneous internal economic area (that is, by completing the internal market, strengthening the European economy's competitiveness, promoting economic convergence, creating a technological community, strengthening the European Monetary System (EMS), and mobilizing the resources needed to set out the objectives defined in the mandate) could not be achieved unless the institutions were "renewed and strengthened." Specifically, it noted the need to extend majority voting in the Council; to restore the Commission's initiating, managing, and implementing roles (the Dutch proposal on the role of the Council in Article 145 was not fully accepted, although key points remain in Article 10 of the SEA); to provide the EP with effective, joint decision-making powers in specifically defined legislative areas; and to redefine its powers on budgetary matters and grant it the right to vote on the investiture of the Commission. All these items were subject to agenda adjustment. Majority voting was limited in line with expanded powers for the EP; the Commission's implementing and managing powers proved so controversial that finalizing details on them was postponed until after the IGC. Acrimonious "commitology" proceedings ensued with the EP seeking the advice of the Court of Justice.

Proposals were made on EP powers by the pro-EP camp, embracing Italy, France, and Germany, and the anti-EP camp of the United Kingdom, Denmark, and Greece. Well in advance of the October 15 deadline for proposals, the German government leaked draft amendments and additions to the treaties, based on the German submission of June 27 to the Milan summit extending "consultation," "collaboration," and "joint legislative action" with the Council. A subtle change in the wording of Article 137, to replace "peoples" with "citizens" (implying federal loyalty divisions), was also included. The German draft drew on EUT proposals and approximated the EUT's suggestions on a first reading and conciliation procedure. However, it deviated in providing for a sole right of decision

for the Council if conciliation failed. This version was to appear in the finally adopted text.

The Commission criticized the German proposal where it suspected that an implicit weakening of its own powers had been foreseen. The Commission put forward alternative proposals based on the "basket approach." Basket 3 referred to the "cooperation procedure" subsequently incorporated into the SEA. Ireland, the Netherlands, and Belgium broadly accepted the cooperation procedure. The other nations were divided. Italy took the high ground and for tactical reasons put forward a proposal based on the EUT and Dooge, advocating full co-decision for most legislation even though it knew that it would not be acceptable. Italy also backed the Commission's fourth basket and generally supported the Commission's proposals. Belgium noted some support as a result. Delors and German representatives had expected that their compromises would appeal to the majority but found negotiations difficult. All but Denmark accepted the idea of EP co-decision on constitutional matters. Co-decision was particularly problematic, and virtually every state had an objection to its application in certain fields—France and Greece on Article 138 on the composition of the EP; France, Germany, and the United Kingdom on Article 201 on financial contributions; France and Ireland on Article 236 on intergovernmental conferences; and Greece on Article 237 on new members.

French proposals sought to combine suggestions from the Commission and Germany. France favored increased EP participation (though not necessarily a colegislative role) on regional development, environment, living conditions, culture, and education. It foresaw increased majority voting and abstention to avert the adoption of decisions when unanimity was required by the treaty.[10] The Dutch proposal sought a consultative role for the EP in the nomination of the Commission president. Little headway was made however. Even a meeting with the EP delegation on October 21 was fruitless. Ministers failed to agree on a new mandate for the preparatory group. The Luxembourg president then took the initiative to instruct the preparatory group to continue and to develop proposals that keep the system as simple as possible (earlier proposals had envisaged up to six readings of draft legislation, to which all the states were opposed). It drafted a compromise derived from Commission proposals on the cooperation procedure and limiting it to nine articles, increasing the Commission's room for discretion at the second reading, and limiting assent to Articles 237 and 238 on new members and associations, respectively. The idea of the conciliation procedure was dropped. (The agenda was adjusted, but the idea surfaced within months of the SEA's coming into effect and received higher profiles during the early 1990s, before the next intergovernmental conferences.)

At this point plurilateralism came into its own. The Benelux countries, Germany, and France said the compromises represented a bare minimum. Denmark still opposed them as too radical. Italy, and to a lesser degree France and Belgium, sided with the EP in suggesting that they were inadequate. The United Kingdom, when the deadlock was taken up by the European Council, indicated that the EP's powers should not be extended. Rather, the EP should be disbanded.

In the event, they produced a compromise for which, through agenda adjustment tactics, they were able to gain broad acceptance. Difficult associated matters on the operationalization of the cooperation procedure were referred to the foreign ministers' meeting for resolution. Denmark and Italy entered reservations against the text for opposite reasons. The EP's resolution on the results of the European Council sought further changes from the foreign ministers. The EP was successful in some respects, and parts of the Commission's original proposal were reinserted. Other problematic points were partially resolved through presidency declarations in the Acts of the Conference and, more weakly, through the Dutch presidency's assurance to the EP in January 1986 that the Council of Ministers' rules of procedure would be amended. The IGC eventually agreed to the EP's being formally called the "European Parliament" instead of the "Assembly" in line with German proposals.

Apart from the EP itself, only Italy and the Commission took a consistently bold line on EP powers. Both did so publicly, thereby indirectly mobilizing elites in a position to pressure national actors. Delors had told the Milan European Council that the EP should be given "genuine and equal power of decision" in limited fields. Spinelli too had intervened in the public debate by publishing an article in twelve European newspapers that condemned the "immobilists" (United Kingdom, Greece, and Denmark) and called for boldness regarding the Union.[11]

A new treaty on the European Union was expected to have a significant psychological impact on the member governments as well as the supranational institutions. The results of Dooge and the IGC fell far short of EUT expectations. They did not have the stature of a new treaty based on the *acquis communautaire*. Rather they amounted to a revision of the existing treaties. EC competence was extended, and the ambiguous position of European political cooperation was rendered slightly clearer by being included in the one document (even though the language of Title III refers not to member states but to high contracting parties).

It was far from obvious from the outset that the result would be a single document that could be seen as a step toward the European Union. Commission President Delors called for a revision treaty comprising a preamble and three sections (joint provisions, revision of the European Economic Community, political cooperation), as reflected in the French proposal of November for a single act. The SEA contained four titles, the first three proposed by Delors and a fourth on final and general dispositions that, by stipulating that the European Court's competence cover only Title II, undermined the import of the rest and of the preamble, where many compromises on contentious issues, like human rights, had been hidden.

Although the European Council meeting on December 2 and 3, 1985, was to lead to agreement among the member states on the internal market, monetary capacity, cohesion, environment and social policy, research and technological development, and institutional reform and political cooperation, several member states expressed important reservations. Thus, the approval of Italy was conditional on support by its national parliament (which espoused the positions of the

EUT and the EP); Denmark and Ireland had deep domestic divisions to overcome; Italy and the United Kingdom entered further reservations about the provisions on the improvement of working conditions at the ministerial meeting in
mid-December. In effect, for political and presentational reasons as much accord
as was possible to secure had been knocked together for the European Council.
Several serious difficulties had been referred back to the working group, but the
quintessential idea of *unicité* was ultimately retained by the treaty amendments'
being presented in a single document, though one that fell short of a treaty on
political union.

Ratification of the SEA fell to the successor to the Luxembourg presidency,
the Netherlands. It, too, had to play an honest-broker, managerial-type role and
was helped heavily by the Commission's legal services at this stage. At the end
of the IGC, the United Kingdom insisted that the veto remain intact and that not
much be changed. Denmark supported the "no loss of sovereignty implied" argument. Mitterrand signaled that the SEA was but the beginning of a longer
process. Belgium noted satisfaction that something, no matter how weak, had
been achieved, and Jan Martens criticized the government for not lining up
boldly with Italy. Portugal spoke out for more power to the EP. Italy's earlier
stand implied that if the EP opposed the package, Italy would prevent its ratification with the result that collapse would be inevitable.

For tactical reasons the Italian position was not quite as watertight as
might seem at a first glance. The EUT formula could after all be invoked leaving
the most procommunitarian state in paradoxical isolation. MEPs wanting to
stick to this line were in a minority. Even so, a good deal of lobbying went on
by the Commission, the Council president, and some member governments to
persuade MEPs to agree to the package. The Dutch Council president made
special representations to the IAC. Eventually, the EP accepted the package but
stressed its inadequacy and recalled that overall, as its resolution of December had
said, it could not be accepted in its present form and, as Mitterrand indicated, the
SEA was but a start. Careful wording of its opposition at this stage meant that
the EP did not imperil ratification. Italy then proceeded with ratification but only
after the issue had been debated by its parliament. Danish ratification was even
more problematic given intense internal divisions. The Danish parliament rejected the package by five votes. Danish Premier Poul Schluter, however, called
a referendum and won a 56 percent majority for the package.

Before the referendum, intense bilateral and plurilateral diplomacy had
occurred. Schluter made swift visits to other governments that, to back him up,
insisted that talks to reform the package could not be reopened. Just over a week
before the referendum, the Dutch called for the package to be signed on February
17 so that general pressure could be put on Denmark. All but Greece and Italy
obliged. The Commission and EP sent their vice presidents to the signing cer-
emony to show their dissatisfaction with its minimalist results. Denmark, Greece,
and Italy added their signatures on February 28. Italy added a lengthy declaration
calling for the SEA's review and expansion (notably in respect to the EP) by 1988.
Court action on the constitutionality of the SEA (lest it infringe Ireland's neu-

trality) delayed but ultimately did not endanger the SEA's implementation from July 1, 1987. Implementation was delayed by the Irish supreme court, which caused a referendum to be held before Ireland could ratify the SEA.

Outcomes

The mixed diplomatic techniques applied during the SEA process showed the advantages of coalition building among the EC states and between blocs within them and EC institutions broadly sympathetic to their views. These coalitions persisted more or less intact throughout the process. Bargaining within them was common and productive. The tactic of isolating the least communitarian member was successful, and the United Kingdom's tactic of trying to divide the big three failed. The EP alliance with Italy maintained maximalist pressure throughout. Others sided with the EP and Italy both for genuine reasons and to take up rhetorically ultracommunitarian positions or to engage in damage limitation exercises when they had been in the minority on other issues. States could afford this tactic particularly when they were certain that this type of minority coalition was unlikely to win the day but was nevertheless an indicator of pro-Union sentiment. The Commission, on whose shoulders the real exercise of drafting proposals fell, adopted procommunitarian, even pro-EP, positions but had to balance suggestions both to suit its own views and especially to facilitate compromise among the states to secure winning coalitions. As necessary, significant inputs were made in the public domain by leading personalities from the EP, the Commission, and member states, such as Spinelli, Delors, Mitterrand, Kohl, Schluter, and Andreotti. The Council presidencies (notably under Luxembourg and the Netherlands) acted as managers and occasionally as front-line mediators.

The knowledge that all the actors had of how each lined up inevitably assisted ultimate compromise and facilitated judicious agenda adjustment. No issue raised during the IGC process disappeared from the EC's agenda. All have been taken up since then and resurfaced in the 1990–91 IGC deliberations; issues dropped from the agenda at the 1991 IGC will resurface at the next IGC. These conferences are unusual and reflect a need to institutionalize major changes in the way the EC operates, in agenda and priority setting, in expanding the EC's policy competencies and institutional capacities, and in creating the necessary legal base for action in new, often highly contentious areas that impinge directly on state sovereignty. Many issues have been highlighted through the IGC process, and, even when only passing reference is made to them on one occasion, new *demarchés* are actually on the short- to medium-term agenda. In short, the pattern of plurilateral diplomacy initiated before the 1985 IGC by the EP has stood the test of time.

Notes

1. Before Spain and Portugal acceded to the EC, forty-five out of sixty-three votes were needed to secure the adoption of a proposal by weighted majority

vote. In some cases, the treaty said that when the Council met without a formal Commission proposal, the qualified majority had to include at least six states—that is, a two-thirds majority (Mathijsen, 1980).

2. *Official Journal of the EC,* C229 (9.9.85), p. 25.

3. *Agence Europe,* No. 4137 (22/23.7.85), p. 3.

4. *Debates,* OJ 2-331 (23.10.85), p. 92.

5. OJ C288 (11.11.85), pp. 105–106.

6. *EC Bull.,* 11-1985, pt. 1.13.

7. COM 1990, p. 26.

8. *Agence Europe* (21.11.85), p. 5.

9. PE 100.758.

10. PE 99.781/Ann 26; Corbett (1986, p. 20).

11. *La Repubblica* (Italy); *De Standaard, La Libre Belgique* (Belgium); *Irish Times* (Ireland); *NRC Handelsblad* (Netherlands); *Tageblatt* (Luxembourg); *Frankfurter Rundschau* (Germany); *Berlingske Tidende, Frederiksborg Amts Avis* (Denmark); *To Vima* (Greece); *El Pais* (Spain); *Diario de Noticias* (Portugal).

Chapter 2

Negotiating the Uruguay Round of the General Agreement on Tariffs and Trade

Gunnar Sjöstedt (Sweden)

This is a study of the Uruguay Round, the great and problematic trade negotiation of the 1980s. The objective is to give an account of its developments and main characteristics: how the Uruguay Round was initiated, how the negotiation was organized, and what patterns of conflict and cooperation materialized. An important part of the analysis will be to elucidate how the structural properties of the context of the General Agreement on Tariffs and Trade (GATT) influenced the negotiation process in all its stages. A comprehensive outcome assessment, which would have completed the picture, was unattainable as the Uruguay Round was still in progress as of this writing (July 1993) and was only concluded six months later (December 15, 1993).[1]

The chapter is organized as follows. The first section deals with the prenegotiations, which were underway long before the Uruguay Round was formally opened. The second part concerns the formal negotiations, which were initiated at the ministerial meeting in Punta del Este in September 1986. Developments are traced until the ministerial meeting in Brussels in December 1990. In the third section a summary description is given of the continuation of the Uruguay Round after the unsuccessful meeting in Brussels. The main theme of this account is the management of failure. The final section contains a few brief observations related to the outcome of the Uruguay Round.

Prenegotiations

The formal point of departure for the Uruguay Round is easily discernible. It was the successful conclusion of the ministerial meeting in Punta del Este, Uruguay,

on September 20, 1986, when almost 100 participating nations agreed to begin a new round of GATT negotiations. This collective decision followed a week of hard bargaining with the outcome remaining uncertain until the eleventh hour (Winham, 1989; Baldridge, 1986). The Punta del Este conference had an important ceremonial function. However, it also represented a genuine decision process in its own right because it determined in considerable detail the agenda of the upcoming Uruguay Round. Although of decisive significance, the Punta del Este meeting was in reality but an episode in a long train of events eventually leading to the start of a new GATT round. The ministerial meeting in Punta del Este not only was the formal starting point of the Uruguay Round but also represented the closure of another process, that of prenegotiations.

Diffuse Origin

It may be disputed exactly when the Uruguay Round began. One reason is that the Uruguay Round did not start on a single occasion. In certain respects it originated in earlier multilateral trade negotiations in GATT, particularly the Tokyo Round, which ended in late 1979. Part of the agenda of the Uruguay Round consisted of leftovers from the Tokyo Round: trade problems that important actors in the GATT process considered to be improperly solved in earlier rounds of negotiation. From a political point of view the most important case is trade in agricultural goods—a matter of particular concern in Washington. Agriculture had been on the agenda in the Tokyo Round but had not been the object of any real liberalization efforts to improve access to closed markets (United Nations Conference on Trade and Development, 1982). With the results of the Tokyo Round in the pocket, Washington found it increasingly urgent to bring agricultural trade under GATT disciplines.

In fact, several trade issues had been only partly settled in the Tokyo Round. For example, the deadlocked negotiations on safeguards (Article XIX in GATT) had been a complete failure. The several celebrated codes on various nontariff trade barriers represented a certain success but had been signed by only a relatively small number of countries, almost all of which were members of the Organization for Economic Cooperation and Development (OECD). Most governments in Third World countries felt that textiles and clothing should be brought under the GATT regime as soon as possible. Numerous governments in the North, as well as in the South, were worried about the increasing use of voluntary export restraints and orderly market arrangements, particularly by the great economic powers in sensitive industrial sectors (Aggarwal, Keohane, and Yoffie, 1987). Thus, in the early 1980s the opinion was widespread that although the Tokyo Round had made impressive headway to free manufactured goods in particular, it had not addressed a number of trade matters that required attention. These needs represented a potential moving force in the initial stage of the process of cross-country consultations that was destined to evolve into the Uruguay Round. Still, the prenegotiations developed into a protracted process full of stumbling blocks.

The political forces, notably the United States, which began to pave the way for new multilateral trade negotiations even before the completion of the Tokyo Round, seem to have been particularly concerned with what became known as the "new" trade issues because they had hitherto neither been covered by the GATT regime nor been on the agenda of the multilateral trade negotiations: trade in services, trade-related intellectual property rights, and trade-related investments. Actually, these issues had not been considered to be trade at all. The new trade issues were, from the very beginning, promoted by the United States and gradually received increasing support from other industrialized countries. The opposition consisted of an initially large group of developing countries, of which Brazil and India stood out as the most influential and assertive. The aim of the opposition was straightforward: to keep the new trade issues outside the agenda of the GATT negotiations (Bradley, 1987; *The Uruguay Round*, 1988).

Thus, the tug-of-war over the new trade issues, so typical of the Uruguay Round, did not first appear at the ministerial meeting in Punta del Este. The patterns of conflict and cooperation in these areas had been crystallized in protracted prenegotiations, which had been going on for several years. Prenegotiations had, in turn, been considerably influenced—indeed conditioned—by earlier GATT rounds. In order to fully understand this continuity from the past it is necessary to consider the great significance that the GATT context has always had for agenda setting in multilateral trade negotiations.

The Uruguay Round was the latest in the series of multilateral trade negotiations that started in Geneva in 1947, when GATT was established. To become a contracting party to GATT a nation had to make certain tariff concessions. In Annecy (1949), Torquay (1951), and Geneva (1955) the GATT membership was widened and the GATT regime consolidated by further tariff reductions agreed on in product-by-product negotiations. Then followed the powerful wave of trade liberalization of the 1960s and 1970s: the relatively unsuccessful Dillon Round (1960–1961), followed by the more impressive Kennedy (1964–1967) and Tokyo Rounds (1973–1979). Together these rounds of negotiation resulted in average tariff reductions on the order of some 70 percent. In the Tokyo Round the agenda was substantially expanded into the area of nontariff barriers to trade—dumping/antidumping, subsidies/countervailing duties, public procurement, tariff evaluation, licensing, and technical trade barriers (Dam, 1970; Golt, 1978).

The point of this short history of GATT is that from a long-time perspective the individual GATT rounds should not necessarily be seen as separate episodes in the evolution of the global trading system. Together they represent a comparatively continuous process. The impact of this continuity seems to have increased over time. The Kennedy Round was partly a result of the inadequacy of the product-by-product approach to attain substantive tariff reductions in the Dillon Round. A consensus emerged among the leading trading nations controlling the GATT system that in future multilateral trade negotiations a new approach of across-the-board tariff reductions would have to be attempted (Dam, 1970). The Kennedy Round has generally been celebrated as a success story, a high

point in the process of trade liberalization after World War II. However, a surprisingly strong protectionist reaction to the outcome of the Kennedy Round manifested itself in many industrialized countries. In many cases increased employment of nontariff barriers compensated for the tariff concessions made in the Kennedy negotiations (Baldwin, 1970, 1986).

Informal preparations for future negotiations of nontariff barriers to trade began in various forums around 1970. A significant part of the necessary analytical work was undertaken in the OECD, the highly competent support organization of industrialized countries. Therefore, when the Tokyo Round formally started in September 1973, draft texts already existed on several new nontariff barriers to be dealt with in the negotiations. The continuity between the Kennedy and Tokyo Rounds was even more clear-cut with respect to the then dominant issue, that of tariffs. In the Tokyo Round the linear, across-the-board approach to tariff reductions was used successfully for a second time. As a consequence, many of the controversies of the Kennedy Round emerged in the Tokyo Round— for instance, the question of whether liberalization efforts should include agricultural goods, the problem of tariff harmonization, and the issue of how to treat the extreme peaks in the tariff wall in the exchange of concessions (Dam, 1970; Winham, 1986).

Against this background the prenegotiations of the Uruguay Round have to be understood. The preparations for the Uruguay Round were firmly rooted in the results of the GATT negotiations of the 1970s and in their unresolved issues. In the area of tariffs as well as with respect to numerous other issues the Uruguay Round was a direct continuation of the Tokyo Round; negotiations in the 1980s took off from where they had been interrupted in the earlier round.

In addition, with respect to the new trade issues there were some backward links from the beginnings of the Uruguay Round to the Tokyo negotiations. The new trade issues were interlinked in various ways, organically as well as tactically or strategically, because of the trade policies of leading countries. Basically, the emergence of the new issues reflected the transformation of the advanced OECD countries from industrialized to postindustrialized societies. This development brought to the forefront new trade problems related to the increasing economic significance of services, information, and knowledge in modern society. However, in spite of these strong interlinkages the new issues were treated separately in the prenegotiations; each had a story of its own.

New Trade Issues

Trade in Services. Trade in services was the most important of the new issues. This area comprises a great number of economic activities—for instance, shipping and other forms of transport, professional services of many kinds, telecommunications, tourism, banking, and insurance. Although earlier they had not been considered part of international trade, service activities as such were not new phenomena in the interchange of nations. When the Uruguay Round began, services had for many years made significant contributions to the economic flows

between nations, which was acknowledged in the work program of the OECD and other international organizations. In the 1970s services had evolved in industrialized countries into the largest economic sector, which was also increasingly internationalized in most countries (Bressand and Calypso, 1989). Therefore, internationally oriented service companies in leading industrialized countries, notably the United States, became increasingly concerned with national regulations and other obstacles hindering access to foreign markets (Feketekuty, 1988).

Already in June 1978 trade in services was suggested as a possible area for multilateral trade negotiations; this was one and a half years before the conclusion of the Tokyo Round. This initiative of the United States had the form of a rather open-ended proposal in the Consultative Group of 18 (CG18) (*Report of the Consultative Group of 18 to the Council of Representatives in GATT*, 1978). This special GATT body neither was involved in the multinational negotiations nor had any formal decision-making authority; but it had a high-level national representation. Therefore, CG18 was an important GATT institution; among other things, it was responsible for strategic planning within GATT. The significance of CG18 was underlined by the fact that in contrast to other GATT bodies it had a restricted membership. The larger developed and developing countries retained a permanent seat in the group, whereas smaller countries alternated as members (Bradley, 1987; Winham, 1986). Later in the same year the United States followed up this initial move with a proposal that trade in services be included in the liberalization program of the OECD. This initiative had an important indirect significance for a future GATT round as it began to identify the exchange of services across national borders as a form of trade.

To begin with, the discussions about trade in services in CG18 did not have any visible impact on the work undertaken in other GATT bodies. However, by March 1981 trade in services had clearly become a politicized and controversial issue. Already at this point the pattern of conflict and cooperation typical for the later, formal prenegotiations for the Uruguay Round was discernible. The United States and other industrialized countries stated that trade in services should be part of the next GATT round. Brazil, India, and other developing countries represented in CG18 argued that, as trade in services was clearly not covered by the GATT regime, it should not be drawn into the multilateral trade negotiations (*Report of the Consultative Group of 18 to the Council of Representatives in GATT*, 1982). At this point the opposition to trade in services as a topic in the multilateral trade negotiations prevented any formal preparatory work on this issue in GATT itself. Therefore, the United States took the initiative in having the OECD secretariat begin gathering information and analysis with respect to trade in services. In the OECD, prenegotiation activities could be comfortably carried out without the disturbing interference of the assertive opposition of Third World countries (*Activities of OECD in 1981*, 1982). In June 1981 the Council of the OECD, meeting at the ministerial level, issued a strongly worded declaration pointing out the need to eliminate obstacles to trade in services and to strengthen international cooperation in this area (*Activities of OECD in 1981*,

1982). This resolution can be interpreted as a political signal showing the determination of industrialized countries, especially the United States, to struggle for the inclusion of trade in services on the agenda of a new GATT round.

Trade-Related Investments. The new issue of trade-related investments was originally initiated in a process that closely resembled early prenegotiation activities related to trade in services. At a meeting with CG18 in April 1979, again before the closure of the Tokyo Round, the representative of the United States urged that trade-distorting measures related to direct, foreign investments should be brought under GATT disciplines. The U.S. delegate had some support from other industrialized countries but, as in the area of trade in services, also met strong resistance from a group of leading developing countries.

At the October 1979 meeting of CG18 the United States continued its offensive to have trade-related investments accepted as a GATT issue. The U.S. delegate insisted that the GATT secretariat be commissioned to make an inventory of investment measures that might have a negative impact on international trade. However, Washington could not, at this point, mobilize sufficient political support for its view that trade-related investments represented a legitimate GATT issue (Bradley, 1987).

Intellectual Property Rights. The assertion that intellectual property rights represented a new trade issue in the Uruguay Round is not correct. During the Tokyo negotiations Washington made an attempt to put this issue on the agenda. In July 1979 the United States and the European Communities (EC) tabled a joint proposal that the problem of counterfeit goods—one of the main topics in the area of intellectual property rights—should be brought into the Tokyo Round (GATT document L/4817, 1979). This initiative was, however, unsuccessful as the Tokyo negotiations had gone too far in the summer of 1979 to permit the extension of the agenda to a totally new issue. Thus, the significance of the U.S.-EC proposal was primarily as a signal for the future, a declaration of intent.

In 1980 and 1981 the United States began a series of bilateral talks over intellectual property rights, notably the alarming problem of counterfeit goods, with a few other key members in GATT. In addition to the members of the EC, these early consultations involved Canada, Japan, and Switzerland: altogether a group of significant and relatively like-minded countries. In the autumn of 1981 the United States and the EC cosponsored extended informal consultations with selected countries. These efforts were still not sufficient to bring opposing developing countries in line. However, gradually, intellectual property rights were drawn into the GATT system. For instance, this problem area was given a certain legitimacy as a GATT issue when the United States and Canada succeeded in having a dispute over patent rights considered by a GATT panel. GATT found that the U.S. exclusion order under dispute with Canada fell under Article XXd (Bradley, 1987). For the purposes of this analysis the significance of this ruling was that for the first time a specific case relating to the infringement of an

intellectual property right was brought before a competent GATT body. To use a metaphor, the ruling of the panel served as a letter of introduction to GATT of the issue of intellectual property rights.

Old Issues

The informal prenegotiation activities related to the future Uruguay Round also included many of the "old" trade issues. One reason is that some of these questions were generally acknowledged leftovers from the Tokyo Round. In some cases formal follow-up measures had been decided in the Tokyo negotiations. These activities represent a significant link between the Tokyo and the Uruguay Rounds. The precise nature of these linking activities depended on the negotiation results that had been attained in the Tokyo Round and could be quite elaborate.

Take, for instance, the case of safeguards (Article XIX), which was a total failure in the Tokyo Round. Because of the great significance of this issue, it could not just be dropped. Therefore, the outcome of the Tokyo Round included a plan for continued discussions. Likewise, the relative failure to bring the so-called multilateral trade negotiations to codes on nontariff barriers to trade could not be permanently accepted. Special bodies had been appointed to supervise the implementation of the codes. The deliberations in these bodies identified unresolved matters that would have to be considered in a new GATT round (Golt, 1978; United Nations Conference on Trade and Development, 1982). In this way the implementation of the Tokyo Round was clearly linked to the prenegotiations of the Uruguay Round.

General Developments

Thus, although the Uruguay Round did not formally start until the second half of 1986, some prenegotiation work began in 1979. The prenegotiation activities were initially diffuse in character and largely invisible. They were split up and carried out in different forums, partly outside of GATT—for instance, in the OECD. Within GATT itself prenegotiation activities were, until 1984, embedded primarily in the ordinary GATT work that is formally unrelated to the multilateral trade negotiations. This early part of the negotiation process was a subtle game in which the United States and its allies were undertaking a variety of measures to enhance the trade status of the new issues and to draw them closer to the legal framework of GATT. At the end of 1981 this campaign began to produce some tangible results. Now, a more comprehensive institutional infrastructure for a prenegotiation process began to emerge. In 1981 plans were developed to convene a GATT ministerial meeting. Conferences at this high political level had hitherto been exceptional events in GATT. The Conference of Contracting Parties, the supreme decision-making body in GATT, normally meets at the level of head of delegation. However, in June 1981 national delegates to CG18 agreed to begin preparations for a ministerial meeting. At its regular

yearly session, the Contracting Parties set November 1982 as the date for the meeting.

The 1982 ministerial meeting was the result of mixed political motives. One reason was the perceived need to make a strong manifestation in defense of the GATT system, which was threatened by the alarming wave of neoprotectionism that was the companion of the deep recession of the early 1980s (Bhagwati, 1988). Another, and related, motive for the extraordinary ministerial meeting was that many governments, particularly in the Third World, wanted to have a formal, political assessment of the results of the Tokyo Round, which ended in November 1979. A widely acknowledged problem was that there were too many "backlog issues" from the Tokyo Round—matters that had been covered by the negotiations but were not part of their results. Here belonged sensitive issues like agriculture, textiles and clothing, and the so-called gray-area measures—that is, import restrictions contrary to the spirit of the GATT treaty (Hufbauer and Schott, 1985). A third reason for the ministerial meeting was that the coalition led by the United States saw it as an instrument to bring the new trade issues further into the GATT processes (Das, 1984).

The declaration of the 1982 ministerial meeting did not call for a new GATT round. In particular, the large coalition of developing countries insisted that the agreements of the Tokyo Round would have to be implemented properly before discussions started about a new round of negotiations. Still, the ministerial meeting represented some movement toward formal prenegotiations for the future Uruguay Round. Ministers agreed on a medium-term comprehensive work program for GATT. This plan covered many issues that were later to reappear on the agenda of the Uruguay Round. It is especially noteworthy that two of the new trade issues were included in the 1982 comprehensive work program: trade in services and intellectual property rights (Bradley, 1987).

After the 1982 ministerial meeting, prenegotiation activities remained informal for some time. Developments with regard to trade in services are illustrative. As this problem area had not yet been given the status of a GATT issue, the secretariat was not authorized to undertake studies related to it. Therefore, the analysis undertaken by the OECD secretariat was essential to the prenegotiation process. Also national studies, particularly those provided by the U.S. and Canadian governments, contributed greatly to the buildup of the necessary consensual knowledge. Partly as a result of these developments, a series of informal consultations could be held in the first part of 1984 concerning the treatment of trade in services in the GATT context (Bradley, 1987). The next step in the U.S. strategy to prepare for the introduction of the new issues into multilateral trade negotiations was to call for a formal GATT working party to deal with trade in services; this strategy was supported by some other countries. This attempt was, however, unsuccessful because of strong opposition by the large coalition of developing countries led by Brazil and India (GATT document C/M 183, 1984).

Also, with respect to intellectual property rights, Washington tried to convert the 1982 comprehensive GATT work program into concrete political action, primarily by proposing a special GATT working party in this area in 1983. As

in the area of trade in services, developing countries blocked the creation of such an institution. In this case their main argument was that intellectual property rights were already the responsibility of a United Nations institution, the World Intellectual Property Organization (WIPO) (GATT document 170, 1983). The lack of a formal working party in GATT made prenegotiations over intellectual property rights difficult but did not prevent them. That work continued is clearly indicated by a substantial background note on intellectual property rights that was prepared by the GATT secretariat in spite of the fact that it had initially lacked a formal mandate to undertake this work (GATT document MDF/W/19, 1985).

In 1984 the prenegotiation process began to change character and speed somewhat, although the United States proposal at the regular Conference of Contracting Parties in November to start preparations for a new GATT round was rejected. However, this outcome represented only a temporary victory for the opposing developing countries. In the longer term it was probably more important that at the same meeting Washington was successful in establishing formal GATT bodies for both trade in services and counterfeiting, which is part of the issue area of intellectual property rights. These working parties were by no means empty shells with merely a symbolic significance, as is clearly indicated by their rate of activity in 1985. The group on trade in services had six meetings, and the working party on counterfeiting, eight (Bradley, 1987).

In February 1985 the intensive discussions about a possible new GATT round were resumed in CG18. Although no formal decision was made, it seems that this meeting firmly anchored the plans for new multilateral negotiations in the GATT context. At the same time the political support for another GATT round was rapidly growing, primarily because of events outside of GATT institutions. A series of informal ministerial meetings involving approximately twenty key trading nations from the South as well as the North was especially significant in this respect. In this context the United States and its allies had an opportunity for direct consultations at a high political level with the nations opposing the plans for a new GATT round, particularly Brazil and India. The general impression was that the ministerial consultations considerably narrowed the differences between the two sides. At the fourth meeting in Stockholm, in the spring of 1985, it was widely believed that an agreement had been reached to launch a new GATT round (Bradley, 1987). Although this assessment proved to be wrong, the Stockholm meeting did have a considerable impact on the prenegotiations as it helped to introduce the discussion about a possible new round in the GATT Council. This development was significant because, in contrast to CG18, the GATT Council is a formal decision-making body (interviews with officials at the Trade Department of the Swedish Foreign Office, Sept. 1986; Bradley, 1987).

While prenegotiations for the Uruguay Round gradually unfolded in the formal GATT institutions, the industrialized countries struggling for a new round continued to put forth their arguments and display their determination in forums other than GATT. For instance, the Council of the OECD and the Group

of Seven expressed strong support for a new GATT round (*Activities of OECD in 1985,* 1986; Bonn Economic Summit Declaration, 1985).

At the meeting of the GATT Council of June 5, 1985, the negotiations about a new round were still deadlocked by a coalition of some twenty developing countries. The necessary consensus looked unattainable, even though at this point a large majority of states were in favor of a GATT round. Then, on July 24 the United States found a way out of the impasse with a tactical move that had hitherto been unusual in GATT. The U.S. delegation called for a vote on its own proposal that the Contracting Parties to GATT be summoned to an extraordinary conference in September in order to plan for a new GATT round. Technically, the U.S. proposal concerned a procedural question, which required only a majority vote to be settled. Therefore, the "dissidents" could not block a favorable decision (Bradley, 1987; Winham, 1989). This defeat was, however, not merely procedural; it broke the veto power of the dissidents with respect to the real bone of contention—whether preparations for a new GATT round should be started.

One significant outcome of the extraordinary meeting of the Contracting Parties in September 1985 was the establishment of a so-called senior officials' group. The mandate of this body was to find a viable compromise between the positions for and against a new GATT round. The senior officials were not able to complete this task, but still they significantly built up momentum in the prenegotiation process. In January 1986 a preparatory committee was established under the chairmanship of the director general of GATT to begin substantive planning for the future Uruguay Round. The preparatory committee worked hard in the spring of 1986 but was not able to fully clear the way for the ministerial meeting that was anticipated to open the Uruguay Round in September.

Had the prepatory committee been successful, it would have presented ministers at Punta del Este with one single draft text for a final declaration. Instead on the eve of the Punta del Este meeting as many as three competing texts were left on the negotiation table. One text was signed by Switzerland and Colombia but was sponsored by some forty industrialized and developing countries. It argued for the immediate initiation of a new GATT round that, among other things would deal with the new trade issues. This text defined the position of the majority. The second draft text expressed the concerns of the dissidents and essentially argued that it was premature to start new multilateral trade negotiations. The third text, presented by Argentina, was an unsuccessful attempt to find a compromise between the two other proposals (Winham, 1989).

Eventually, in September 1986 ministers met in Punta del Este to decide whether a new GATT round should be launched. The outcome of the week-long meeting remained uncertain until Friday night. The meeting involved a complex distribution of work. During most of the week a conference took place in which the 100-odd participating countries presented formal position papers, which had been prepared in advance. No real bargaining could take place in this body. Therefore, the chair of the ministerial meeting—the foreign minister of Uruguay—organized a heads-of-delegation group to function as a supreme negotiat-

ing body during the Punta del Este meeting. Generally nations were represented by their trade ministers. In this supracommittee politically responsible delegates could concentrate on the sticking points of the negotiation in all issue areas. Special working parties were set up to deal with the most difficult issues—trade in services and agriculture. By the middle of the week many of the controversies had been settled.

To deal with the remaining and more difficult problems, a restricted group of some twenty key countries was set up including main dissidents like Brazil and India. In order to be able to work in secrecy, without media attention, they held meetings outside Punta del Este. With this organization of the negotiations one problem after the other could be eliminated during the week. Still on Friday evening, when negotiations were supposed to be closed, there was no generally accepted text for a final declaration of the ministerial meeting. During the week the Swiss-Colombian text had been generally accepted as a draft, even by the developing countries that were trying to prevent or delay new multilateral trade negotiations. However, they submitted a long list of amendments to the Swiss-Colombian text that reflected their position but could not be easily incorporated into the proposal. Hard bargaining on Friday night and Saturday morning was eventually successful. Early Saturday morning all secretarial resources available were fully mobilized. On Saturday afternoon the final declaration of the Punta del Este meeting was communicated to the media. Prenegotiations were over; the Uruguay Round had formally started (Finger and Oleschowski, 1987; Winham, 1989).

Functions

This account demonstrates the complexity of the prenegotiations of the Uruguay Round. In certain respects they originated in the Tokyo Round, but in others they started much later. Initially, prenegotiations were split up into a number of subprocesses, some of which took place outside the GATT context. The OECD played a particularly important role in this respect. Gradually, the various subprocesses became more and more integrated and increasingly channeled into GATT institutions. At first, prenegotiation activities unfolded in GATT bodies that were not directly related to the multilateral trade negotiations. Later on, special institutions were established for the preparation of the Uruguay Round. Essentially, the cumbersome prenegotiations served two functions: to build up a political platform to support the proposal for a new GATT round and to delimit and clarify the agenda of these negotiations. Setting the agenda implied the establishment of a common outlook for the Uruguay Round.

Evolution of the Political Platform. Before the Uruguay Round a political platform for multilateral trade negotiations had evolved. The United States had taken the first initiative by inviting its main trading partners and competitors to consultations about a new GATT round. Before the Tokyo Round these discussions had been conducted among the big three in the GATT system: the United

States, the EC, and Japan. A number of selected middle powers in the issue area of trade were then allowed into the prenegotiations. These states were invariably industrialized nations and members of the OECD: Canada, the European Free Trade Association (EFTA) group, and Australia and New Zealand with respect to trade in agricultural goods. After they reached a general agreement to launch a new GATT round, an invitation was issued to other trading nations—primarily the Contracting Parties to GATT—to take part in the formal prenegotiations (Golt, 1978; Winham, 1986).

This familiar pattern of interaction reemerged in the Uruguay Round, but only partially. As in the past the United States was the initiator of the prenegotiations and conducted privileged consultations with its main trading partners. From the start, however, a large coalition of developing countries led by Brazil and India had been involved in the prenegotiations, they tried to prevent a new GATT round in the near future as proposed by the United States and other industrialized countries (Strange, 1984). This coalition of dissidents was particularly hostile to the idea that the agenda of the multilateral negotiations should include the new trade issues—trade in services, intellectual property rights, and trade-related investments. The new element in the prenegotiations as compared with earlier rounds was the open confrontation between two blocks in which the new GATT round itself was at issue. However, because of defections the balance of influence between the two sides shifted gradually to the disadvantage of the coalition of developing countries. The veto power of the dissidents gradually weakened as a number of export-oriented countries in Southeast Asia and Latin America changed their position and became favorable of a new GATT round. Still, the deadlock in the prenegotiations remained until the summer of 1986— only a few months before the official opening of the Uruguay Round.

If the protracted impasse of the prenegotiations was a new feature in the multilateral GATT negotiations, so also was the process through which this deadlock was broken. In earlier GATT rounds the great powers, especially the United States, had exercised decisive leadership of the prenegotiations. At the end of the prenegotiations of the Uruguay Round a growing coalition of middle powers and small states partly took over some of the leadership role. The most concrete manifestation of the accomplishment of this coalition was the Swiss-Colombian submission that was eventually accepted as a draft text for the Punta del Este meeting. The origin is to be found in extended cooperation among a number of OECD countries with "free-trade" commercial policies, notably Canada, the EFTA nations, Australia, and New Zealand. This group, commonly called G9, invited a number of developing countries to join in its effort to draft a viable text for a ministerial meeting opening a new trade round. Initially, some twenty developing countries took part in this work, but in the end almost fifty participated (Bradley, 1987). Thus emerged the large coalition of small and middle powers that was able to build up a tenable middle ground between, on the one hand, the United States and the other two great powers (the EC and Japan) and, on the other, the dissidents led by Brazil and India.

Delimitation of Issues. Prenegotiations were partly about whether the Uruguay Round should be held at all. They also included a confrontation over which issues should be included in the agenda. This process of issue selection was closely related to what may be called "the game of issue clarification." Some of the issues to be dealt with in the Uruguay Round were leftovers from earlier GATT negotiations; prenegotiations picked up these issues in the shape they had been in when the Tokyo Round was terminated. As a rule, negotiators were familiar with these backlog issues and the positions taken by key countries. The issue of the safeguard clause is a good example. However, some of these old GATT issues required clarification—notably, trade in agricultural goods, one of the high-policy issues of the Uruguay Round. Early in the prenegotiations key countries agreed that agriculture should be covered by a new GATT round but could not agree on the terms. For example, the United States wanted to phase out all production and export subsidies, a proposal that many other countries, including the EC, could not accept. In order to argue for a position, each side needed an analytical model to aggregate and compare different types of subsidies. For this reason, prenegotiations in the area of agricultural trade were to a large extent a struggle among the United States, the EC, and other leading countries about which analytical concepts and methods should be used in the negotiations (Finger and Oleschowski, 1987).

The prenegotiation struggle over the new trade issues was still more dependent on issue clarification. Take the case of trade in services. Under this new heading a number of well-known economic activities were hidden—for example, shipping, air transport, banking, and insurance. The problem was, however, that these issues had hitherto not been considered part of international trade. The framing of the international exchange of services as a trade issue required new concepts and new data, including basic statistics. Furthermore, a careful analysis was needed to clarify how existing GATT rules could be applied to trade in services with due consideration given to the great differences among sectors. For instance, only some services are transferred across national borders as if they were goods. In other cases the export of a service requires the establishment of a firm or a branch in the importing country (for example, in the sector of insurance) or temporary migration (for example, construction) (Bressand and Calypso, 1989).

To become negotiable, trade in services, as well as other new trade issues, required extensive as well as innovative analysis. The development of the Uruguay Round was seemingly considerably influenced by the fact that the secretariat of GATT was not able to fully undertake this task in the early stages of prenegotiations. One explanation was the lack of necessary analytical capacity—the staff of the GATT secretariat had been recruited primarily to manage the existing treaty. A second reason was that it was not until late in the process of prenegotiations that the GATT secretariat was authorized to study the new trade issues. Therefore, the prenegotiation work became heavily dependent on the analytical work undertaken by the OECD and individual industrialized countries. Leading industrial countries like the United States, the EC, and Canada were in a very

good position to shape the consensual knowledge necessary for negotiations on the new issues so that it was in line with their own particular interests. This analytical dominance was strongly resented by developing countries, particularly larger nations like Brazil and India with aspirations to influence negotiations. It is very likely that this asymmetry with respect to analytical capacity and influence over the building of consensual knowledge hardened the position of the coalition of dissidents.

Formal Bargaining

Once the Punta del Este ministerial meeting had succeeded in formulating a final declaration, there was an immediate qualitative change in the process of the Uruguay negotiations. A number of goals were set. The main objectives agreed on were to strengthen and broaden the GATT system, further liberalize the growth of world trade, strengthen and improve rules governing international trade transactions, and increase the responsiveness of the GATT system to changes in its international environment. Through these goals negotiations were given a clear direction that, in turn, made it possible to set up an elaborate institutional machinery.

Organization of the Negotiations

Leaning on the experience gained in earlier GATT rounds, participants established an organizational structure for the Uruguay Round soon after the closure of the Punta del Este meeting. Among the Uruguay Round institutions the Trade Negotiations Committee (TNC) had the highest authority. Its tasks were to supervise and coordinate negotiations in all issue areas. Below TNC were two main bodies, one of which was the Group on the Negotiations on Services (GNS). As the result of a compromise made at Punta del Este, GNS was technically outside the GATT framework. It was to be decided at a later date whether the outcomes of its negotiations were to be incorporated in GATT. The second main body under TNC was the Group on Negotiations on Goods (GNG), whose responsibilities covered everything negotiated in the Uruguay Round except trade in services. Real negotiations were to take place in fourteen negotiating groups reporting to the GNG and concerned with the following issue areas: tariffs; nontariff barriers to trade; natural resources; textiles and clothing; agriculture; tropical products; GATT articles; multilateral trade agreements negotiated in the Tokyo Round; safeguards; subsidies and countervailing duties; intellectual property rights; trade-related investments; dispute settlement; and functioning of the GATT system. All these negotiating bodies were, in principle, open to all countries that were formal participants of the Uruguay Round (Finger and Oleschowski, 1987).

In addition to dealing with all these issues, the parties engaged in the Uruguay Round had committed themselves to undertake standstill and rollback measures. The essence of standstill was a promise not to impose any new trade-

restrictive measures even though they were not clearly prohibited by GATT (for example, so-called voluntary export restraints) as long as the Uruguay negotiations went on. Rollback meant that negotiating parties were to begin phasing out existing trade-restrictive measures of this type. The implementation of the standstill and rollback commitments, which represented a particularly great grievance for developing countries, was to be supervised by a special surveillance body (United Nations Conference on Trade and Development, 1982).

The institutional structure created for the Uruguay Round indicates the general character of the negotiation process. The large number of negotiating groups gives support to the assertion that the Uruguay Round represented the most ambitious multilateral trade negotiations attempted so far. In particular two properties of the process should be emphasized; first, the complexity confronting negotiating parties and, second, the compartmentalization of the agenda. Each negotiating group in reality represented a quasi-autonomous negotiation process in its own right with its own particular problems, sticking points, conceptual framework, and to some extent national representation. Take, for instance, the negotiating group on trade in agricultural goods, which, among other things, was given the mission of dissolving the almost structural conflict of interest in this area between the United States and the EC. Or consider the negotiating group on textiles and clothing, which had the task of eliminating a regime of managed trade (the Multi-Fibre Agreement) that had frustrated a great number of developing countries for many years (GATT document MTN/TNC/11, 1989). These two cases indicate the magnitude of the purely political difficulties that confronted negotiating parties in the Uruguay Round.

The new trade issues were not only politically problematic but also represented another type of complexity because of the lack of sufficient knowledge and information about the issues. Although progress was considerable with respect to issue clarification in the prenegotiations, this work was not sufficient. The buildup of consensual knowledge had to continue in the formal negotiations. This necessity complicated negotiations, as some developing countries that were acknowledged stakeholders in the issue area concerned were handicapped in this continued process of issue clarification. Their only means to influence the process was to obstruct or delay it.

An overview of the main problems dealt with in the negotiating groups gives an idea of the complexity and magnitude of the agenda of the Uruguay Round.

- NG1. *Tariffs.* Reduction of tariff rates; formula (related to across-the-board reductions) versus request/offer procedures (related to bilateral negotiations); tariff escalation.
- NG2. *Nontariff barriers.* Continued dismantling of nontariff barriers negotiated in the Tokyo Round; procedures for assessing the equivalence of offers/requests.
- NG3. *Natural resources.* Product coverage; tariff escalation; quantitative restriction; the problem of secure supply.

- NG4. *Textiles and clothing.* Integration of the Multi-Fibre Agreement into the GATT regime.
- NG5. *Agriculture.* Improved market access through elimination of special import measures; changes in the GATT rules on subsidies.
- NG6. *Tropical products.* Product coverage; tariff escalation under generalized special preferences (to developing countries) or multilateral trade negotiation (nondiscrimination) principles; reciprocity or nonreciprocity for developing countries.
- NG7. *GATT Articles.* Revision of Article 2.1a, tariff bindings; Article 24, customs unions/free-trade areas; Articles 12, 14, 15, and 18, balance of payments; Article 28, modification of tariff schedules; Article 17, state trading; Article 21, national security; Article 25, waivers; and the protocol for provisional application of GATT.
- NG8. *Multilateral trade agreements and arrangements.* Elaboration and clarification of the codes negotiated in the Tokyo Round; increased participation of developing countries.
- NG9. *Safeguards.* Selectivity with respect to the use of safeguard measures; transparency; objective criteria for safeguard action; retaliation; structural adjustment to preempt the need for safeguard action.
- NG10. *Subsidies and countervailing duties.* Definition of subsidy; disciplines with respect to export subsidies; review of Articles 6 and 16.
- NG11. *Trade-related intellectual property rights (TRIPs).* Integration of trade rules pertaining to TRIPs; consideration of international cooperation and regimes related to other international organizations, especially WIPO.
- NG12. *Trade-related investment measures.* Elaboration of GATT rules that help eliminate the adverse effects of investment measures on trade.
- NG13. *Dispute settlement.* Effective enforcement of GATT panel rulings through, for instance, increased transparency and improvement of procedures.
- NG14. *Functioning of the GATT system.* Procedures for the surveillance of trade policies; enhanced decision making through ministerial involvement; better coordination between GATT and the International Monetary Fund and the World Bank.

In addition, GNS was responsible for a considerable number of issues including statistical reporting on trade in services, the conceptual framework for the integration of trade in services in GATT, coverage, and analysis of individual service sectors (Finger and Oleschowski, 1987; *The Uruguay Round*, 1988).

In order to cope with this extensive and complex agenda an overall plan of action was agreed on, including a timetable (Finger and Oleschowski, 1987; *The Uruguay Round*, 1988). By December 1986 all negotiating groups had begun to implement this general plan in their respective areas of responsibility. As agreed, a midterm review was held at the ministerial level in Montreal in late December 1988. The main purpose of this meeting was to take stock of activities, although a few negotiation results were codified already at this point with respect

to the issue areas of dispute settlement and functioning of the GATT system. For instance, at Montreal it was decided that ministerial meetings should be held more frequently than before and that reviews should recurrently be made of the trade policy of individual countries (GATT document MTN/TNC/11, 1989). In the summer of 1990 another comprehensive stocktaking took place, although this time at the level of head of delegation. The ambition, not realized, was to establish one single draft for an agreement in each negotiation group by the end of July. These texts were then to be polished during the autumn so that a ministerial meeting in Brussels scheduled for early December could terminate the Uruguay Round (GATT document MTN/TNC/15, 1990). This plan of action was essentially implemented.

Steered by this strategic plan, all negotiating bodies worked in approximately the same way. They were all serviced by the GATT secretariat on equal terms, although GNS formally remained outside GATT. The secretariat has no formal authority to take initiatives or otherwise steer negotiations. Still, the secretariat exercised a certain influence. The input into the Uruguay Round made by the secretariat consisted of background information and analyses, summary records of negotiation sessions, and syntheses of country positions. In particular, in the later part of the negotiations, when there was stalemate in important issue areas, the director general of GATT tried to act as mediator.

Continuously serviced by the secretariat, the average negotiation group worked approximately as follows during the Uruguay Round. Early in the negotiation active nations for the most part submitted papers discussing the issues at hand and the problems or the tasks they would like the particular negotiation group to address. The secretariat was asked to provide background information— for example, about the work undertaken by other international organizations. In the following stage of the process nations began to submit discussion papers to the negotiation group that directly expressed their interests and ambition. Eventually, draft texts or elements thereof began to be tabled. Hence, activities in the negotiating groups in many ways resembled committee work within a national administration. All nations that were formal members of the negotiating groups did not take an active part in the negotiations. For instance, many developing countries were mostly absent from the sessions or were passive observers. Active states behaved quite differently. In order to understand the working processes in the various negotiating groups their performance as actors—nations—has to be considered.

Actor Performance

Sometimes multilateral negotiations lead to an exchange of measurable concessions. In the GATT context the typical example is negotiations on tariffs. Bargaining over this type of issue, which can be distributed with the help of a clean quantitative measure, can be handled easily through an offer/request procedure. In the GATT process offers and requests with respect to tariffs have been made in two different ways, either product by product or with a formula for across-the-

board reductions. In the GATT negotiations the offer/request procedure had been used in other issue areas as well as in tariffs issues. For instance, in the Tokyo negotiations on government procurement a formula was found that permitted an exchange of concessions; the measurable unit was the number of state agencies to be covered by agreed-upon liberalization measures (Winham, 1986).

However, for most of the issues on the agenda of the Uruguay Round it was not possible to find, or invent, quantifiable bargaining chips. Instead, the exchange of concessions in most issue areas took place through a process that may be described as "editing diplomacy": the establishment of a convention text. The objective of this kind of bargaining was to reach agreement on the creation or modification of regime elements—principles, norms, rules, procedures—related to a particular issue area. In editing diplomacy bargaining does not concern the immediate distribution of a certain value—for example, market access as indicated by the size of an import duty. Instead negotiations concern the establishment of conditions, in the form of "rules of the game," that influence the disputed distribution of values in a more diffuse way in the longer term.

Editing diplomacy strongly characterized the negotiation process in the Uruguay Round by conditioning the tactical and strategic considerations of participating nations. Typically, editing diplomacy evolved in two stages. The first was characterized primarily by the negotiation task of issue clarification, an activity that usually started early in the prenegotiations. In this stage there was little bloc building; instead nations tried to express their individual concerns in the process of agenda setting. Typical submissions tried either to explain the nature of the issue or to design general approaches to the resolution of negotiation problems. In complex trade negotiations such editing is a demanding kind of diplomacy requiring a high degree of professional skill and access to the necessary technical expertise and information. These qualified demands help explain the relatively low degree of active participation in the Uruguay negotiations. Approximately 70 percent of the formal participants were passive, or almost passive, in the negotiations following the Punta del Este meeting.

The second stage in the process of editing diplomacy was characterized by text consolidation. This stage entailed the beginning of movements of convergence in the many negotiating groups toward a few dominant positions followed by the search for a single text. These developments coincided with the emergence of coalitions of nations supporting the various main proposals or texts.[2] In this connection noteworthy new patterns of conflict and cooperation emerged that had not been present in the Kennedy and Tokyo Rounds. In these two earlier GATT rounds the relationship between the United States and the EC, be it cooperative or conflictual, had been the axis around which negotiations had rotated. The key issue area of trade in agriculture is a good example. In the Tokyo Round the conflict of interest, and recurrent confrontation, between the United States and the EC set the terms for the bargaining process and for coalition building. In several cases the U.S.-EC dispute over an issue was the main reason that it had been put on the agenda in the first place. A common strategy for each side was to try to build up a winning coalition before the end game started. The

U.S.-EC confrontation contributed considerably to delimiting the strategic options of other countries. Thus, one policy choice many countries had to make was whether they should basically support the U.S. position or the EC position. It is interesting that the rapidly rising economic power of Japan was one of the nations keeping a conspicuously low profile throughout the negotiations. Some of the middle powers in the issue area of trade saw an opportunity to act as creative mediators between the United States and the EC. One example is the so-called Swiss formula, which helped to settle the transatlantic dispute over tariff harmonization. Developing countries were essentially kept outside the negotiation process until the last stage, when their options were limited to accepting or rejecting draft agreements worked out by industrialized countries. As a result a large protest alliance appeared at the very end, when active nations thought that the time was ripe for the signing of the agreements reached in the negotiating groups. The closure of the Tokyo Round was delayed several months, and still only a handful of developing countries signed the codes on nontariff barriers to trade (Winham, 1986).

The pattern of state interaction in the Uruguay Round had many similarities with that of the Tokyo Round. There were, however, also significant differences in this respect. Recall from the above account that many developing countries asserted themselves in the earliest stages of the prenegotiations and then remained active players in the process. The significance of the participation of developing countries is indicated by the fact that representatives of the Third World were elected chairpersons in several of the negotiating groups, including the controversial and politically important GNS. In earlier rounds the governments of industrialized countries had retained a firm control over all significant negotiating groups.

At the early prenegotiations the North-South confrontation that had disturbed the end game of the Tokyo Round reappeared and threatened to block the process. However, the Uruguay Round never developed into full-scale, ideological trench war between developed and developing countries. One explanation is probably that leading countries like Brazil and India abstained from taking grand ideological stands. Instead they tried to defend their own national interests in the negotiating groups of most significance to them. This posture was contrary to the principles of a solidarity policy, which would have been to keep the large coalition of Third World countries together. As a result the Third World alliance gradually shrank as prenegotiations proceeded. A growing number of members of this group chose, or were forced, to pursue national strategies. One result was that developing countries increasingly chose to form or take part in coalitions created to defend narrow sectoral interests related to market access for a certain product group such as bovine meat.

Thus, in contrast to earlier GATT rounds there emerged a few issue-specific coalitions made up only of developing countries. One example is the surprisingly assertive coalition concerned with tropical products that was made up largely of poor and weak West African countries. A second case is the "tiger coalition" in the negotiating group on safeguards, which included newly indus-

trialized countries in Southeast Asia, notably the members of the Association of Southeast Asian Nations and Hong Kong and Korea (Hamilton and Whalley, 1989). A third example of a "pure" coalition of developing countries was the Group of Ten of the Uruguay Round, the consolidated coalition of Third World countries, led by Brazil and India, that was striving to block or at least delay the preparations for new multilateral trade negotiations. Although it shrank over time, this coalition continued to oppose the inclusion of the new trade issues on the agenda of the Uruguay Round long after prenegotiations were formally concluded at Punta del Este.

Another noteworthy development was the emergence of issue-specific mixed coalitions consisting of both developed and developing countries. The Cairns group, originally established in early 1986, is the most well-known example. It included thirteen or fourteen countries that were competitive exporters of agricultural goods: Argentina, Australia, Brazil, Canada, Chile, Colombia, Fiji (part of the time), Hungary, Indonesia, Malaysia, New Zealand, the Philippines, Thailand, and Uruguay. The Cairns group developed into a key actor in the important sector of trade in agricultural goods (Hamilton and Whalley, 1989).

Besides the issue-specific alliances an important mixed coalition of industrialized and developing countries emerged that did not limit its activities to a particular issue area but tried to influence the Uruguay negotiations generally. This was the de la Paix group, a continuation of the coalition of middle and minor trading nations that had paved the way for the Punta del Este meeting.[3] Originally the de la Paix group consisted of Australia, Canada, Colombia, Hungary, Malaysia, New Zealand, the Philippines, Singapore, South Korea, Sweden (as a representative of the Nordic group), Switzerland, Thailand, Uruguay, and Zaire. This grouping of states did not present position papers in its own name. Rather, the members of the de la Paix group strove collectively to promote negotiation solutions at the table, which was a movement toward liberalization and nondiscrimination in the issue area concerned. It is noteworthy that the de la Paix group included neither any of the great industrialized actors (the United States, the EC, or Japan) nor any of the dissident countries from the South (for example, Brazil, India, or Mexico) that confronted the industrialized states in several issue areas, notably with respect to the new trade issues (Hamilton and Whalley, 1989). This make-up permitted the de la Paix group to play a role in the negotiations that can be described as a mixture of leadership and mediation.

The End Game

In the summer of 1990, negotiations in the Uruguay Round had certainly moved forward from the situation at the time of the Punta del Este meeting. Issues had been considerably clarified. Negotiations generally concerned two, or a few, proposals for a document defining the outcome of the work in the negotiating groups. But still many of the basic negotiation problems remained unresolved. In several areas the conflict of interest between the main contenders had attained the character of a zero-sum game. This was notably the case in the most proble-

matic conflict: that between the United States and the EC with respect to trade in agricultural products. The transatlantic dispute over agriculture—as well as over other issues—was, however, by no means the only remaining serious conflict. For instance, a group of Latin American countries delayed the signing of the declaration from the midterm review in Montreal for several months on the grounds that sufficient results had not yet been attained in the area of agriculture and in other areas of interest to developing countries (GATT document MTN/TNC/11, 1989). Among the new trade issues, trade in services remained especially controversial during the Uruguay Round.

Therefore, it is not entirely surprising that the results of the grand stock-taking exercise in the summer of 1990 were disappointing. The initial goal was to have a draft for a single text ready in all negotiating groups at this point. When, in the spring of 1990, it became obvious that this objective was unrealistic the new concept of a "profile" was introduced. A profile was not a single text, but it described its main elements. However, by the end of July delegations had not been successful in producing such profiles in all negotiating groups. In some areas stocktaking had to substitute for a profile (GATT document MTN/TNC/15, 1990). Part of the reason was that unfinished bargaining over relatively minor details remained in the would-be single text. However, in other sectors unresolved principal bones of contention prevented the drafting of a single text. One notable example is trade in agricultural products; another is textiles and clothing. The problem was that these difficult areas held back progress in other sectors where it would probably have been possible to reach an agreement if negotiations had been conducted autonomously. The basic conflicts of interest among the key actors were, hence, not resolved and eliminated from the agenda. They were rather swept under the carpet—a strategy that in the end proved to be self-defeating (Winham and Kizer, 1993).

Preparations

In early December 1990 ministers from the nations participating in the Uruguay Round met in Brussels in order to close the negotiations before the end of the year. Intensive preparations for the Brussels meeting went on in all negotiating groups from September onward. According to plan, the work was to be devoted to hammering out the details of the remaining unresolved differences. The results, scheduled to be codified in Brussels, would be separate texts from all negotiating groups and a single final text summarizing the total outcome of the Uruguay negotiations. Autumn was a hectic period with recurrent meetings in all groups. However, in November it was clear that the Brussels meeting would not merely be ceremonial. Instead, the outcome of the Uruguay Round clearly depended on the ability of the ministers to conduct and terminate real negotiations in the most difficult areas like agriculture, textiles, dispute settlement, and the new trade issues. This task was highly complicated because negotiation work in relatively manageable areas was severely restrained by the outstanding politically sensitive problems in other areas. Part of the reason is that some negoti-

ation problems can be resolved only in a final and decisive exchange of concessions. The dilemma is that negotiating parties will not engage themselves fully
in bargaining over such outstanding matters until they are certain that negotiations are, in fact, in the process of being terminated once and for all.

Thus, when the ministers arrived in Brussels, they were confronted with
a heavy work load and a highly uncertain outcome to the negotiations. In was,
hence, not possible to bring the Brussels meeting to a successful end. The meeting
was organized in a constructive and effective way. Working parties were set up
under the leadership of selected ministers to deal with the outstanding issues.
Progress was made in many areas, and minor movements of position by principal
actors were discernible in some difficult areas. However, it was impossible to
eliminate the main sticking points in sensitive areas—for instance, those pertaining to agriculture. The key actors were unwilling to yield sufficiently to pave the
way for an agreement. After a week of intensive, more or less continuous, negotiations the ministers had to leave Brussels without having been able to bring the
Uruguay Round to a successful end.

Management of Failure

There seems to have been a wide consensus that it would have been disastrous
to acknowledge and accept the failure of the ministerial meeting in Brussels
officially. Accordingly, the outcome of the Uruguay Round was left indeterminate. No formal decision was taken to continue negotiations after Brussels. However, in his concluding speech the Uruguayan foreign minister chairing the
meeting offered the suggestion that the director general of GATT undertake a
thorough evaluation of progress made in the various sectors during the meeting,
a proposal to which no nation objected.

Thus, in early 1991 the staff of the GATT secretariat started to analyze by
sector the progress made in Brussels. The criterion was the texts produced for the
ministerial meeting. Arthur Dunkel, the director general of GATT, had a proposal accepted for a new system of negotiating groups in which some of the older
bodies were integrated into one. Formal decisions to that effect were taken in the
three main bodies of the Uruguay Round on April 25, 1991 (GATT, *News of the
Uruguay Round of Multilateral Negotiations* 047). The new groups were to deal
with the following issue packages: market access (tariffs, nontariff measures,
natural resource–based products, tropical products); textiles and clothing; agriculture; trade-related investments and rule making (subsidies and countervailing
duties, antidumping, safeguards, preshipment inspection, rules of origin, technical barriers to trade, import licensing procedures, customs valuation, government procurement, and a number of specific GATT articles); trade-related
intellectual property rights; institutions; and trade in services (GATT, *News of
the Uruguay Round of Multilateral Negotiations* 047).

Some of these new groups had initial meetings in April. These sessions
dealt essentially with minor procedural matters but were still politically important as they signified that the Uruguay Round had now been formally re-

launched. However, the rate of activity was low in the formal negotiation machinery. In the summer of 1991 a new stocktaking exercise took place in Geneva, where the progress made in Brussels and thereafter was formally assessed and consolidated in most areas. A new plan of action was agreed on for continued negotiation; it was implemented in the autumn. The overall objective was to terminate the negotiations before the end of the year. Therefore, October and November were scheduled to serve as a deal-making stage. The new revision of the Final Act, originally prepared for the ministerial meeting of December 1990, was scheduled to be finished by early November 1991 (GATT document MTN.TNC/W/35.1; GATT, *News of the Uruguay Round of Multilateral Negotiations* 050).

Some progress was made in these consultations, as indicated by several meetings of TNC during 1991. For instance, a seemingly viable general agreement on trade in services was worked out in this period. Also, in other areas some progress was made with respect to the technical problems. At a meeting of TNC on November 7, 1991, it was decided that negotiations were going to be sped up to ensure the conclusion of the Uruguay Round in December. From then on the chairpersons of all the remaining negotiation groups were to conduct "continuous and simultaneous negotiations." In his main stocktaking speech Director General Dunkel of GATT, functioning as the chair of TNC, said that this November represented "the best available window of opportunity" for making constructive deals (GATT, *News of the Uruguay Round of Multilateral Negotiations* 050). However, Dunkel also reported that "the chairmen of the negotiating groups have informed me that progress so far has not been such as to offer a sufficient basis for compromise solutions on the essential substantive issue" (GATT, *News of the Uruguay Round of Multilateral Negotiations*, 050, pp. 2–3).

Again the pessimistic assessment of the situation proved to be the realistic one. In December 1991 a draft Final Act had been accepted including texts covering all areas negotiated on in the Uruguay Round. Furthermore, the draft Final Act also included a revised proposal that GATT be transformed into a multilateral trade organization. However, negotiating parties had not been able to agree on commitments regarding market access in any of the three main areas—industrial goods, agricultural products, and trade in services ("GATT inför Uruguay-rundans slutförhandling," 1992).

In January 1992 TNC met to take stock of the situation in order to relaunch the end game of the Uruguay Round. It was agreed that henceforth the negotiations would be conducted on four parallel tracks. The first two tracks concerned the difficult negotiations on market access with respect to, first, industrial products and agricultural goods and, second, trade in services. On the third track a detailed, final examination was to be conducted of all the texts that had been negotiated in the Uruguay Round. Finally, the fourth track was reserved for the eventual renegotiations of particular elements of the outcome and trade-offs at the decisive stage of the end game. The new target date for the conclusion of the round was mid-April 1993 ("GATT infür Uruguay-rundans slutfürhandling," 1992). However, when, at the stipulated time, TNC had an informal

meeting, it could note only that the end game had never actually taken off. Participants felt that "despite efforts at the highest political levels in key capitals, little or no concrete progress had been achieved since January and that tracks 1, 2, and 3 were, in effect, blocked" (GATT, *News of the Uruguay Round of Multilateral Negotiations* 052, pp. 2–3).

During the summer and early autumn of 1992 TNC held no formal meetings, although several informal discussions took place. Of these the unsuccessful bilateral talks between the United States and the EC on trade in agricultural goods were crucial. The unresolved transatlantic conflict of interest blocked the negotiations in all issue areas. At the time of the presidential elections in the United States a new meeting of TNC was devoted primarily to crisis management (GATT, *News of the Uruguay Round of Multilateral Negotiations* 052). After having noted the seriousness of the situation, "an overwhelming majority of participants" expressed their "deep concern and helplessness" in the face of a deadlock in the Uruguay Round because of the incapacity of the United States and EC to resolve their conflict of interest (GATT, *News of the Uruguay Round of Multilateral Negotiations* 052, pp. 2–3). These same nations voiced their dissatisfaction with this state of affairs and turned to the United States and the EC "to urge their cooperation in restarting multilateral negotiations in Geneva"— that is, within the formal, multilateral negotiation machinery of the Uruguay Round (GATT, *News of the Uruguay Round of Multilateral Negotiations* 052, p. 4). The chair of TNC, the director general of GATT, was commissioned to communicate these deep concerns to the EC and the United States.

When TNC reconvened on November 26, Director General Dunkel reported on his meetings with the authorities in Brussels and Washington, who, according to Dunkel, had responded in the most positive and constructive terms, even more so because they "were already engaged in a process of intensive consultations" (GATT, *News of the Uruguay Round of Multilateral Negotiations* 054, p. 1). Therefore, Dunkel, widely supported by the majority of the participants in the negotiations, proposed the reactivation of the Uruguay Round on the basis of the same four-track approach that had been established in January. Also, in other respects the GATT secretariat elaborated a renewed negotiation plan (GATT, *News of the Uruguay Round of Multilateral Negotiations* 054). This ambition was seemingly supported by the EC and the United States. On the eve of the Christmas vacation the chair of TNC received a formal message from the highest authorities of the United States (the president) and the EC (the chair of the Council of Ministers and the president of the European Commission) stating that "the aim should be to conclude a balanced and comprehensive agreement by the middle of January" (GATT, *News of the Uruguay Round of Multilateral Negotiations* 056, p. 1). However, once more the target date was further advanced with a remaining hope that, in the best of all worlds, negotiations would be concluded before the extended mandate of the U.S. executive expired in March 1993. This deadline too has past. Thus, the final outcome of the Uruguay Round still remains uncertain.

Outcome

It may be argued that whatever eventually came out of it the Uruguay Round was a failure, at least in terms of its own objectives. The essence of the negotiation after the unsuccessful ministerial meeting of December 1990 was the management of failure. The Uruguay Round was seemingly too vast an enterprise to be permitted to flounder. It should be stressed, however, that failure is relative. Even if the negotiated results of the Uruguay Round appear meager, its total outcome may still have some significance. According to the "bicycle theory" a round of multilateral trade negotiations supports the international trade regime by just being conducted, particularly in times of economic recession like the early 1990s (Winham, 1986). The analytical work and the bargaining that have taken place in the Uruguay Round have paved the way for future trade negotiations, not least with regard to the new trade issues. However, these various contributions do not conceal the fact that after the Brussels meeting no significant breakthrough occurred in the main political controversies. The organizational plan for the end game had to be redone repeatedly, and the date for the conclusion of the negotiation was only finally set, by the fear of total failure, at the end of 1993.

This story does not provide a clear answer to the question of why it was so much more difficult to bring the Uruguay Round to a successful end than earlier GATT negotiations. It does, however, offer a few suggestions. Seemingly some of the answers relate to the complexity of the agenda and the distribution of power between trading nations. One dimension of complexity is simply the number of items on the agenda. According to this criterion the Uruguay Round was, no doubt, more complex than any of its predecessors, as is indicated by the sheer number of formal negotiating bodies. Furthermore, the agenda dealt with in some of the fifteen negotiating bodies in operation before the Brussels meeting was extremely vast. For instance, trade in services pertains to a sector that makes up 60 percent or more of the economy in many developed countries and includes a multitude of highly different activities such as professional services, transportation, insurance, and banking. The agenda of the Uruguay Round was also highly complex from a qualitative point of view. Several of the issues required the gathering of a considerable amount of information as well as an extensive technical analysis to become negotiable. This was typically the case with the new trade issues.

One result of the extensive agenda was that the Uruguay Round meant different things to different governments. Some governments, especially in the Third World, were concerned primarily with the consolidation of the results of the Tokyo Round and the old trade issues. Others were interested primarily in bringing the new trade issues into the GATT regime. These countries were also usually active in most negotiation groups. In contrast, many developing countries were seriously engaged in only a few sectors because their interests as well as their negotiation capacity were limited. Thus, the Uruguay Round was characterized by a wide variety of diverging interests even for a multilateral negotiation. The traditional GATT procedure for handling this particular kind of

complexity was to conduct the negotiations in the various groups independently of each other until the end game at the highest political level started. However, when constructive cross-sectoral trade-offs could not be worked out, the unmastered issue linkages turned into major obstacles to a comprehensive agreement.

It seems that the success of earlier GATT rounds had been due partly to assertive and effective U.S. leadership. For various reasons the United States was not in a position to perform the same role in the Uruguay Round. First, the two great economic powers, the EC and Japan, counterbalanced the U.S. leadership and had more influence in these negotiations than in earlier multilateral trade negotiations. For instance, one of the problems in the crucial agricultural sector was the total inflexibility of the EC—and of Japan—in the face of strong U.S. demands. In earlier GATT rounds the same kind of conflict of interest had been at hand, too, but in the end U.S. pressure had produced a compromise.[4]

Second, the power relationships among the leading nations had become more symmetrical by the Uruguay Round; the number of active players had increased considerably since the Tokyo Round. The reason was the higher and more assertive participation of several developing countries. Thus, while U.S. hegemony was definitely gone, the problem of leadership had become more pronounced. At the same time as single actors were no longer able to confront the negotiation process, the leadership function had become more demanding than in earlier GATT rounds, since there were more significant interests that had to be adjusted to one another. Thus, a disturbing observation is that the increasing "democratization" of GATT talks occurring in the Uruguay Round—the participation of more countries in informal negotiation groups—is not entirely beneficial. It seems that multilateral processes tend to become unmanageable unless some critical decisions can be taken by small groups of leading countries.

Notes

1. The Contending Analyses section of this book (Part Two) does not cover the whole process of negotiations in the Uruguay Round, which is still underway. The authors of the theory chapters were able to follow developments only until about the time of the Brussels meeting in December 1990. The assessment of the Uruguay Round at that point as basically a "failure story" has, however, not been gainsaid by later events described at the end of this chapter.

2. This assessment is based on an overview of the submissions made by active participants in the various negotiating groups. See GATT documents MTN.GNG/NG1-14/W and MTN.GNS/W. The Contending Analyses section of this book relies partly on the same sources.

3. This group initially had its meetings at the Hotel de la Paix in Geneva, hence its name.

4. Seemingly, the gradual decline of U.S. leadership coincided with weakening support for the multilateralism represented by the GATT regime.

PART TWO

CONTENDING
ANALYSES

Chapter 3

Decision Theory
Diagnosing Strategic Alternatives and Outcome Trade-Offs

Bertram I. Spector (USA)

The essential task in analyzing any international negotiation process is to understand and explain modifications in the initial positions and interests of nations that facilitate eventual convergence on mutually acceptable outcomes. These shifts imply national preference adjustments and are usually related to strategic and tactical trade-offs on alternative negotiation outcomes (Raiffa, 1982; Spector, 1983). Decision analysis is a methodology that facilitates the evaluation of such preference adjustments and trade-offs based on systematic and quantitative techniques. The purpose of this chapter is to demonstrate the utility of this analytical approach in explaining these significant process dynamics specifically in the context of multilateral negotiation.

The value of decision analysis as a systematic framework by which to understand multilateral negotiation may be somewhat problematic however. The technique is distinct from other analytical methods applied to negotiation in that it is typically used in a normative, prescriptive mode. Decision analysis is applied most often as a practical consultative tool to help negotiators diagnose strategic alternatives and outcome trade-offs prior to or during negotiations and less often as a technique to analyze, understand, and explain how and why negotiating strategies were selected after the fact.

Moreover, decision analysis is a methodology inherently formulated to deal with one decision-making unit at a time. Trade-offs are assessed against a

I wish to thank Daniel Druckman, I. William Zartman, James Sebenius, and several anonymous reviewers for their many thoughtful comments and suggestions on earlier drafts of this chapter.

singular preference structure for a particular actor. Thus, a bilateral negotiation requires comparison of two preference structures—only a slight complexity. Multilateral negotiations, on the other hand, involve multiple interacting preference structures; the identification and comparability of theses structures introduce significant methodological complexities.

One of the purposes of this chapter is to bridge the gap between decision analysis as a consultative tool and as an analytical vehicle. Fortunately, this issue can be reduced to a discussion of how the decision analytic model is populated with data, not its inherent methodological attributes. The chapter focuses on the central issue of identifying ways decision analysis can be used to evaluate international multilateral negotiations effectively.

Applying Decision Analysis to Negotiation

Decision analysis is a methodology typically used to support decision makers actively assessing alternative courses of action. Generated from statistical decision theory, decision analysis was developed in the field of business administration as a practical approach to assist corporate managers in weighing their options and designing logical solutions in a systematic fashion. It is usually applied in a consultative mode with decision makers, helping them work through immediate decision problems (Ulvila and Brown, 1982).

Decision analysis is a normative technique that seeks to prescribe for decision makers appropriate courses of action that coincide with their values and preferences. Behavioral decision theory, as reviewed by Slovic, Fischhoff, and Lichtenstein (1977) and described by Kahneman and Tversky (1986), is the broader theoretical structure within which decision analysis falls. It comprises both the normative/prescriptive approaches and descriptive theories of how individuals incorporate their beliefs and values into their decision calculus. These descriptive theories seek to explain how people perceive, process, and evaluate decision situations and decision options, given uncertainty, risk, and interactions with other stakeholders. The main psychological concepts encompassed in these theories include the logic of probabilistic reasoning, choice, inference, heuristics, biases, adjustment, and framing/reframing. This chapter focuses in particular on the decision analysis because it has been applied to the negotiation environment specifically and is a distinctive technique that can be used to understand the bargaining process.

Decision analysis tools—in particular, multiattribute-value (MAV) analysis models—have been applied prescriptively with negotiators and policy makers to assist in prenegotiation strategy development regarding U.S. military bases in the Philippines (1978), the Panama Canal (1974), and international oil tanker standards (1978) (Raiffa, 1982; Ulvila and Snider, 1980; Ulvila, 1990). In these cases, decision analysts supported negotiating teams by eliciting practitioner preferences and values, generating models based on these subjective judgments, calculating the decision analytic results, and feeding these results back to the negotiators to help them evaluate alternative strategies. In these cases, decision

analysis was used as an analytical support technique and was meant to guide policy makers and influence the course of the negotiations not to explain retrospectively why certain negotiation strategies were selected or why the process turned out the way it did. Typically, decision analysis has not been used to diagnose or evaluate the negotiation process after the fact, but there is no reason why it cannot be applied this way.

Decision analysis focuses on several critical elements of the decision-making process, suggesting that they are the keys to making and understanding effective choices. Central to all these elements is the concept of preference. Kahneman and Tversky (1986) indicate that preferences are the filters through which decision makers frame and reframe—perceive and define—their national interests and salient issues as well. The decision maker's values or preferences are incorporated into decision analysis models along with objective inputs. If these preferences can be defined and elicited directly from involved negotiators concerning particular interests, then the technique can be applied proactively as a supportive tool. If one is attempting to explain the process in an historical case, however, one usually relies on indirect means of gathering data on preferences. Herein lies the difficulty in using decision analysis as an analytical research technique for negotiation processes. Some ways to overcome this data collection problem are presented later in this chapter.

Decision analysis applied to the negotiation process can be helpful in understanding strategy and outcome. The methodology is geared to evaluating alternative strategy options based on trade-off analyses that take into account the expected value of the projected outcomes. Probing evaluations of strategy decisions are accomplished in decision analysis primarily by looking at negotiator's preferences. The technique can help one understand why particular strategies were selected and others rejected on the basis of negotiator preferences, the attractiveness of strategy options, the perceived likely outcomes of alternative strategies, and the probabilities of the occurrence of other-party strategies and other uncontrollable events. Applied in the prenegotiation phase, an integrated family of related decision-analytic methods can provide effective support to negotiators, facilitating situational diagnosis, planning, and strategizing (Spector, 1993a).

Decision-analytic models offer the capability of disaggregating the decision rationale for selecting one strategy over another by evaluating negotiator preferences, criterion by criterion. In so doing, it is possible to understand not only the genesis of a country's bargaining interests and why certain outcomes are seen as attractive but also the genesis of compromise formulas that provide an improved distribution of benefits to all parties.

From Consultative to Analytical Tools

One of the primary features of decision analytic approaches is their highly subjective nature; they depend on the decision maker's perspectives, preferences, and values. In a typical application of decision analysis, the preferences of the negotiator are elicited directly in the immediate negotiation environment. After the

fact and without direct access to the negotiator, indirect means are required to reconstruct these preferences. Several approaches can be used to perform this reconstruction.

1. *Cognitive Mapping Approach.* Cognitive maps attempt to represent the belief structure of individual decision makers as a series of interrelated causal links (Bonham, 1993). Decision makers behave within the context of this network of beliefs. If cognitive maps could be constructed for each negotiator in a multilateral setting, their preferences and alternative proposed outcomes could be inferred and put into a decision analysis model. A practical problem in using this approach is that developing a comprehensive cognitive map for each negotiator would be much more difficult than identifying preferences on a limited number of specific negotiation issues and would be somewhat out of proportion to the task.

2. *Expert Analysis or Content Analysis Approach.* In this approach, richly descriptive case study material or transcripts of the targeted negotiation process are required. This textual material is presented to coders, who examine it and code relevant passages into categories on specified actor preference scales. In the case of expert coding, substantive experts are asked to reconstruct or role-play the negotiating actors and code their presumed preferences on structured actor preference scales that are then used in the decision analytic models. Ulvila (1990) reports on the coding of preference data for the 1978 U.S.-Philippine base negotiations using case study material and statements of the negotiation parties; his resulting decision analysis is based on preference data gathered by only one coder. Ulvila and Snider (1980) collected preference data for other parties to the international tanker standards conference based on expert coding. In this case, the U.S. negotiating team served as a panel of experts to code the perceived preferences of the other parties to the negotiation. Two potential difficulties with this approach are obtaining sufficiently rich descriptive material on the case and intercoder reliability.

3. *Nonquantitative Approach.* A third approach avoids preference ratings of the negotiating parties altogether. Instead, the graphic representation of the decision tree can be used to display the sequence of offers, counteroffers, and intervening situational factors without the probabilities and value judgments. Although this approach results in a much watered-down application of decision analysis, it requires much less information to implement and can still yield a longitudinal depiction of the negotiation process from a strategy perspective. Such an analysis might also provide a useful way of studying stages in the negotiation process.

Table 3.1 compares these three coding procedures according to ease of data collection, the ability to utilize the features of decision analysis fully, and data validity. Overall, the cognitive mapping approach is not attractive because of the difficulty of coding preferences and the extensive time required. The nonquantitative approach is also attractive because it severely limits the researcher's ability to fully utilize the analytical features of decision analysis. The content analysis technique, although it has several drawbacks, is the preferred approach for cod-

Table 3.1. Comparison of Indirect Coding Procedures.

Procedures	Ease of Data Collection	Utilization of Decision Analytic Features	Data-Validity Level
Cognitive Mapping	Low	High	Medium
Content Analysis	Medium	High	High
Nonquantitative	High	Low	High

ing negotiator values. Although it requires considerable time and resources to collect the data and intercoder reliability may present some problems, the resulting information can be used fruitfully within the decision analysis algorithm.

Friedheim (1991) describes an interesting empirical analysis of national and coalition interests and preferences in the United Nations Conference on the Law of the Sea (UNCLOS III). Although the case does not include development of a decision analytic model, data on an issue-by-issue basis of the type required for a modeling effort were collected systematically on the conference proceedings using content analytical procedures.

Preference data for the two multilateral negotiation cases analyzed in this chapter were collected using the content analysis approach. Based on this retrospective coding of negotiator preferences, we can run the decision analysis model and conduct sensitivity tests as if the negotiators had provided their preferences directly. The trade-offs of one negotiation strategy over another can be evaluated in relation to these preferences. In so doing, we can draw inferences about the reasoning used by the practitioners in the negotiation situation—why they preferred certain negotiation strategies and outcomes and why they rejected others—and how shifts in these preferences over the course of the negotiation made certain outcomes mores likely than others.

Analyzing Multilateral Negotiation

Ulvila's (1990) study of the Philippine-base negotiations is a good example of the use of decision analysis to understand strategy development in a bilateral situation. As indicated previously, a content analysis procedure was used to code the negotiator preferences. Two MAV models were developed—one for each actor—by weighing the multiple issues in the negotiation and rating the perceived attractiveness of positions on each issue. A compromise position that fell within the range of negotiating positions was also rated in terms of relative attractiveness. Using these quantified models, Ulvila was able, first, to identify the attractiveness of alternative packages of agreements across all the key negotiating issues for each negotiating party. Many alternative packages were simulated across the issue areas and attempts were made to analyze their overall attractiveness to each party. Ulvila was able, second, to identify an agreement space in which both sides

could maximize their gains in the negotiation. The points along the optimal frontier were explainable in terms of the actors' issue weights and position preferences. Raiffa (1982) describes a similar application of decision analysis to the bilateral Panama Canal negotiations.

In the context of multilateral negotiations, multiple decision analytic models can be built, each attempting to replicate the perspective of each negotiating party. One can assume that the model structures (the inventories of interests and outcomes) are the same but that actor preferences and priorities vary. Players that are closely aligned with each other—with high interest commonality—have similar interest preferences: they perceive and frame the negotiating problem in a similar manner, and their model weights are likely to be highly correlated. However, players with strong interest divergence are likely to have different perspectives on the criteria weights and the hierarchy by which courses of action are evaluated; their decision calculus is different and thus may be framed differently when modeled. In either case, it is possible to compare and analyze both the assumptions of the analysis (weights, scores, probabilities) and the decision results directly—that is, the prioritization of decision alternatives across actors.

From a bureaucratic-politics perspective, decision analysis models built and assessed as described above to simulate preferences of the various parties to a multilateral negotiation can be meaningful as well in uncovering significant milestones in the decision-making process within each party, identifying the elements that were critical and examining the process of option selection and modification. The models and their fine-tuning through sensitivity testing can help to mirror historical negotiations from the perspectives of domestic stakeholders, national parties, or coalitions of parties. The "trueness" of each model can be validated by comparing the prioritized alternatives to historical accounts or memoirs of the participating practitioners. If the model is valid, the analyst can look back at the premises in the model—the hierarchy of criteria, the weights, scores, and probabilities—to understand how and why decisions were made.

Negotiation processes are dynamic, meaning that many decisions on multiple issues are made and modified by each negotiating party over time. For each issue area, different decision analysis models may be required. However, if countries have a consistent policy concerning their national objectives and interests within a negotiation, one can assume that the underlying evaluation criteria and weighting schemes will remain invariant—that they will be similar across decision phases and episodes. What will change over time, however, are the preferences for particular proposals under debate; in this area flexibility can occur.

Ulvila and Snider (1980) provide an interesting case of the use of decision analytic models not only to support a particular negotiating team in an upcoming multilateral negotiation but also to explain some elements of the process. They used an MAV modeling consultative mode with the U.S. negotiating team to the 1978 International Conference on Tanker Safety and Pollution Prevention to prepare alternative strategies and consider trade-offs among them during the prenegotiation phase. In building the decision analytic model, U.S. negotiation

interests had to be compared with the interests of the other countries that would participate in the conference. This comparison was accomplished by having the U.S. team role-play their counterpart teams from twenty-one other countries.

A common set of criteria and negotiation was identified for the MAV model structure, and a common set of scores was elicited from the U.S. team for rating each proposal package against each criterion. In building the model, the authors assumed that this basic structure of the negotiations was essentially equivalent across participants. However, the relative importance given to the various criteria were conceived as different across participants—that is, each country's interests, while comprising the same set of issues, were prioritized differently.

By analyzing the model and examining its component elements, the researchers and the U.S. negotiating team were able to highlight some issues that were likely to be contentious in the negotiations and to develop compromise solutions. They were able to explain, in terms of the differential interests of various countries on particular issues, why a specific U.S. strategy was not likely to be successful in yielding agreement in the upcoming multilateral conference.

Friedheim (1993), while not implementing a formal decision analytic model, used country-by-country and issue-by-issue preference data to produce graphs indicating where consensus existed and where opportunities for compromise were possible in the UNCLOS III talks. His analysis used these data creatively to track changes in preferences and issue salience over time, coalition formation and modification, and the potential for the development of multi-issue formulas for all nations participating in this multilateral conference. Based on a set of assumptions, Friedheim was able to track position adjustment and forecast likely multi-issue agreements but was unable to explain systematically why these preference shifts came about. As demonstrated later in this chapter in two case analyses, the application of decision analytic models using preference data can extend the types of assessments that were produced by Friedheim from simple descriptions of position modification to identification of the principal factors underlying changes in position.

Spector (1993c) demonstrates a contingency decision analytic approach that enables detailed probing of multilateral prenegotiation while the process is still in progress. Using the preparatory committee meetings of the United Nations Conference on Environment and Development during 1990 and 1991 as the case, Spector structured several MAV models on several of the key negotiation issues using tentatively assessed interest profiles of various emerging coalitions as model criteria. In this approach the MAV analysis is performed to identify the relative preferences of these different coalitions to the negotiation proposals identified. Sensitivity analysis is also conducted to determine the degree to which the various coalitions must adjust their preferences to achieve agreement on potential mutually acceptable compromise proposals. Because the interest profiles and tabled proposals are dynamic during the prenegotiation, the analysis is conducted using different coalition and outcome structures, where the analytical results are contingent on these assumed structures. This approach is considered useful both

from a perspective of understanding movement in positions and interests and in supporting the United Nations secretariat for the conference in promoting its understanding of the likely implications for agreement on various proposals.

Case Studies

The following application of decision analysis to both negotiation cases—the Single European Act and the Uruguay Round of the General Agreement on Tariffs and Trade (GATT) talks—is based on the research by Ulvila and Snider (1980) and Spector (1993c), and the content analysis approach for coding preference data. Because of the multi-issue complexity of these negotiations, only one key issue area is examined for each case.

Several procedures were followed in the analysis. First, national interests in the negotiation were identified. Second, alternative negotiation outcomes, including the final compromise, were defined. Third, the extent to which these outcomes satisfied each of the national interests is assessed. The result of these first three steps was an MAV model structure that can be used to evaluate context-specific strategy development on a particular issue within a multilateral negotiation. Fourth, the relative weights, suggesting the importance attributed to interests by each negotiating party, were then identified. These weights were applied to the model structure to develop an alternative model for each negotiating party. Finally, these models were analyzed to compare the differences among and evolution of national preferences across negotiating outcomes. Comparative analyses across parties on the possible outcomes help in assessing the determinants of shifting preferences that result in compromises.[1] Because we know the actual outcome of the negotiations, we can use the methodology to analyze and diagnose how and why these initial positions and preferences were modified during the course of the negotiations to arrive at the compromise outcomes. To perform this analysis, a weighted deficiency index is calculated to measure the preference adjustment dynamic, the difference between an actor's initial preference and the total acceptance or endorsement of a formula. This procedure is described more fully later in the chapter. A brief methodological appendix is also given at the end of the chapter.

Data were coded to conduct the decision analyses based on content analysis of the two case studies in this volume as well as additional papers written about these negotiations by Winham and Kizer (1993), Winham (1989), Lodge (1986d) and Moravcsik (1991). In particular, the coding was conducted on the targeted negotiation issues to answer these questions: What are the national interests, goals, or preferences that guide or motivate the actions of each national actor or coalition? What is the importance or salience of each national interest, goal, or preference relative to the others held by each nation or coalition?

Inputs to the decision analysis model are the going-in preferences of the negotiating participants. Each mention of preference or salience in the case study texts was coded and then corroborative information sought from other sources. This cross-checking approach extends a degree of reliability to the data. Although

numerical values were assigned to the preference weights, no engineering precision is implied; in fact, an ordinal ranking was assigned first that provided a relative degree of magnitude in importance before an interval scale was applied. For the purposes of this type of decision analysis, an ordinal ranking is probably more appropriate and realistic than an interval scale; it suggests a limited range of values for each preference rather than a precise figure. However, to facilitate the calculations in this chapter, specific numerical values are used.

The analyses that follow are intentionally a simplification of the negotiation cases evaluated. Issues are viewed as representative packages, and actors are regarded as coalitions or marker countries that represent a certain point of view. Analysis could have been carried out on a country-by-country basis, demonstrating internal divisions within coalitions but at the cost of a geometric increase in the complexity of the analysis. We view these cases solely through the lens of decision analysis, seeking to understand how preferences and values influence negotiation behavior. Although these are certainly significant factors that can reveal critical aspects of the process, they do not make up a comprehensive theory of multilateral negotiation by themselves. Such a theory may be achieved only by combining the strengths of several diverse theoretical perspectives in a synthetic way.

Uruguay Round of GATT

Model Development. Trade in services was one of the issues successfully resolved in the Uruguay Round by the end of the Montreal midterm review in 1989. The debate concerning trade in services revolved around four national interests:

- *Transparency*—accessibility of foreign markets to national corporations. This interest manifested itself in two basic forms: transparent (foreign markets are made accessible) and highly restricted (barriers are instituted to restrict and regulate foreign entry into a domestic market to protect the domestic industry).
- *Sectoral reciprocity*—the manner in which foreign corporations are treated in a domestic market. This interest took two forms: national treatment (foreign entities are treated the same as domestic corporations in the same market) and foreign standards (foreign entities are allowed to operate under the standards by which they would conduct business in their home countries).
- *Treatment of developing countries*—the extent to which a country's level of development may be taken into account when applying liberalized standards for trade in services. This interest took two forms: preferential treatment (exceptions to standards are made for developing countries) and uniform standards (all countries are treated the same regardless of their level of development).
- *Enforceability*—the extent to which standards are considered a legal GATT

obligation. This interest manifested itself in two ways: legal obligation (acceptance implies a legally binding GATT obligation for the accepting country) and informal acceptance (acceptance implies no legal obligation).

These interests served as the criteria to structure the MAV model.

Four alternative negotiation outcomes were identified, including two extreme options and two compromise proposals:

- *Minimalist Option.* The outcome at one extreme was to exclude trade in services altogether as a valid area within GATT. However, if it were to be included in GATT, the following provisions would be incorporated: preferential treatment for developing countries, foreign standards applied, domestic service industry protected as much as possible, no legal obligation implied within GATT to observe the standards, and labor intensive employment services, such as those the developing nations might export, covered.
- *Compromise/Transparency Option.* This compromise was close to the minimalist option except it emphasized easy access to foreign markets and the positive impacts of establishing trade in services as a valid GATT area. It included the following provisions: trade in services incorporated into GATT (but no legal obligation implied), preferential treatment given to developing countries, and foreign standards applied.
- *Compromise/National Option.* This compromise included the following provisions: establishment of trade in services as a GATT area with no legal obligation implied, preferential treatment for developing countries, and national standards applied to foreign enterprises. This was the compromise finally agreed to by the parties to the GATT.
- *Maximalist Option.* The preferred outcome at the other extreme was to establish trade in services as a GATT area, institute uniform treatment for all countries, apply national standards for foreign entities, and make GATT arrangements legal obligations for signatories.

Table 3.2 identifies the extent to which each alternative outcome satisfies the criteria for an acceptable conclusion to the negotiation. As defined earlier, the criteria are the national interests at stake in the talks. The quantitative assessments were made based on the cited case material. These assessments reflect the content of each negotiation formula.

The compromise national option indeed bridges the gap between the two extreme proposals put forth by the developing countries and the United States. Making the agreement less than a legal obligation within the GATT framework and offering preferential treatment to developing countries—positions viewed as favorable by the developing countries—are traded for accessibility to foreign markets and national treatment for foreign companies in the host market—positions favored by the United States. The European Communities (EC) held positions somewhat in between the two extremes.

Table 3.3 presents the relative importance of these national interests from

Table 3.2. Trade in Services: Outcomes Scored on Each Criterion.

Criteria	Minimalist	Compromise/ Transparency	Compromise/ National	Maximalist
Transparency				
Transparent	20	100	100	100
Highly Restricted	80	0	0	0
Sectoral Reciprocity				
National Treatment	0	0	100	100
Foreign Standards	100	100	0	0
Treatment of Developing Countries				
Preferential	100	100	100	0
Uniform	0	0	0	100
Enforceability				
Legal Obligation	0	0	0	100
Informal Acceptance	100	100	100	0

Table 3.3. Relative Importance of National Interests by Country/Group: Trade in Services.

Criteria	United States	EC	Developing Countries
Transparency	33	35	7
Transparent	100	100	20
Highly Restricted	0	0	80
Sectoral Reciprocity	25	24	7
National Treatment	100	0	0
Foreign Standards	0	100	100
Treatment of Developing Countries	9	12	14
Preferential	0	50	100
Uniform	100	50	0
Enforceability	33	29	72
Legal Obligation	100	100	0
Informal Acceptance	0	0	100

the perspectives of three major participants/groups in the negotiation—the United States, the EC, and the developing countries. Although there were certainly other actors, these are the only ones considered in the analysis for the sake of simplification. As described earlier, these importance weights were assessed based on the case material cited.

The United States and the EC shared similar preferences in terms of their national interests. Development of a formula that dealt effectively with issues of

transparency and enforceability was high on the list of these participants. The regulations and standards under which their companies would operate in foreign markets was also a major interest. Developing countries, however, were much more focused than the United States or the EC on the issue of enforceability—whether trade in services should even be incorporated into the GATT framework at all and, if so, how strict the obligation to abide by these standards should be.

Model Results. Given this structure and set of preferences, the results of the decision analysis are presented in Figure 3.1 as priority scores on each potential outcome for each actor. These results are calculated in the decision analysis model by multiplying the outcome scores on each criterion by the relative importance weights for each criterion. The products are then summed for each actor on each outcome option.

Based on the initial going-in preferences of the parties, each country/group shows a high preference for its own desired outcome—the United States and the EC for the maximalist option and the developing countries for the minimalist option. If this were not a negotiation in which the parties were required to search for a mutually agreeable outcome, each actor would clearly have chosen the option with the highest priority score. These findings coincide with Sjöstedt's (Chapter Two) and Winham and Kizer's (1993) descriptions of the early negotiations on the trade-in-services area: that there was extreme disagreement on the original single text used.

Figure 3.1. Prioritization of Negotiation Outcomes for Trade in Services.

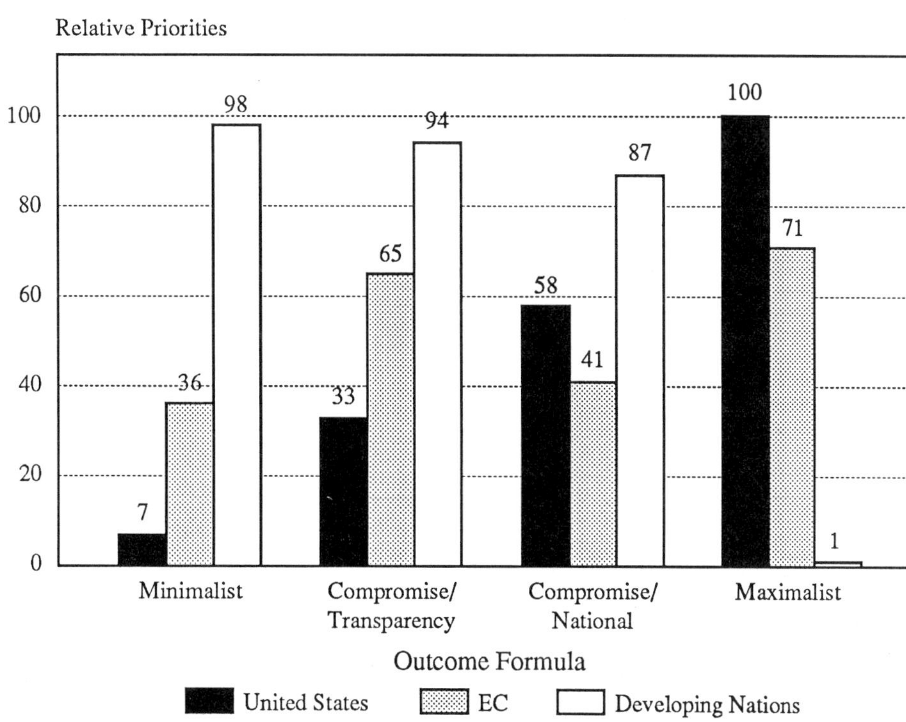

Relative Priorities

Each participant's preference for the final compromise (compromise/national) option, as one would suspect, is always less than for its own proposal but not the lowest among the range of options. The result suggests that each party over time showed some flexibility in its interest preferences, with the goal of achieving a commonly acceptable agreement. However, in examining the values by country/group across the various alternative outcomes, one can infer that more compromises had to be made by the United States and the EC countries than by the developing nations to reach the final compromise option. Specifically, there is much more variation in the preference figures of the United States and the EC between their own proposals and the final compromise agreement (differences of 42 and 30, respectively) than of the developing countries (a difference of only 11 preference points). However, the final compromise actually represents an optimal solution among the given options, equivalent to the Nash (1950) solution when the product of the outcomes is maximized. Decision analysis allows this point to be identified.

If these outcome priorities represent the initial position of each party, a process of position modification must ensue if the final compromise outcome is to be reached. Decision analysis can help to explain this preference adjustment dynamic by decomposing the decision logic of each actor and specifying which criteria were most likely responsible for the modification in interests. The analytical procedure is rather simple: it compares the negotiator's initial weighted preferences on the final compromise formula, interest by interest, with the maximum preference for that same compromise formula (measured as a weighted preference score of 100). The remainder, obtained by subtracting 100 from the going-in preference, is defined as the *weighted deficiency,* the distance between the actor's initial preference for or position on a particular formula (partial acceptance) and its undisputed acceptance of that formula. This score represents the degree to which the actor's preference must change from its going-in position to reach endorsement of the formula.[2]

Table 3.4 presents the results of this preference adjustment analysis for the trade-in-services issue. The values in the weighted deficiency column can add to –100 only in the extreme case, if total preference modification is required across

Table 3.4. Preference Adjustment Between Final Compromise and Ideal: Trade in Services.

	Interest	Weighted Deficiency	Percent of Total Deficiency
United States	Legal obligation	–33	80
	Uniform standards	– 8	20
EC	Legal obligation	–29	50
	Foreign standards	–24	40
	Uniform standards	– 6	10
Developing Countries	Foreign standards	– 7	56
	Highly restricted access	– 6	44

all interest areas for a given actor. An example of such an extreme case would be if negotiators finally capitulated to an agreement that was diametrically opposed to their initial interests. Thus, high negative values in this column suggest that major preference adjustments were needed, while low values indicate that minor modifications in preference were required.

For the United States, the biggest preference adjustment that had to be made to enable its acceptance of the final compromise formula was on whether to make trade in services a legal obligation within the GATT framework. This adjustment accounted for 80 percent of the total weighted deficiency between the compromise agreement and the ideal case for the United States. The next most important area of preference adjustment for the United States was on the uniform treatment issue, which accounts for only 20 percent of the total weighted deficiency. Thus, position modification for the United States essentially revolved around the legal-obligation issue. For the EC countries, movement on the legal obligation issue was almost equally matched by movement on the foreign standards issue; together they accounted for 90 percent of the deficiency in the compromise agreement. Position modification on the uniform standards issue again was required but was of minor importance.

For the developing countries, preference movement to come to agreement on the compromise option was required on the foreign standards and restricted market access issues. It is interesting to note how low weighted the deficiency values were for the developing countries. This analysis suggests that the final compromise was cognitively easier for these developing countries to accept than for either the United States or the EC nations. Developing nations had a shorter distance to span between their going-in position and the final compromise; they had to make fewer compromises that contradicted their national interests.

The developing countries were in this position because the dominant element in their decision logic was, by far, enforceability, which received an overall importance weight of 72 percent (see Table 3.3). In the final compromise agreement, the developing countries' position on enforceability—to ensure an informal, nonlegally binding interpretation of trade in services as an area within GATT—was satisfied. The next most important factor in their decision calculus was gaining preferential treatment; this goal too was achieved in the final compromise. Only on criteria of low importance did the developing countries concede. For the United States and the EC, however, the concessions and successes in satisfying their national interests were more of a mixture. Some interests given high importance were abandoned in the compromise agreement, while others were satisfied. Overall, the developing countries were much more successful in satisfying their high-importance interests through the negotiations than either the United States or the EC, as demonstrated in the results of the decision analysis model. The ability of these three actors to satisfy their interests appears to be inversely related to the asymmetry in their resource-based power. The distinctive advantage of effectively applied behavioral power by the ostensibly weakest party is borne out in this case.[3]

Implications. How has decision analysis modeling enhanced our comprehension of the negotiation process in the GATT trade-in-services case? First, the analysis codified and evaluated the extreme divergence of positions of the key parties at the beginning of the negotiations. The model not only identified and compared each actor's relative priorities toward the proposed formulas but also facilitated a probing analysis of the component national interests and of the preferences that resulted in the prioritization. The graphic device used to display these results demonstrates fairly dramatically the size of the bargaining space that must be bridged in the subsequent negotiations.

Second, the decision analytic model helps in diagnosing how that bridging dynamic came about. All parties in the trade-in-services case modified their interest during the course of the negotiation, some more than others. The extent of preference adjustment required to achieve a successful outcome to the negotiation was measured and assessed through the decision analysis. The developing countries, for example, conceded little in order to satisfy their highly coveted interests of preventing trade-in-services agreements from becoming legally binding obligations within GATT and gaining preferential treatment when applying liberalized trade-in-services standards. The degree of adjustment to preferences required of these countries was assessed by the decision analysis model as being very low. However, the United States and the EC conceded dearly on their demand for establishing trade-in-services regulations as a legal obligation within GATT; this was a highly valued interest for both parties. As a result, the decision analysis indicates that extensive preference adjustment was required of both the United States and the EC to achieve the final compromise formula, primarily because of this failed interest as well as the EC's "costly" concession on maintaining foreign standards. Thus, this modeling approach offers useful insight into the key drivers of position modification; it tracks the type and degree of trade-offs required to achieve accommodation and compromise.

Single European Act of the EC

Model Development. The negotiations on the Single European Act (SEA) covered many different issue areas, but one that was particularly central to the goals of the EC and many of the EC member states was institutional reform regarding the power and authority of the European Parliament (EP). The issue revolved around whether additional legislative powers should be granted to the EP, a supranational body, and the relationship of the EP to the Council of Ministers, an intergovernmental institution in which the individual countries can demonstrate their national sovereignty and exercise greater control than in the EP. Two principal national interests emerged as pivotal from the debates. First, *national sovereignty* related to the fear that increased powers for the EP would erode national authority. Second, *institutional reform* related to the development of improved institutional rules and procedures by which EC organizations, especially the EP, conduct business and interact with other EC units. These two interests are used as the criteria for the MAV model structure.

Three negotiation outcomes can be identified:

- *Maximalist Proposal.* This outcome would establish full co-decision for the EP with the Council of Ministers for most areas of legislation, thus expanding the power of the supranational parliament.
- *Compromise Proposal.* This compromise includes provisions for increased cooperation with the Council of Ministers on a variety of issues and incorporates a limited ability for the EP to amend legislation. It expands the use of qualified majority voting in the Council of Ministers but only on certain noncontentious matters related to the internal market, thus excluding fiscal and social regulation. On other issue areas, majority voting is limited by the maintenance of national veto rights. This proposal constituted the final agreement achieved by the SEA negotiation.
- *Minimalist Proposal.* This formula would offer no colegislative role for the EP. It would extend some collaborative and consultative actions to the EP relative to the Council of Ministers but would clearly maintain the existing power imbalance in the Council's favor. The right to veto would be maintained in the Council when "very important national interests" were at stake.

Table 3.5 presents an assessment of the extent to which each alternative outcome satisfies the national interest criteria. The quantitative values were assessed based on the case study material describing the negotiation. The maximalist formula pushes institutional reform ahead, seeking expansion of EC activities and rapid movement toward European federalism and the expense of a perceived loss of national sovereignty. The minimalist formula does just the opposite. The job of the compromise formula is to build a bridge between these extremes by extending new and real effectiveness to the EP while at the same time encouraging institutional reform in an evolutionary manner so as not to alarm countries fearing the implication of European federation.

Table 3.6 displays the relative importance of these national interests for the three major national actors and leaders in the negotiation—Germany, France, and the United Kingdom. Moravcsik (1991) describes the preferences of these countries on the procedural reform issue: Germany was in favor of strengthening the EP's role, was opposed to the right to veto, and was in favor of increased majority voting. France was opposed to strengthening the EP's role, was opposed

Table 3.5. Institutional Reform: Outcomes Scored on Each Criterion.

Criteria	Maximalist	Compromise	Minimalist
National Sovereignty	30	70	100
Institutional Reform	100	60	30

Table 3.6. Relative Importance of National Interests by Coalition: Institutional Reform.

	Germany	France	United Kingdom
National Sovereignty	5	25	85
Institutional Reform	95	75	15

Figure 3.2. Prioritization of Negotiation Outcomes for Institutional Reform.

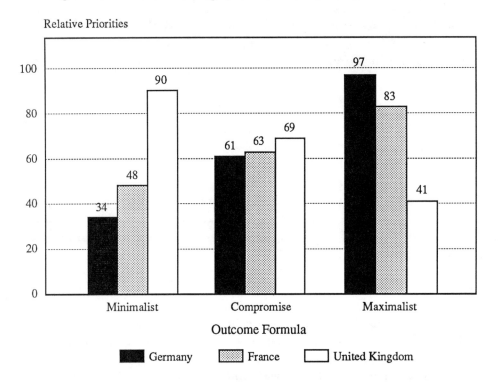

to the right to veto, and was in favor of increased majority voting. The United Kingdom was in favor of the veto right and was in favor of informal efforts to facilitate increased but limited majority voting. From Table 3.6 it can be seen that the preferences of the three actors are different from each other. Given the clear lines along which these priorities are drawn, one would expect the debate to be extremely caustic and divisive with little hope of resolution.

Model Results. The results of the decision analysis model are presented in Figure 3.2. As in the GATT case, each actor indicates divergent priorities across the available formulas. The compromise proposal always holds the middle ground, representing similar calculated preference scores for the three actors. The attractiveness of the compromise proposal is enhanced by the fact that the dis-

tance to be bridged between the most preferred option and the compromise one is roughly equivalent across the three actors. (However, this is not a product maximizing solution.)

An analysis of the preference adjustment that occurred for each negotiating actor is presented in Table 3.7. How far off from an ideal formula is the compromise outcome for Germany? By far, the greatest deficiency is in institutional reform, which exhibits 96 percent of the total deficiency. France, taking a somewhat more moderate position on procedural change, required movement on institutional reform interests that account for 80 percent. However, for the United Kingdom, preference adjustment must come on its national sovereignty position, representing 81 percent of required movement to make the compromise viable. Overall, across the three major negotiation actors, agreement on the compromise formula requires the greatest adjustment to Germany's interests on institutional reform.

Implications. How, in the case of negotiating institutional reform in the SEA, did decision analysis modeling help to understand the process? As Lodge (Chapter One) indicates, the initial interests of the principal actors in this issue were widely divergent; this divergence is reflected quite clearly in the outcome priorities in Figure 3.2. Germany was very much the maximalist leader and the United Kingdom, the minimalist leader, leaving France in between, though more closely aligned with the maximalists. The decision analysis, thus, provides a useful map of the initial bargaining space and the gap that must be bridged on this issue.

The methodology provides meaningful insights, as well, in decomposing the process by which compromise was achieved. As indicated in Table 3.7, the United Kingdom conceded little in the final compromise on its demands for minimal institutional reform; according to the model, the United Kingdom needed to make only minor adjustment to its preferences on institutional reform. The Germans and French, however, were required to make major modifications to their initial interests to achieve the compromise formula. As Lodge puts it, the compromise represents the lowest common denominator on institutional reform;

Table 3.7. Preference Adjustment Between Final Compromise and Ideal:
Institutional Reform.

	Interest	*Weighted Deficiency*	*Percent of Total Deficiency*
Germany	Institutional reform	−38	96
	National sovereignty	− 2	4
France	Institutional reform	−30	80
	National sovereignty	− 8	20
United Kingdom	National sovereignty	−26	81
	Institutional reform	− 6	19

it was viewed by the main proponents of this issue, the French and Germans, as the bare minimum and obviously inadequate. The United Kingdom, however, had to modify its interest and make concessions concerning national sovereignty in a major way to be able to achieve the compromise. Thus, trade-offs were made by each party and an agreement was struck, but at a cost to all. The model helps to identify the type and extent of these costs and benefits in the preference adjustment analysis.

Conclusions

Although it often has been applied in a prescriptive mode to assist a single decision maker on a single issue at a time, decision analysis can be a potent analytical methodology to explain multilateral negotiations. The technique is best suited to address the process by which negotiators consider trade-offs across multi-issue formulas and modify their preferences, thus yielding a convergence of interests and compromise agreements. In the two cases reviewed in this chapter, decision analysis has provided a meaningful approach to understanding the dynamics by which the negotiating coalitions made concessions that resulted in agreements on compromise formulas. Negotiator preferences and priorities for major national objectives and interests in the negotiation are the currency by which decision analysis provides this understanding.

Negotiation is a dynamic process in which positions are modified by the principal parties over time, enabling the development of an agreement. When more than two parties are engaged, as in multilateral negotiation, this process of position modification and search becomes complex to track and explain. Decision analysis models provide a tool that can assist researchers in this regard. As demonstrated in this chapter, they facilitate measurement of the bargaining space—the distance between actor priorities and preferences for alternative outcome formulas—and specification of the criteria most responsible for the modification of interests.

The decision analytic approach, however, is not well equipped to address other key dimensions of the negotiation process, such as structure, the effects of situation, power, and strategy. Thus, decision analysis can be useful in evaluating certain aspects of multilateral negotiation and can enhance a larger analysis of such negotiation processes in collaboration with other approaches.

Decision analysis offers several substantial benefits that help researchers in evaluating multilateral negotiations: First, the methodology is capable of examining multiple negotiating parties using a single model structure. In this structure all participant interests are arrayed, and the range of possible outcomes or formulas are represented and scored against these interests. The model thus depicts the feasible bargaining space and the major gaps that must be bridged in the negotiations. The scores of outcomes on criteria are invariant across actors because the outcomes possess certain properties regardless of the actor. Unique preference sets representing the relative importance of each interest for each negotiating participant are required for insertion into the model.

Second, by developing the models using the actors' initial sets of preferences and the range of possible outcomes, including the final negotiated agreement, decision analysis can assist in understanding not only a static but a dynamic negotiation environment. As demonstrated in the cases described in this chapter, the decision analysis model can be used to analyze the process of preference adjustment and position modification across negotiation stages. By juxtaposing the initial going-in position with final or compromise outcomes, one can evaluate movement in actor preferences over time. The development of several models that essentially provides snapshots of preference modification at different stages allows production of a moving picture of the incremental dynamic of the negotiation, and feedback and learning that can be traced from round to round.

Third, the factors that leverage this adjustment can be pinpointed throughout the analytic approach. The decision analysis allows researchers to dissect the preference structure of each actor on each proposed formula, interest by interest, to identify the relative satisfaction each alternative outcome provides to the participants and why. The preference adjustment calculation decomposes the decision rationale used by actors, as represented by their criterion weights, and identifies the relative significance of each criterion in achieving the adjustment between the going-in position and the final accepted agreement. As a result, the methodology provides a level of granularity that enables meaningful substantive understanding of the case in context, despite the reductionist tendencies of such an analytical technique.

Fourth, the methodology can be used in a "what if" mode, enabling practitioners to question the effects of changes in national interest profiles or different negotiation proposals on the extent of preference adjustment required by the various actors to achieve agreement and the likelihood of agreement overall (Spector, 1993c). The approach can help negotiators diagnose the current situation and play out alternative situations in which coalitions or interests change.

Fifth, several generalized decision analysis software packages are commercially available and easy to use; they can help negotiation researchers design MAV models and decision trees.[4] Specialized negotiation software using decision analysis methods, such as MCBARG (Bronisz, Krus, and Lopuch, 1988), are also being developed to analyze multicriteria bargaining problems. These packages are easily adaptable to the specific circumstances of particular negotiation cases.

Nevertheless, some problems exist in the application of the methodology. Decision analysis can help to track, disentangle, and diagnose the preferences and interests of multiple parties on the same issue, but it stops short of explaining why the parties adjust their preferences. What stimulates movement? Why are some parties willing to go further than others in modifying their positions and, thus, move toward mutual convergence? Decision analysis can only hint at answers to such questions.

Decision analysis models do not deal well with multiple issues simultaneously. They can process one issue area at a time. The linkage and interaction of issues must be handled outside of the approach. Moreover, the validity and reliability of data collection procedures for negotiator preferences require further

refinement. Systematic techniques using content analysis of transcripts, cognitive mapping approaches, and expert panels need to be tested for intercoder reliability, and taxonomies to facilitate preference coding are required. Examination of these methodological questions is likely to enhance the utility of decision analysis as a valuable tool for multilateral negotiation research.

Appendix

The development and use of an MAV model to evaluate interest dynamics in negotiation require several steps.

1. *Criterion Structure.* The range of national interests for all parties concerning the issue under debate must be identified. These interests are represented in the model as the criterion structure, the set of factors by which national policy makers evaluate the costs and benefits of each possible negotiated solution.

2. *Outcome Structure.* The range of possible negotiated outcomes must be specified and arrayed. This structure will include all the proposals currently on the table as well as additional options that can be identified and may be generated in the future.

3. *Outcome Rating.* Data must be gathered to estimate the extent to which each possible outcome satisfies each interest in the criterion structure.

4. *Criterion Weighting.* For each nation or coalition, the relative importance of each criterion must be assessed.

5. *Model Exercise.* The MAV calculations can now be performed for each nation or coalition; they yield a prioritization of alternative negotiated outcomes for each entity. The calculation is simply the sum of all outcome ratings multiplied by criterion weights for each possible outcome by actor. Comparisons across entities can be assessed to evaluate the extent of convergence or divergence on the various possible outcomes. These comparisons can also pinpoint opportunities for logrolling across the set of possible options.

6. *Sensitivity Analysis.* The dynamics of preference adjustment can be analyzed through sensitivity analysis. Prominent outcomes that are identified as the most preferred by the key nations or coalitions are the basis for the analysis. The objective is to evaluate the extent to which each principal actor must adjust its interests and preferences to be able to accept these prominent outcomes. To make this evaluation analytically, the initial weighted preference on each prominent outcome, interest by interest, is compared with the maximum possible preference each actor can have (equal to a weighted preference score of 100). The difference between these two values is defined as the *weighted deficiency,* the distance between the actor's initial preference for the outcome and its undisputed acceptance of that solution. This score represents the degree to which the actor's preferences must change from its going-in position to reach total endorsement of the outcome option. Because this sensitivity analysis is calculated on an interest-by-interest basis, it is possible to specify which interests must be adjusted more than others by each actor in order for a prominent outcome to be acceptable.

For each issue to be analyzed, a separate model must be structured. For

multilateral negotiation analysis, it is possible to develop a single model structure for each issue, varying only the criterion weights for each actor, thereby enabling direct comparison of preferences.

Notes

1. As in Ulvila and Snider's (1980) case study, it was decided not to use probabilistic distributions in the MAV models developed for this analysis. Such probabilistic assessments might be useful in a prescriptive application where there is informational uncertainty and utility in simulating alternative transitions from one negotiation stage to the next. However, when preferences and negotiation proposals are known, as in the case of an historical multilateral negotiation, uncertainty and probabilities play a much smaller role.

2. This measure provides a novel perspective on flexibility in negotiation. While many negotiation analyses compare actor preferences with a baseline defined as their best alternative to no agreement, this weighted deficiency measure facilitates a comparison with the optimal alternative. Rather than focusing negatively on how far an actor is from walking out of a negotiation, this index highlights positive movement toward the actor's most preferred position.

3. Rubin and Zartman (1994) present an interesting collection of cases concerning the effects of power asymmetry on the negotiation process and outcome.

4. The decision analyses conducted in this chapter utilized a software package for personal computers developed by James Huttinger at Booz, Allen and Hamilton Inc., Bethesda, Maryland. Similar packages are available from the Decision Analysis Unit of the London School of Economics and Political Science.

Chapter 4

Game Theory
Focusing on the Players, Decisions, and Agreements

*Steven J. Brams, Ann E. Doherty,
Matthew L. Weidner (USA)*

Game theory assumes that each player in a game, in formulating its own best course of action, takes into account the possible actions of the other players. It assumes that negotiations that may lead to the settlement of a dispute depend on the rational actions of all players.

Decision theory also assumes that players act rationally, but it does not make the strategic interactions of players its focus. Rather, it postulates that these interactions, as well as other forces that may affect the rational choices of decision makers, can be summarized for a single decision maker by probabilities that certain events will occur. This decision maker plays a "game against nature," or a one-person game, in an uncertain environment.

One reason for making explicit strategic information about the choices of all players, who may have partially cooperative and partially conflicting interests, is that real-life decision makers seem to factor such choices into their calculations in deciding what course of action is rational. They often ask themselves: What is so-and-so likely to do if I do such-and-such? Depending on the answer, they may decide that such-and-such is a sensible thing to do, compared with the possible consequences of other actions they may consider. The assumption of rationality underlying this kind of calculation is by and large realistic in the study of negotiations: players *do* bargain to achieve certain goals, knowing that other players may try to help or thwart them. But beyond its descriptive powers, does game theory offer insights that other theories or perspectives do not?

In modeling negotiations, game theory has been used primarily, but not exclusively, to study two-person strategic situations (Brams, 1990; Raiffa, 1982).

95

What we shall endeavor to show here is its applicability to two n-person situations, one of which culminated in an agreement and the other of which did not. In the first case, we use *cooperative* game theory, which assumes that a binding agreement can be imposed that ensures all parties of some value. We then ask how this value (in this case, voting power) will be distributed among the parties but not whether it is in their interest to stick with the agreement were it not imposed. In the second case, we use *noncooperative* game theory, which assumes that a binding agreement cannot be imposed if it is not in the players' interests to adhere to it. But if it is individually rational for the players to make such an agreement, then it will perforce be self-enforcing and, therefore, need not be imposed. In brief, cooperative game theory asks how value will be divided, whereas noncooperative game theory asks what strategies rational players will choose in situations of conflict.

We begin by using the cooperative theory to study the voting power of members of the European Communities (EC) Council of Ministers. Looking beyond the assigned weights of the twelve members of the Council, we next analyze the effects of giving de facto vetoes to France and Germany and also consider how grouping members into plausible coalitions affects their powers. We then investigate the power of the Council to act under qualified-majority, simple-majority, and unanimity decision rules.

Our analysis of both the formal and informal decision rules sheds light on how the Single European Act (SEA) came to be adopted. The SEA, it seems, was a response to outmoded rules, which no longer served most members' interests. For example, the veto that all members had on matters they deemed vital to their national interests had sometimes frustrated the will of the majority. By contrast, the more realistic distribution of power under qualified-majority voting—and weights under this rule that would allow both France and Germany to have vetoes—suggests why these two countries supported the SEA. The United Kingdom probably also benefited, in part because it was able to gain concessions from France and Germany that more than counterbalanced giving up part of its sovereignty under qualified-majority voting.

We use noncooperative game theory to analyze the dynamics of negotiations on two major issues—agricultural price supports and access to markets—related to the liberalization of trade. Disagreement on the first issue was the principal reason for the breakup of the Uruguay Round of the General Agreement on Tariffs and Trade (GATT) in December 1990, whereas the second issue has been a bone of contention among the United States, the EC, and Japan for some time.

We postulate a three-person game among these players, based on their positions on both these issues (or platforms). We assume that the players begin by supporting only their most preferred platforms, lending their support to lower-ranked platforms, if there is no consensus, until they reach a point at which they would prefer impasse to further compromise. This dynamic negotiation model illustrates both the conditions that led to the conflict and the compromises needed to overcome it.

Whereas the cooperative model applied to voting on the EC Council is most useful in drawing out quantitative implications of the formal and informal rules of the voting game, the noncooperative model applied to trade negotiations gives one insight into the actual jockeying for position among the main players as each strives to attain its preferred positions in extended negotiations. Although the viewpoints provided by game theory are quite different in each case, both highlight nonobvious consequences of strategic interaction among players in an n-person game.

Voting Power in the EC Council of Ministers

The SEA was approved by the EC Council of Ministers in December 1985 and ratified by the member states in early 1986. When it came into force in July 1987, it committed its members to the progressive establishment, by the end of 1992, of an internal market, defined as "an area without internal frontiers in which the free movement of goods, persons, services and capital is ensured." The SEA has been called "the most important amendment to the Treaty of Rome since the latter was adopted in 1957," primarily because "it rejects the national veto" (Sandholtz and Zysman, 1989, pp. 115–116) by extending qualified-majority voting to Council decisions pertaining to the internal market. Indeed, Cameron (1992, p. 56) claims that this extension may represent the "most important" aspect of the SEA.

Although qualified-majority voting was increasingly invoked from 1966 until 1985 (Moravcsik, 1991, p. 51), its scope was circumscribed by the Luxembourg compromise. Under pressure from France, which had boycotted EC proceedings for six months in 1965, the other five EC countries reluctantly agreed in January 1966 that France would be able to veto proposals of the Council that it declared infringed on its "very important" national interests, which was a right later invoked by other governments.

The expansion of qualified-majority voting (the decision rule is fifty-four out of seventy-six votes on the Council, or 71 percent) under the SEA has greatly reduced use of the veto. To be sure, the SEA allows for certain exceptions relating to the internal market: fiscal (primarily tax) issues, the free movement of people, and worker rights. But except in these areas qualified-majority voting can be invoked relatively easily. If the Commission of the EC unanimously agrees that a matter is pertinent, then a simple majority of the Council weighted votes (thirty-nine out of seventy-six) can sanction a qualified majority of the Council to act on the matter (Garrett, 1992, p. 550). As is usual in such cases, the procedural threshold to decide that a matter is pertinent (thirty-nine votes), if unchallenged by any member of the Commission, is lower than the substantive threshold (fifty-four votes), necessary to act on this matter. The Council, acting unanimously, may amend a Commission proposal, and the European Parliament (EP) may in turn approve, reject, or amend a Council decision. Other intricate relationships among the Council, Commission, and EP—as well as the Court of

Justice and the national courts—are discussed in Garrett (1992), who offers an informal strategic assessment of their effects.

Here we shall focus on the more formal implications of weighted voting in the Council itself, based on a game-theoretic measure of voting power. Then we shall modify this measure to take into account the de facto vetoes that France and Germany allegedly exercise on the Council. We shall also consider likely groupings of members, which reduce the number of players from twelve to three, and analyze the power of the Council to act under different decision rules.

Brams and Affuso (1976, 1985a, 1985b) applied the Banzhaf index of voting power (Banzhaf, 1965) to the original EC Council of six member (1958) and the later expanded Councils of nine members (1973), ten members (1981), and now twelve members (1985). They discovered striking anomalies of weighted voting that have arisen, including:

- Luxembourg's "dummy" status from 1958 to 1973 (that is, it had zero voting power).
- The "paradox of new members" (Luxembourg increased its voting power in 1973 and again in 1981 when new members were added, despite the fact that it had an increasingly smaller proportion of the vote total).
- The failure of differently weighted members to have different voting power (from 1981 to 1985, Luxembourg with two votes had the same voting power as Denmark and Ireland with three votes each).

Brams and Affuso attributed these bizarre effects to the "capricious nature of constitution writing—done mostly by lawyers uninformed as to the significance of the weights and decision rules they set down—even today" (Brams and Affuso, 1976, p. 52).[1]

Because Banzhaf voting power is defined formally in Brams and Affuso (1976, pp. 32–34), among other places, we shall give only an informal definition here. This measure has been compared with other game-theoretic of voting power—Shapley and Shubik (1954) and Johnston (1978)—in Brams and Affuso (1976), Brams, Affuso, and Kilgour (1989), and Brams (1975, 1985, 1990). Because these other measures generally attribute greater voting power to larger players than does the Banzhaf index, we probably err in being too conservative in our later estimate of the voting power of the big four (France, Italy, Germany, and the United Kingdom) and of the even more substantial influence of France and Germany when they have vetoes.

The Banzhaf power of a member is based on the number of winning coalitions (WCs) in which it is critical—that is, in which its defection would cause such a coalition to become losing. The (normalized) *Banzhaf voting power* of a member is the number of WCs in which it is critical divided by the total number of critical defections of all members (including this member). The sum of these proportions for all members is, of course, one.

Table 4.1 shows the Banzhaf powers of the twelve current members of the Council under qualified-majority rule (Brams and Affuso, 1985a).[2] To illustrate

the Branzhaf calculation, consider the case of Luxembourg, which has two votes. A qualified majority of fifty-four out of seventy-six is required in order for the Council to act. Luxembourg will be critical if the sum of the votes of the other members of a coalition is fifty-two or fifty-three because then the addition of Luxembourg's two votes will give these members, together with Luxembourg, at least fifty-four votes, the minimum required to be a WC. It turns out that Luxembourg is critical in exactly forty WCs,[3] whereas all countries combined have a total of 2,222 critical defections, giving Luxembourg 1.8 percent of the voting power, or a Banzhaf index of 0.018, as shown in Table 4.1.

What is the rationale behind the decision rule of fifty-four out of seventy-six? Note that not only does no single country have a veto, but not even two of the big four (with ten votes each) do. At a minimum, a blocking coalition, whose opposition prevents the Council from acting, must comprise two large countries plus one other country with at least three votes, which excludes Luxembourg. For this reason Luxembourg has significantly less voting power than either Denmark or Ireland, each of which has three votes and therefore can be critical in many different blocking coalitions with other members that have exactly twenty other votes.

Interestingly, the Banzhaf values for Denmark and Ireland, as well as for the nine larger countries, are roughly proportional to their voting weights. However, the weights—and therefore the Banzhaf values—are not proportional to the populations: the populations of the largest countries, especially that of a united Germany today, are disproportionately greater than their weights, which would seem to give the advantage, in relative terms, to the smaller countries on the Council.

To explore this question further, we next consider how the vetoes of two members and plausible coalitions of other members that might form affect the Banzhaf values. We then define a new index that is used to measure the power of the Council as a whole to act, with and without the possibility of vetoes.

Table 4.1. Banzhaf Voting Power in EC Council of Ministers Under Qualified-Majority Decision Rule.

Class of Member	Banzhaf Power
Each Ten-Vote Member (France, Germany, Italy, United Kingdom)	0.129
One Eight-Vote Member (Spain)	0.109
Each Five-Vote Member (Belgium, Greece, Netherlands, Portugal)	0.067
Each Three-Vote Member (Denmark, Ireland)	0.046
One Two-Vote Member (Luxembourg)	0.018

Vetoes, Coalitions, and the Power of the Council to Act

In calculating the "criticalness" of members, the Banzhaf index assumes that all minimum winning coalitions (MWCs) are equally likely. Surely this is not the case in most voting bodies, including the EC Council. We shall posit likely coalitions of members—based on their apparent common interests—later, but first we recalculate the Banzhaf values to take into account the fact that the numerical weights of members, and the qualified-majority decision rule, may not give an accurate picture of members' influence on the Council.

In point of fact, the big four are not all equal: "Where EC bargaining is concerned, it is axiomatic to assert that no major initiative can proceed without the consent of France and Germany. This is true even though qualified majority voting in the Council does allow for other coalitions' formations. Politically, however, it would be most unlikely for a major development to go ahead without their endorsement. This "rule" does not apply to Italy or the United Kingdom" (Lodge, 1991, p. 7). In a similar vein, after noting that France and Germany have almost half the total EC output, Garrett (1992, pp. 546–547) argues that they effectively have vetoes; because they can afford to "go it alone," they have an exit option, whereas the United Kingdom, in particular, does not.

To take into account this informal rule, we can modify the weights of France and Germany and the qualified majority necessary for the passage of acts so that each country has a veto. Specifically, consider a hypothetical Council in which France and Germany have 23 votes each (instead of 10) but assume the weights of all the other countries are as given in Table 4.1, which gives a new total of 102 votes. In addition, change the decision rule to a qualified majority of 80 out of 102 votes.

Now the ten other countries, plus either France or Germany (but not both), have a total of seventy-nine votes, which is one vote shy of the new qualified majority. Consequently, France or Germany each has a veto—either's exclusion from a coalition that includes all other members causes that coalition to lose.[4] In other words, the presence of both countries is necessary in every WC, but—as in the present Council—they are not sufficient by themselves. In the hypothetical Council, their combined 46 votes must be supplemented by an additional 34 votes to reach the decision rule of 80 (when the total is 102). In the actual Council, their combined twenty votes must also be supplemented by an additional thirty-four votes to reach the decision rule of fifty-four (when the total is seventy-six). This equality in additional votes needed to form a WC means that the WCs in the hypothetical Council completely overlap those in the actual Council, but the actual Council contains 54 WCs (out of a total of 342) without France, Germany, or both countries that the hypothetical Council does not contain.

How do France and Germany's de facto vetoes change the distribution of power in the hypothetical Council? The new Banzhaf values are given in Table 4.2 and show that these two countries have 60 percent more power (0.184 versus 0.115) than Italy and the United Kingdom, their ostensibly equal partners on the actual Council. With the exception of Luxembourg, which has the same Banzhaf

Table 4.2. Banzhaf Voting Power in EC Council of Ministers,
When France and Germany Have Vetoes, Under Qualified-Majority Decision Rule.

Class of Member	Banzhaf Power
Each Twenty-Three-Vote Member (France, Germany)	0.184
Each Ten-Vote Member (Italy, United Kingdom)	0.115
One Eight-Vote Member (Spain)	0.092
Each Five-Vote Member (Belgium, Greece, Netherlands, Portugal)	0.055
Each Three-Vote Member (Denmark, Ireland)	0.036
One Two-Vote Member (Luxembourg)	0.018

power as before (0.018), all the smaller countries suffer a power loss but not, relatively, as much as Italy and the United Kingdom do. We conclude that the Banzhaf power values given by the de jure decision rule (Table 4.1) change significantly when the de facto vetoes of France and Germany are incorporated into the calculation (Table 4.2). Not only are the de facto Banzhaf values probably a better reflection of the actual power of the players on the Council, but—more germane to negotiating the SEA—these values may better mirror the degree to which France and Germany, rather than Italy and the United Kingdom, achieved their goals in the SEA.

Garrett (1992) reaches a similar conclusion, based on locating three different groupings of EC countries in an ideological space of two dimensions, one based on "political authority" and the other on "economic principles." Thus, for example, he locates the United Kingdom as favoring the national veto on the political dimension and favoring mutual recognition—but not full economic integration and social harmonization—on the economic dimension. In fact, Greece, along with the United Kingdom and Denmark, favored the national veto (Moravcsik, 1991, p. 39; Lodge, 1991, p. 6). Following Garrett (1992)—except for Greece, which he puts in group C (see below)—we call this group of countries group A (total votes: eighteen). Group B comprises France, Germany, and the Benelux countries, all of which supported a qualified-majority decision rule (total votes: thirty-two). Group C, which favored a simple-majority decision rule, comprises Ireland, Italy, Portugal, and Spain (total votes: twenty-six). In this three-person game, only coalition BC, with a total of fifty-eight votes, has a qualified majority of at least fifty-four votes, giving both B and C a Banzhaf power value of 0.5. Whether France or Germany—and therefore group B—has a veto would not change this result; because B and C are both necessary in the only WC, each has a veto. Group A, by contrast, not only has no veto but also is a dummy, with zero power.

Insofar as the present Council is a mirror of power relationships that existed before the adoption of the qualified-majority rule, group A could not have prevented enactment of the SEA. (In fact, because BC is the only WC, the SEA would presumably be a compromise between B and C.) Group A's dummy status perhaps helps explain why the United Kingdom, as the dominant actor in A, decided in the end not to go it alone. Not only did its group not have veto power, which requires at least twenty-three votes in the present Council, but it could not combine with either B or C to produce a qualified majority of at least fifty-four votes.

The United Kingdom's acquiescence on the qualified-majority issue may have enabled it to wring concessions out of the other members on issues that it considered more important. Indeed, Moravcsik (1991, p. 41) argues that the United Kingdom was the real winner in a "victory for the minimalists" because it had "little to lose from qualified majority voting on the internal market plan, which it favored in general." In effect, Margaret Thatcher may have successfully postured on the political dimension in order to get concessions on the economic dimension (for example, liberalization of financial services or a reduction in the United Kingdom's contribution to the EC budget), which is a well-known tactic in bargaining theory that has an evident rational basis (Brams, 1990).[5]

One consequence of the compromises hammered out to secure passage of the SEA is that whereas "bargains initially consisted of bilateral agreements between France and Germany, now they consist of trilateral agreements including Britain" (Moravcsik, 1991, p. 26). In fact, Moravcsik (1991, p. 49) claims that Britain is the country "most satisfied with the final outcome." Notwithstanding possible "inside" agreements among the big three (Italy's interest tend more than this triumvirate's to echo those of the poorer, mostly southern countries), Cameron (1992, p. 56) is undoubtedly right that "the broader application of majority voting has changed the political calculus of Council of Minister members, who must increasingly search for allies in majoritarian coalitions. Moreover, in its broader application majority voting implies that national preferences are more likely to be overridden and, as a result, that national sovereignty might be eroded."

To shed further light on this "political calculus," we compute a final measure, the power of a collectivity to act (Coleman, 1971), under both qualified-majority voting and the alternative decision rules considered. This power is measured by the proportion of coalitions that are winning. If there are n members of a voting body, and each member either favors or opposes a measure, then the total number of coalitions favoring the resolution—or complementary coalitions opposing—is 2^n, which is also the number of ways of partitioning the voting body into two subsets.[6]

Because there are twelve members of the EC Council, there are $2^{12} = 4,096$ partitions. Under a decision rule of unanimity, in which each country has a national veto, only the grand coalition can pass a resolution. Hence, the power of the Council to act under this decision rule is a minuscule $1/4,096 = 0.000244$, given that all partitions, or divisions of the body, are equally likely. Under

simple-majority rule, by contrast, the power to act is $1,800/4,096 = 0.439$ because, for every partition, the favorable coalition will win in half (2,048)—except for the 248 (= 2,048 - 1,800) partitions that lead to a 38-38 tie, in which both coalitions are blocking but neither is winning.

Less obvious is the power of the Council to act under its qualified-majority decision rule. It turns out that there are only 402 WCs under this decision rule (342 are minimal WCs in the sense that the defection of at least one member would cause them to be losing), so this power is $402/4,096 = 0.0981$. By comparison, if both France and Germany have de facto vetoes, there are 288 WCs (all are minimal because all include France and Germany, whose defections make them losing). Thus, the power of the Council to act in this case is $288/4,096 = 0.0703$. This is a relatively small reduction (28.4 percent) from the Council's power to act under the qualified-majority rule without the two vetoes. Far more striking, a qualified-majority rule, with or without the vetoes, vastly increases the Council's power to act—by factors of about 300 to 400—compared with a unanimity rule (0.000244).

True, the national veto has rarely been invoked; but, on the important occasions on which it was—for example, Charles de Gaulle's veto of the 1966 Common Agriculture Policy (CAP), which occasioned the Luxembourg compromise—it blocked a consensus on the part of all the other members. By comparison, under qualified-majority rule—with or without vetoes by France and Germany—blocking coalitions are still far more numerous than WCs (more than 90 percent of the total), but the WCs no longer require a heroic effort if there is a fairly broad consensus and some spirit of compromise.

The winning coalitions that form will obviously depend on the issue, at least if the very different alliances that were put together in negotiating the SEA are any indication (Lodge, 1991). Consequently, a purely formal "issue-independent" power analysis can never perfectly reflect political realities; depending on the issue, members will have partially overlapping and partially divergent interests, making some coalitions more likely than others.

For this reason, we have tried to show how the special prerogatives of members, like France and Germany, or likely groupings, like those given by A, B, and C, might alter the de jure power calculations. Additionally, it is illuminating to view the Council as a whole and compare its power to act under different decision rules. Unanimity, by a wide margin, is the most stultifying rule, suggesting that the Council made a radical shift toward democratic rule in permitting a 71 percent majority to prevail. Because this majority still requires a preponderance of weighted votes, the Council's greatly enhanced power to act will, one might hope, be power used to serve the interests of most citizens of the EC countries. But the Council, of course, is not directly elected by these people, so the "democratic" character of its rule can be questioned.

Presumably, the decision rule of qualified majority institutionalized by the SEA reflected, at least to some degree, the bargaining power, skills, and interest of the players in the preceding negotiations. Not only do our game-theoretic results quantify the relative powers of the players on the Council—depending on

which assumptions about individual and collective players, with and without
vetoes, are most accurate—but they also offer a precise notion of the ability of the
Council, as a body, to act.[7]

Preferences of Players in the Uruguay Round (and Beyond)

Founded in Geneva in October 1947 by twenty-three countries, GATT is now an
organization with 108 countries; it has sponsored eight rounds of negotiations.
These multilateral talks have dramatically influenced international economic
relations since World War II, primarily through liberalizing international trade
by lowering tariff barriers on the order of 70 percent (Sjöstedt, 1990, p. 5). It is
variously estimated that between one-third (Bentsen, 1991) and two-thirds ("Free
Trade Loses a Round," 1990) of world trade is covered by GATT rules, with total
trade amounting to about $4 trillion annually (Greenhouse, 1991; Silk, 1991a).

The latest negotiations have been dubbed the Uruguay Round because
they began in Punta del Este in September 1986. Scheduled to last four years, they
collapsed in Brussels in December 1990 (Farnsworth, 1990). Although they resumed in February 1991, an agreement even on procedural aspects of the talks was
not in sight two years later, lending credence to the rueful GATT appellation,
General Agreement to Talk and Talk. As of fall 1993, the full reinstatement and
successful conclusion of the Uruguay Round still faced formidable obstacles. The
increase in bilateral trade negotiations, the rise of regional trading blocs, and a
new debate about free versus fair trade all may undermine an already shaky
international trading regime riddled with protectionist proclivities. But the most
immediate obstacle has been the conflicting interests of the three major players
in the current trading round—the United States, the EC, and Japan, which Oxley
(1990, p. 88) calls the "big three." Of course, there are other influential players,
most notably the so-called Cairns group (Higgott and Cooper, 1990), an association of fourteen developed and developing agricultural-exporting countries that
pushed for lower agricultural barriers. Newly industrializing countries, like
South Korea and Taiwan, and developing countries, like Brazil, India, and the
members of the Association of Southeast Asian Nations, also played a role in the
Uruguay Round.

The impasse, however, is due primarily to differences among the big three
on agriculture, which Winham and Kizer (1993, p. 43) characterize as "the pivotal
issue" and Sjöstedt (1990, p. 3) calls "the most important" unsolved problem.
Although less consequential to the outcome of the Uruguay Round, the issue of
market access also pervades discussions of trade liberalization. Hence, we include
the positions of the big three on this issue—the "and beyond" allusion in the title
of this section—as well as the agricultural issue:[8]

1. Support of agriculture through price supports or export subsidies
   (favored by the EC, opposed by the United States and Japan).[9]
2. Barriers to foreign market entry (favored by Japan, opposed by the United
   States and the EC).

The "barriers" in issue 2 do not necessarily apply to intraregional trade, such as between the United States and neighbors like Canada and Mexico. In fact, issue 2 more and more may be interpreted as the issue of supporting regional pacts by limiting outside access to internal markets (as the EC has done), which may undermine the universality of GATT and which we shall say more about later. Issue 2, of course, is related to issue 1 if agriculture is the sector being restricted.

Japan, at least for its national market, is more restrictive than either the United States or the EC. It therefore seems fair to say that Japan "favors" barriers, whereas the United States and, to a lesser extent, the EC oppose them. That the nature of Japanese restrictions is sometimes heavily governed by culture and practice—not comparative advantage in resources or even wages—is illustrated by the case of automobiles (Prestowitz, 1991, p. 28):

> Even if U.S. and Japanese automakers attained the same quality and production costs, U.S. producers would likely lose out. Why? Because it takes dealers to sell cars. Establishing a national dealer network from scratch in a country the size of the United States is an expensive and time-consuming task—as it is in Japan because of stratospheric real estate prices. But Japanese automakers selling in the United States don't have to build from scratch. They can piggyback onto existing, GM, Ford, and Chrysler dealers because U.S. antitrust laws stipulate that producers must allow dealers to carry other lines. In contrast, by custom and because the Japanese do not enforce antitrust laws, outside firms find it extremely difficult to hook up with dealers in Japan.

In the face of such barriers, the United States and the EC have become increasingly less content to be unilateral free traders. For example, the United States and the EC have used import quotas and antidumping provisions—sometimes in retaliation against restrictions of Japan and other countries (or each other)—or they have negotiated export restraints that evade GATT rules.[10]

At the same time, Japan has not been totally recalcitrant and seems to be improving (Sanger, 1991). It has, under pressure, lifted restrictions in certain areas, like its beef market (Oxley, 1990, p. 68) and semiconductor-chip trade (Prestowitz, 1991, p. 26) with the United States; the semiconductor-chip agreement, which was in effect from 1986 to 1991, was extended for three years (Bradsher, 1991). Currently, however, not only does Japan have a blanket prohibition on rice imports (Farnsworth, 1990), but its rice farmers also benefit from subsidies and have, consequently, become "the most protected farmers in the world" (Passel, 1990).

Other prominent issues debated during the Uruguay Round include intellectual property rights, financial and other services, and textile trade (Winham and Kizer, 1993). An agreement by developing countries to protect trade in intellectual property and services in return for reduced barriers on food and textile imports by developed countries will presumably be part of any eventual settle-

ment, which is the kind of pattern that has been established in previous successful North-South negotiations (Zartman, 1987).

But here we shall focus on issues 1 and 2 among the big three, in part because the trade-offs are not so apparent. Call the positions on issues 1 and 2:

>A (for agricultural supports) and $\bar{A}$ (against supports)
>B (for barriers) and $\bar{B}$ (against barriers)

Positions on both these issues define four possible platforms: AB, A$\bar{B}$, $\bar{A}$B and $\bar{A}\bar{B}$. We assume that the players can order these platforms from best to worst, based on "primary" and "secondary" goals. A player's (1) primary goal distinguishes its two best from its two worst platforms, whereas a (2) secondary goal distinguishes between its two best platforms and between its two worst platforms. Thus, if (1) were $\bar{A}$ and (2) were $\bar{B}$, the player would order the platforms, from best to worst, as follows: $\bar{A}\bar{B}$, $\bar{A}$B, A$\bar{B}$, AB.[11] We, in fact, assume this ordering to be the preferences of the United States. We summarize below the goals, and the preferences they imply, of the other players as well:

>United States: (1) $\bar{A}$ and (2) $\bar{B}$ ($\bar{A}\bar{B}$, $\bar{A}$B, A$\bar{B}$, AB).
>EC: (1) A and (2) $\bar{B}$ (A$\bar{B}$, AB, $\bar{A}\bar{B}$, $\bar{A}$B).
>Japan: (1) $\bar{A}$ and (2) B ($\bar{A}$B, $\bar{A}\bar{B}$, AB, A$\bar{B}$).

Because of its pivotalness in the Uruguay Round, we make the issue of agricultural supports primary for all players. It is certainly possible that the players' positions on the market-entry issue—and regional versus worldwide pacts, like GATT, which this issue raises—will assume greater importance in the future than they now have. Indeed, the ultimate failure of the Uruguay Round may lead to trade agreements by continental blocs, such as the Americas, Europe, and Asia (Passel, 1991), which some analysts view with alarm (Silk, 1991b) and others consider salutary (Prestowitz, 1991), but which may actually be strategic: "By preparing the ground for a series of bilateral trade deals with every country in Latin America," the United States and its potential partners may be "quietly hedging their bets" ("Hedging," 1990). Conceivably, however, the "minilateralism" of such blocs may evolve into the multilateralism of GATT, facilitating rather than undermining world trade; but this consequence is hotly debated (Belous and Hartley, 1990; Uchitelle, 1991; Milner, 1993; Yarbrough and Yarbrough, 1992).

Observe that each of the three players has a different first, second, third, and last preference, suggesting a lack of social consensus. Nevertheless, if we compare, for each pair of platforms, which is socially preferred (that is, by a majority of two of the three players), we obtain the social preference ordering shown in Figure 4.1. (Later, however, we shall indicate that social preferences based on majority rule probably do not describe how negotiation outcomes are determined.)

Notice that, as indicated by the three arrows emanating from $\bar{A}\bar{B}$, two of

Figure 4.1. Social Hierarchy of Majority Preferences for Platforms.

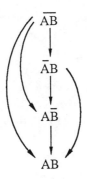

Note: Arrows emanating from a higher platform to a lower platform indicate that the higher platform is socially preferred (that is, by a majority of two of the three players) to the lower platform.

the three players prefer $\overline{A}\overline{B}$ to each of the other three platforms. The fact that these other platforms can also be ordered so that all social preference relations flow "downward" from $\overline{A}\overline{B}$ to $\overline{A}B$ to $A\overline{B}$ to AB establishes the existence of a social hierarchy of platforms.[12] Even $\overline{A}\overline{B}$, however, if pitted against each of the other platforms, would always be opposed by one of the three players. Thus, if each of the players is able to veto the social choice of a platform, the fact that there exists a social hierarchy based on majority preferences does not establish that a social consensus will develop around $\overline{A}\overline{B}$ at the top of the hierarchy. Quite the contrary: each of the platforms would be vetoed by the player who prefers another. Hence, if unanimous consent is required (as is probably the case among the big three in the Uruguay Round), it will not be achieved.

A Dynamic Negotiation Model

Now consider a negotiation model in which players begin by supporting only their first preferences. If there is no agreement among these, as in our example (they differ for all three players), we assume players next lend their support to their second preferences as well.[13] At this second stage, observe that $\overline{A}B$ would have the support of the United States and Japan, as would $\overline{A}B$. Only if the players—at least the EC—then give their support to their third preferences will a consensus (unanimous support) form around $\overline{A}\overline{B}$—but not around any of the other platforms. The required support by the EC of $\overline{A}\overline{B}$ (as a third preference) is what led to the breakup of the talks in December 1990, when the EC failed to alter significantly its position on agriculture. Resolving this sticking point, according to our model, would end the conflict and produce unanimous consent for $\overline{A}\overline{B}$. Moreover, having all the players pledge support for all platforms down to the third preference would not induce unanimous support for any other platform.

The United States or Japan would have to dip down to their last preferences to cement unanimity for either AB or A$\bar{\text{B}}$.

We next introduce a player's N threshold, or point at which it would prefer no agreement (N) to any lower-ranked platform. Assume the EC is adamant in its position on issue 1; unalterably opposed to $\bar{\text{A}}$, it insists on agricultural supports and so puts N in third place. Assume the United States puts N in fourth place: it will not give up on both its primary and secondary goals. Then the only way that unanimous consent can be achieved is if Japan puts N in fifth place. If this is the case, support for the various alternatives will evolve to the following:

United States: ($\bar{\text{A}}\bar{\text{B}}$, $\bar{\text{A}}$B, A$\bar{\text{B}}$, N | AB).
EC: (A$\bar{\text{B}}$, AB, N | $\bar{\text{A}}\bar{\text{B}}$, $\bar{\text{A}}$B).
Japan: ($\bar{\text{A}}$B, $\bar{\text{A}}\bar{\text{B}}$, AB, A$\bar{\text{B}}$ | N).

By the time the players have lowered their support to the points indicated by the vertical bars—where they will stop because, by assumption, they prefer N to further concessions (that is, support for lower-ranked platforms, if there are any)—there will be unanimous support for A$\bar{\text{B}}$.

Yet both $\bar{\text{A}}\bar{\text{B}}$ and $\bar{\text{A}}$B beat A$\bar{\text{B}}$ in the hierarchy! $\bar{\text{A}}\bar{\text{B}}$ and $\bar{\text{A}}$B platforms "lose," once we insert N in the preference rankings, because of the EC's hypothesized intransigence—it will not support $\bar{\text{A}}\bar{\text{B}}$ and $\bar{\text{A}}$B because they rank below N on its preference scale. The diminished intransigence we hypothesize for the United States—and still less for Japan—ensures that A$\bar{\text{B}}$ rather than $\bar{\text{A}}\bar{\text{B}}$ will be the outcome (the reverse would be the case if Japan ranked N fourth and the United States ranked it fifth). In this manner, a player's higher placement of N induces the choice of a preferred platform, even though this platform may fall lower in the social hierarchy, based on majority-rule voting, than others (Brams and Doherty, 1992; Brams, 1993, Chap. 7).

Time will tell, if our hypothetical attribution of preferences for the players is correct and the unanimity rule is operative, whether the EC's N threshold is higher than that of the United States and of Japan. The U.S. and Japanese N thresholds also matter, as we have just shown, and also may not be as we have hypothesized. Indeed, the fact that the big three have disagreed since 1990 suggests that one or more of these players ranks N higher than we have hypothesized. The hypothesized preferences of the big three (for N as well as for the different platforms), the unanimity decision rule, and negotiations that unfold in the manner of our model certainly do not capture all the nuances of any end game that may be played out in the Uruguay Round and later. Other preferences and rules, and even new players, might be incorporated into the analysis if doing so offers a more realistic portrayal than our model of the current trade-negotiation game.

The game-theoretic methodology that we have introduced for analyzing negotiation processes, simple as it is, is the main contribution of this section. We believe it offers an enlightening way of viewing the unfolding of positions and possible changes in support patterns, as players offer compromises—specifically, by progressively supporting lower-ranked platforms, at least up to some point

N.[14] A model in which players respond to each other over time provides, we think, an innovative and compelling way to explicate the dynamics of negotiation processes.

Conclusions

Multilateral negotiations can often be reduced to bilateral negotiations, or a series of bilateral negotiations, but sometimes they resist such a simplification. This seems to be the case in both the SEA and the Uruguay Round negotiations, in which there were at least three major players and a reduction of either set of negotiations to two-person games would do violence to reality. It is true that there has been a serious two-person conflict between the developed and developing countries on the Uruguay Round, but these collective players also have intersecting interests on which reasonable compromises seem possible. The fact that they have yet to be fashioned after several years of negotiations suggests that more basic conflicts divide other players. Also, the existence of the Cairns group, comprising both developed and developing countries that share an interest in lowering barriers to agricultural imports, is testimony that the North-South division may not be the fundamental one.

   We were thus led to analyze a three-person game among the big three, in part because their positions on agriculture, the most contentious issue, were divergent. But the issue of market access also seems salient, even if it is not so relevant to the Uruguay Round but is instead part of a larger game.[15] The issue of market access, should it become paramount, may be instrumental in restructuring the players into regional blocs and altering the fundamental nature of the trading game. Our analysis of the game among the big three, reflecting their positions on both agriculture and market access, indicates not only that their preferences differ but also that they all will have to make significant compromises to reach a consensus. Our dynamic negotiation model showed that a consensus will not be achieved if the EC considers a continuing impasse preferable to compromise on its primary goal of maintaining agricultural supports.

   The SEA was successful in redistributing power, based on qualified-majority voting, in a way that probably mirrored the strengths of the negotiating positions of the main players, especially France, Germany, and the United Kingdom. The United Kingdom, even though it did not have a veto and therefore could be isolated, nevertheless probably managed to attain most of its goals by posturing on some issues in order to get concessions on others. In particular, qualified-majority voting, which it opposed, probably was never a dire threat to its sovereignty, so it could afford to compromise on this issue in order to get its way on other issues, such as the liberalization of financial services or a reduction in its contribution to the EC budget. To be sure, we did not explicitly model these trade-offs but rather focused on the power-related consequences of voting. One of the more revealing quantitative findings is that the Council enhanced its power to act by a factor of between 300 and 400 by renouncing national vetoes on most questions. At the same time, a 71 percent majority is not trivial to muster,

especially if France and Germany have de facto vetoes, so precipitous action that threatens major national interests seems improbable.

We view the SEA as a major step toward democratic rule, despite the fact that the compromises reached so far may have a lowest-common-denominator ring. Like the 69 percent majority needed to ratify the U.S. federal constitution (nine of the thirteen original states), or the 75 percent majority (again, of states) needed to ratify constitutional amendments, the 71 percent EC Council majority is of the order of magnitude to make possible important and necessary changes without trampling on the rights of individual members, who are likely to remain the key actors even if most are dispossessed of their national vetoes.[16]

It is hard to say at this point whether a compromise agreement will eventually be worked out on what seem to be the most divisive issues in the trade talks, both inside and outside the Uruguay Round. If not, failure will occur because an agreement, at least in the eyes of some players, is worse than no agreement. Our game-theoretic analysis, we believe, illuminates why this is the case and why a different game, in which regional blocs become the new players, may supplant the present game.

Notes

1. Actually, the rationale of the weights and of the decision rule of the Council today is quite transparent, leading to a good fit of weighted votes and Banzhaf power values. But, as we shall show, a different story emerges when we factor in the apparent special prerogatives of certain members as well as take into account the likely coalitions.

2. Under a simple-majority decision rule of thirty-nine out of seventy-six (used mostly for routine procedural matters), the Banzhaf values are: ten-vote members, 0.134; eight-vote member; 0.107; five-vote members, 0.064; three-vote members, 0.040; two-vote member, 0.024. Clearly, the decision rule matters, benefiting the largest four members and the smallest member—vis-à-vis the seven intermediate members—compared with qualified-majority voting (Table 4.1).

3. There are no nonwinning coalitions (NCs)—without Luxembourg—with fifty-two votes, but there are forty NCs without Luxembourg with fifty-three votes, in which case Luxembourg's two votes are, therefore, critical:
- Four with members (10, 10, 10, 10, 8, 5)—four different countries may be the included "5."
- Sixteen with (10, 10, 10, 8, 5, 5, 5)—four different countries may be the excluded "10," and four different countries may be the excluded "5."
- Twelve with (10, 10, 10, 10, 5, 5, 3)—six different countries may be the two included "5s," and two different countries may be the included "3."
- Eight with (10, 10, 10, 5, 5, 5, 5, 3)—four different countries may be the excluded "10," and two different countries may be the included "3."

4. Other weights could accomplish the same end, but these are the smallest that do so.

5. Cameron (1992, p. 62) also believes that British intransigence on certain

issues may have enhanced its bargaining position, although the specific concessions it gained are by no means clear. The budgetary rebates the United Kingdom received, for example, may not have been in return for British support of qualified-majority voting but instead for concessions on internal-market issues.

6. These complementary coalitions include the coalition with no members (ϕ) and the grand coalition with all members. Thus, if $n = 2$, the four partitions, indicated by a slash, are $\phi/12$, $1/2$, $2/1$, and $12/\phi$. If the coalition to the left of the slash favors a resolution, and the decision rule is simple majority, the favorable coalitions in the first three partitions are losing and only 12 in the last partition is winning. The favorable coalitions in the two middle partitions, 1 and 2, are blocking (as well as losing) because neither side of the partition is winning.

7. It should be noted, however, that many of the Council's decisions are, in fact, reached without actually taking a formal vote. Yet this fact does not detract from the thrust of our analysis, which is intended to establish a kind of power baseline against which actual negotiations are played out. Moreover, as the EC faces the possibility of expansion in the future, such an examination could become critical not only because the proper distribution of power is important but also because the enlargement of the membership is likely to lead to more frequent use of formal voting procedures. Thus, despite its somewhat ambiguous role in the daily proceedings of the Council, members' formal voting power probably reveals important facets of Council negotiations, both now and increasingly in the future.

8. Thereby we add "quantity" issues (for example, the volume of trade or its management in particular sectors), which are not generally subjects of GATT, to "quality" issues (for example, rules that allow market forces to operate), which are subjects of GATT, as part of the negotiation game analyzed.

9. Paradoxically, the SEA has led to liberalization of agricultural trading within the EC through the EC's CAP, "which protects 8 million EC farmers against nearly 300 million farmers in the poor countries" (Bhagwati, 1991, p. 8). CAP, incidentally, is estimated to cost more than $35 billion annually (Greenhouse, 1991), with total subsidies running between $100 billion ("A Big Win-Win on Trade," 1991) and $300 billion (Silk, 1991a).

10. U.S. retaliatory actions have been sanctioned by what are known as the regular, special, and super 301 sections of the 1988 Omnibus Trade and Competitiveness Act, which were largely a response to U.S. trade and budget deficits (an earlier trade act was passed in 1974 with weaker provisions). These actions have been argued to be "GATT-illegal," on the one hand, and to be necessary for the proper functioning of the world trading system by penalizing noncompliance with a GATT tenet, reciprocity, on the other (Bhagwati and Patrick, 1990).

11. See Hillinger (1971) and Kadane (1972) for an analysis of the effects of combining different positions into platforms. The use of primary and secondary goals to order platforms is an example of a lexicographic decision rule, whereby outcomes are first ordered on the basis of a most important criterion, then a next-most important criterion, and so on (Fishburn, 1974); such goals are used to define games in Brams (1983).

12. Such a hierarchy will not exist if the players' individual preferences lead to cyclical majorities, whereby social preferences cycle because no platform is preferred to all others; for an example, see Brams (1975, pp. 55–57). Such a cycle creates a paradox of voting, which may aggravate the problem of achieving a consensus—or, for that matter, reaching an agreement in the dynamic negotiation model described in this chapter.

13. The negotiation model to be described, with one significant difference, is illustrated with another example—involving cyclical majorities—in Brams (1991) and developed fully in Brams and Doherty (1992) and Brams (1993, Chap. 7). The significant difference in this other model is that it assumes that the players have incomplete information about each other's preferences, which is revealed only as they progressively indicate support for lower-ranked alternatives during the negotiation process; also, the model does not assume an impenetrable "no agreement" but allows players to breach this threshold if doing so may prevent an inferior alternative from being selected. For more on games of incomplete information as well as models relevant to negotiation analysis, see Siebe (1991), Sebenius (1991), and P. Young (1991).

14. We are hampered, however, by having insufficient information to test whether support patterns evolved in the manner predicted by the model. In fact, we are not even sure what the "true" preferences of the players are, which is why we claim only to have illustrated a methodology, not rigorously tested a model.

15. Clearly, the identity of the players and of the games being played is not always evident. Most problematic in applying game theory is ascertaining the preferences of the players, not so much on the broad issues we have discussed but on specifics, to which we are simply not privy.

16. With respect to democratic rule, however, it should be recalled that the Council (unlike the EP) is not elected, though it represents elected governments. Also, the U.S. qualified majorities we refer to in the text apply to the enactment and amendment of the U.S. Constitution; amendments to the Treaty of Rome still rquire unanimity. Perhaps a more appropriate comparison is to the two-third majorities of the U.S. House of Representatives and the Senate that are needed to override a presidential veto.

Chapter 5

Organization Theory
The Interface of Structure, Culture, Procedures, and Negotiation Processes

*Deborah M. Kolb (USA),
Guy-Olivier Faure (France)*

The study of negotiations of either the bilateral or multilateral sort has long been dominated by models of individuals or small groups (or both). Most of our theorizing provides a picture of freelance individuals, or combinations of individuals, conducting their negotiations unfettered by organizational expectations or constraints. Yet organizations often figure prominently in negotiations. Many negotiations are explicitly conducted under the auspices of a particular organization with a structure and culture that undoubtedly influences the form and course of a negotiation. Furthermore, negotiators are often agents of organizations that have constituents they represent and must satisfy. Thus, organizational issues influence and affect negotiation in potentially important ways.

Negotiation theory, however, has been virtually silent on this interface between organizational structures, cultures, and procedures and negotiation. The same can be said for a strain of organization theory, called *negotiated order*, where negotiation is seen as a major organizational process (Strauss and others, 1963). Negotiation from this perspective serves merely as another term for interaction, and so scholarship on negotiated orders has contributed little to our understanding of how negotiations are affected by the organizational setting in which they are located. Although this state of scholarship is generally regrettable, it is even more problematic in the international sphere, where most multilateral negotiations actually take place within formal organizational structures.

An *organization* is a difficult entity to define because the elements one identifies often depend on the theory one consults (Morgan, 1986). At a minimum an organization can be defined as "a formal social grouping which is established

113

in a more or less deliberate or purposive manner for the attainment of (a) specific goal(s)" (Mouzelis, 1967, p. 4). From the perspective of formal structure, an organization can be described on the basis of the roles assigned to individual members, the specialized functional areas among which the organization's tasks are allocated, and the mechanisms for control and integration of effort. These characteristics include hierarchical reporting relationships, the rules and procedures that guide organizational activity, and goals and objectives toward which members work (Etzioni, 1964; Mintzberg, 1979).

All organizations develop informal structures, a set of norms and taken-for-granted understandings about how decisions are made and work gets done, which complement (and sometimes modify) formal structures. Organization analysts diagnose these dimensions of organizational activity by attending to the structure and politics of decision making, the informal social and work networks that form around particular activities both within organizations and across organizational boundaries, the organizational culture and subcultures that form among different functions and subgroups, and the areas of conflict and modes of resolution (Crozier, 1964; Pfeffer, 1982; Schein, 1985; Silverman, 1971). We think that a consideration of organizational structure in both the formal sense and the informal sense can be used to explain the dynamics of international multilateral negotiations.

International multilateral negotiations differ in many respects from their counterparts in a national setting. First, these negotiations actually take place in organizations. Both the European Communities (EC) and the General Agreement on Tariffs and Trade (GATT) are organizations that serve as the background for negotiations that take place under their auspices—in this case, the negotiations for the Single European Act (SEA) and the Uruguay Round. The EC has an elaborate organizational structure composed of a Council on Ministers, the European Parliament, and the Commission—an organization of some 16,000 members. Similarly, GATT has a structure of a secretariat and various standing committees; it has also developed sets of policies and procedures to handle disputes arising among members. These structures continue in place even though there are no active rounds under way. The second distinguishing feature of multilateral relations in the international setting is the cross-cultural character of these organizations as well as of the negotiations. Both characteristics mean that it is impossible to explain, much less understand, what occurs in these international multilateral contexts without reference to the organizational issues that permeate them.

The purpose of this chapter is to explore the contributions an organizational perspective makes to the understanding of multilateral negotiations. There are two major ways that the organizational perspective is used in this chapter. The first is to treat GATT and the EC as organizations and to show how the structures in these two organizations set the context for the Uruguay Round and the SEA negotiations. The second is to use concepts from organization theory to analyze basic features of the actual negotiations. From this dual focus we arrive at an understanding of multilateral negotiations as organizational systems

Figure 5.1. Perspectives of Organizations and Negotiations.

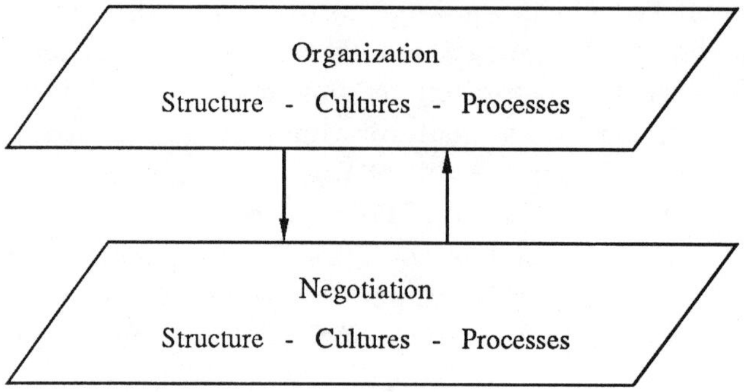

(Figure 5.1), an understanding that contributes significantly to explaining the process and outcomes of the Uruguay Round and the SEA.

The first section of the chapter describes two theoretical models of organizational structure and process, which we have labeled structural and actionist perspectives of organizations. These models are used to develop three major dimensions of organizational function and process that seem most salient to the workings of the EC and GATT. These dimensions are formal structure, decision-making mechanisms, and conflict-resolution procedures. In the second section, the two organizations are compared according to these thematic dimensions. We find that GATT conforms more closely to an actionist model, in which structure is primarily coalitional, decision making political, and conflict resolution achieved on an ad hoc basis. In contrast, the EC has a formal, well-defined structure, a shared culture, longstanding relationships, and an extensive set of policies and practices for managing decision making and conflict. The negotiation processes and the ways the two organizations respond to problems during bargaining can be explained, in large part, by the different structures of the convening organizations.

In the third section of the paper, the focus is on the ways in which the Uruguay Round and the SEA negotiations accord with their respective organizational context. Specifically, the discussion is on how decision making is structured in the negotiations and the ways conflicts and problems are handled. Although there are some similarities, we conclude that the well-developed organizational structures and strategies that had evolved over time in the EC institutions prepared it to meet the challenges of the SEA negotiations better than the loose structure of GATT prepared it for the Uruguay Round. Furthermore, we contend that negotiation processes replicate the rationale of the organizations in which they take place and can be viewed as organizational processes. Ultimately, we want to show how organizations or organizational settings (or both) influence negotiations and lead to specific outcomes.

There are several caveats in this enterprise. First, the topic of organization and negotiation has not been well developed either in theory or in practice. Thus, we view this enterprise as a beginning, and, as in any new approach, much of

what we propose will require further refinement and testing. Second, there is always a danger in talking about organizations as singular entities. The tendency is to reify them, make them appear more unified in purpose and more functional than experience and research suggest that they are. We are not immune from these charges; much of what we report reflects some notion about "ideal" rather than actual types. Third, as organizational consultants and researchers, we realize how difficult it is, given the complexity of organizational processes, to attribute causality to a particular set of factors. Thus, we have chosen to be modest in our claims about the degree to which organizational attributes determine negotiation outcomes. Despite these potential limitations, we believe that an organizational approach merits further consideration, and we anticipate that the reader will concur.

An Organizational Approach to Multilateral Negotiations

Organization theory is rife with debates on the nature and structure of organizations. One of the central debates concerns the question of whether organizations are more accurately described as functionally rational and technically constrained systems or as socially constructed, meaningful embodiments of individual action (Astley and Van de Ven, 1983). In the managerial wing of organization theory, structural theory has been most dominant. In this view, organizations are seen as integrally linked to the environments in which they operate. This link suggests both a contingent relationship between environment and technology and formal features of structure such as roles and specialization of function (Lawrence and Lorsch, 1967; Perrow, 1967). Here the focus is on the formal dimensions of structure—that is, the allocations of tasks, formal roles and responsibilities, hierarchical decision making, the relationships between various elements of the organization, and the development of rules and procedures for handling recurring problems. The argument runs that the degree of formal structure and hierarchy reflects, among other factors, the nature of the technology involved and the environments in which the organization operates and that these structures channel and control behavior in the interest of goal achievement (Emery and Trist, 1965; Thompson, 1967; Williamson, 1975). These theories are labeled *structural theories* to highlight their attention to formal structure and the efficiency of decision making. We use these structural theories in this chapter as a means to define organizations according to the degree to which these attributes characterize their functioning.

An alternative perspective, the *actionist view,* defines organizations not as formal systems but rather as interacting individuals and groups who seek to reach their own goals and do so using whatever influence and control they have (Astley and Van de Ven, 1983; Silverman, 1971; Strauss, 1978; Weick, 1979). From this perspective, organizations are joined together less by formal structure and hierarchy and more by the individual choices actors make and the immediate actions they take. Thus, environment is not so much a determining factor but rather a constraint over which members have more or less control and which influences

their decision making. Furthermore, structures are not presumed to have an existence apart from what actors give them. In the actionist view, meanings and interpretations are important because they influence the degree to which actions can be aligned, and these recurring patterns of alignment constitute structure. Thus, structure according to the actionist theories is informal, adaptive, and continually changing. Decision making in this approach tends to be political and highly conflictual. Indeed, organizations that have these kinds of characteristics, and they are often ones where professionals or other independent actors dominate, are the ones that are described as negotiated orders (Strauss, 1978). Again, it is possible to label an organization as actionist to the degree that its major characteristics approximate those associated with the actionist view.

These two models of organizations, the structural and the actionist, can be used to diagnose and analyze any organization. Indeed, the models highlight different aspects of an organization and so elucidate different dimensions, some formal and structural in character, others more informal and political (Morgan, 1986). However, it is also possible, given the history, size, goals, strategies, and functions of an organization, that one or the other model does a better job describing that organization and the kinds of actions and strategies it uses to deal with new situations. Part of this descriptive "fit" is that each model suggests some of the ways institutions will strive to structure a new set of negotiations that take place under their aegis.

Three major dimensions of organizational process seem to be most relevant to the two organizations of interest here and to the negotiations that they oversee. The first is the formal definition of the organization and its structure. Structure concerns the design of an organization and the degree to which its arrangements, specifically its goal-setting processes and control mechanisms, are elaborated and formalized (Mintzberg, 1979). The second dimension is the decision-making process. Here the focus is on the institutionalized procedures for making decisions as well as the informal political contexts and cultural values that influence the bases on which decisions are made (March and Simon, 1958). The conflict-management function is the third major dimension we will consider in organizations. Specialization of organizational functions and responsibilities, the need for innovation as well as the routine requirements for integrated effort, and the sheer complexity of integrating the efforts of diverse stakeholders create the seeds of conflict and make the need for management mechanisms pressing (Kolb and Bartunek, 1992).

Structural Dimension

Formal Mechanisms. Organizations differ according to the degree to which their structures and procedures are formalized and institutionalized. Organizations develop formal structures and procedures to allocate work, to differentiate tasks and functions, and to control and regulate activities across functional boundaries (Thompson, 1967). The challenge for the leadership of an organization is to balance differentiation and integration in such a way that

critical tasks are performed but that efforts are controlled and coordinated in ways that promote the achievement of an organization's goals (Lawrence and Lorsch, 1967).

The challenge is met in different ways in organizations. In large-scale organizations formalized and bureaucratic structures, procedures, and rules channel and control major aspects of activity (Mintzberg, 1979; Pugh, Hickson, Hinings, and Turner, 1968). These large-scale organizations operate in (and create) environments that they exert more or less control over rather than the reverse. They allocate tasks to specialized units, which develop their own subgoals and modes of operating; these subgoals and processes may or may not support the explicit mission of the organization. Furthermore, these specialized units have access to information and the resources to process that information that others do not have (March and Simon, 1958; Pfeffer and Salancik, 1978), which sometimes makes integration of their efforts difficult. There is obviously a political dimension within organizations as well. Departments carry out their functions in such a way as to increase internal leverage, expand their purview and jurisdiction, and so manage behind the scenes to achieve their own agendas. These patterns of behavior become institutionalized, hence formalized, even when circumstances change (Zucker, 1977).

A major problem that bureaucratic organizations face is the problem of innovation. Given centralized and formal structures, it is difficult for new ideas to be communicated and receive support. Thus, less hierarchical structures are necessary to meet new challenges (Galbraith, 1973). Again politics is important here as well. Organizational units that are well positioned to anticipate change can exert influence in the design of lateral structures and increase their own leverage on the outcomes (Pettigrew, 1973).

The formality of the convening organization's structure and the leverage of specialized subunits have a number of potential impacts on negotiations. First, an organization that has a well-articulated formal structure for managing the routine elements of its work will be able to use its standard approach in the design of negotiations in ways that make it likely that the process and outcomes it favors will result. When innovation is required to meet changing circumstances, units with specialized expertise and political leverage can use their experience and position to take a dominant role in the design of alternative structures and processes (Pettigrew, 1973). Second, organizations with well-articulated formal structures are partially insulated from interference from constituent or client groups (Blau, 1955). Thus, in the design of negotiated processes, they can exert more influence than members, who are less organized. Organizations that lack such structures will typically find themselves buffeted by their stakeholder groups and have difficulty exerting authority over the course of the negotiations.

Role of Culture. In order to achieve their goals, organizations need to control and coordinate the diverse activities that occur within them. Clearly, formal structures and procedures provide one means for doing so. However, informal structures and norms develop among members that have important

impacts on how an organization functions (Dalton, 1959). The actionist perspective calls attention to the kinds of patterns and routines members develop through interactions with each other (Silverman, 1971). In large-scale organizations, these networks of relationships become essential for getting work done. As these activities recur, they become institutionalized and part of the normative order of the organization and influence behavior as surely as the formal mechanisms (Zucker, 1977).

In this context culture refers to the informal behavioral norms and rules that bind members of the organization (Schein, 1985). The degree to which a culture can be said to be shared is always an issue in organizations and affects the kind of control that is possible in negotiations. In international organizations, the notion of shared culture is problematic. First, these organizations are mosaics of national cultures, which make communication, interpretation, and coordinated action always a matter of translation (Hofstede, 1984). Second, as in any large organization, the tasks of different units give rise to subcultures with different interpretations of time, goals, and norms of work accomplishment. Third, members enter organizations with different backgrounds and professional experience, which also shape their interpretations of behavior. Thus, lawyers and accountants have professional subcultures that may be at odds with those of other groups in the organization (Van Maanen and Barley, 1985; Lang, 1993). The referential cultures of the actor influence the way he or she interprets all levels of organizational activity, but especially conflict and its potential resolution (Faure and Rubin, 1993). Shared culture tends to focus effort, whereas diverse subcultures contribute to conflict and make the tasks of decision making and negotiation considerably more challenging.

Negotiations take place in the context of a set of institutional procedures and cultural rules that are part of the established structure and routines (Walton and McKersie, 1965). These cultural understandings and procedures lend a degree of certainty and control to the negotiation process. Thus, in the absence of any challenge to these procedures, negotiations will be conducted according to these norms (Tolbert and Arthur, 1988). When an organization finds itself negotiating in a new arena, its approach generally conforms to the existing practices. However, if the new arena is sufficiently different, members of the organization strive to find at least satisfactory ways of responding to the challenge (March and Simon, 1958). A shared culture and a rich network of past relationships facilitate the required changes.

Decision-Making Dimension

Mechanisms. Organizations are decision-making entities. Actionist and structural models of organizations portray decision making differently. In the structural view, decision-making procedures are guided by considerations of technical rationality and are designed to be responsive to the strategy of the organization and environment in which it operates (Williamson, 1975). Studies of decision making in action suggest a rather different picture in which organiza-

tions strive to reduce complexity in their decision making. They do so in a variety of ways (March and Simon, 1958). They develop elaborate repertoires, or standard operating procedures. Decision makers seek to frame problems in ways that make them similar to those they have handled in the past (March and Olsen, 1976). Furthermore, the tendency is to divide a problem and assign pieces of it to specialized individuals (roles) or to parts of the organization (functions) as a way to minimize discussion and conflict. Given the segmentation of problems, it follows that issues will be treated sequentially rather than simultaneously (Cyert and March, 1963). The outcome of these efforts to reduce complexity is that optimization is rarely achieved.

Typically, in international multilateral negotiations numerous demands of many different types need to be decided. Some relate to economics, others to governance, others are time related, and still others may have ideological overtones. In addition demands present different challenges to potential agreement making. Some will be distributive in that there is an implied winner and loser. Others will contain integrative potential because the parties have different preferences regarding them. And for some of the demands the parties' interests may be overlapping. These characteristics of negotiated demands require that parties have the skills to manage complexity in situations in which the outcomes are always uncertain. Where decision making is compartmentalized and simplified in organizations, it is much less likely that opportunities for joint gains will be naturally discovered in negotiation. Organizations that can structure decision making in more satisfactory ways and that have cultures that support such framing heighten the possibility that more integrative solutions will be discovered.

Goals. One of the characteristics that define organizations and differentiate them from other collectivities is their goals. Organizations are presumed to be goal-directed even though the nature of the goal-setting process is subject to some debate (Perrow, 1961). Structural models envision goal setting as a rationalistic and deliberate process in which a small number of strategic and consistent objectives guide the organization. Even within formal structures, goals are fragmented as subunits set their own goals, which do not necessarily support those of the organization.

The actionist framework focuses on the process of goal setting; it sees goals as the outcomes of a complicated negotiation process (Cyert and March, 1963). Goals are never finally set but are subject to continual revision as negotiations occur among different stakeholders. New goals emerge from interactions in which neither party is necessarily aware that it is actually involved in the setting of goals. Implicit action also leads to goals that are not formally articulated. As organizations develop procedures and rules to manage uncertainties in a task, the means of task accomplishment can become elevated to a goal. And, finally, any number of unofficial goals are understood to exist but cannot be formally expressed because they challenge the mission of the organization.

The variability in the ways goals are set leads to inevitable problems of consistency among them. Different processes may lead to a proliferation of goals,

many of which are in conflict with each other. This is likely to be the case especially where certain units are zealous in pursuing their own goals without regard to those of the organization. One of the outcomes, particularly in large-scale organizations that respond to multiple constituencies, is that organizations often get paralyzed because there is no centralized procedure or uniform process for setting goals or resolving conflicts among them. Without such processes, it is difficult for an organization to act in a concerted manner in negotiations, which in turn gives rise to political jockeying. Organizations that have formal decision-making structures and procedures in place may be more likely to be in a position to pursue more consistent goals in negotiation.

Even with structures in place, goal setting and decision making are highly political processes. Certain groups and individuals come to acquire and exert influence over decisions in ways beyond the formal positions they hold (Pfeffer and Salancik, 1978; Bacharach and Lawler, 1980). This influence may come about in several ways. Members or groups in the organization control resources that the organization needs. These resources may be money or new recruits or essential information (Pfeffer and Salancik, 1978). Control over critical uncertainties affecting the functioning of the organization also gives members influence (Crozier, 1964). Or members may become powerful because they have the ear of key people in the organization or because they know the nature of power relations (Kanter, 1977; Pettigrew, 1973). Use of these various sources of power can become critical when organizations are in flux or transition (Pettigrew, 1973).

When organizations face new situations and challenges, they are forced to adapt themselves through innovations in structure and process in order to enhance their decision-making capacity. Under these circumstances, certain individuals and groups are likely to emerge as influential. Individuals who occupy strategic roles that span units either within the organization or across its boundaries take on responsibility for integrating efforts that were previously separate. Boundary spanners play a critical role in gathering and disseminating information and in representing the organization to its outside constituents (Adams, 1976). Specialized units and task forces that bring together people with particular information and expertise are created and buffered from the rest of the organization and so accrue influence.

Complementing these formal structural adaptations may be activities in the informal structure that promote change and innovation and provide windows onto power politics in action. Members can act individually; they try to usurp formal channels by gaining access to strategic information that would normally not be available to them. They also apply unofficial or unsanctioned criteria in making decisions. Strategic alliances, including coalitions, are formed behind the scenes with people external to the organization (Tolbert, 1985). Through these means the decisions that move the organization in new directions may be made without any formal public consideration of the issues.

How an organization handles decision making affects the negotiations that occur under its auspices. From what we know about decision making in organizations, the possibility of deliberate and rational decision making is slim.

First, the tendency for organizations to reduce complexity will have an effect on the possibilities of finding mutually beneficial outcomes. Second, political posturing means that unless otherwise controlled, negotiated outcomes will reflect the individual interests of those in power. Finally, the complications of cross-cultural organizations make communication and the possibility of understanding the interests of others that much more difficult.

Conflict Dimension

The hierarchical structure of most organizations and the requirement for integration of task and effort usually contain the seeds of conflict (Kolb and Bartunek, 1992). In international organizations, the potential is increased. First, diverse cultures and national groups complicate communication and increase the chances for miscommunication and misunderstanding. Real differences in interests and positions can be exacerbated by these cultural differences, which make decision making considerably more contentious than it would otherwise be.

Second, more or less conflict occurs to the degree that innovation and change are present. The structural mechanisms that keep conflict in check— hierarchical authority, division of labor, standardized rules and procedures—are of necessity violate when change is the aim. Structures for innovation and adaptation, in contrast with normal structures, tend to be flatter, less hierarchical, requiring increased teamwork and flexibility (Kanter, 1983). These structures breed conflict, indeed view conflict as essential to the innovation process. However, in order for these structures to produce the innovation they promise, mechanisms of conflict resolution more elaborate than usual are also required (Lawrence and Lorsch, 1967). Mediation-type functions are essential to making these kinds of systems operate.

Mediation can become institutionalized in several ways. First, the organization can explicitly design a dispute-resolution system to handle the recurring conflicts that surface. One of the problems, however, is that these systems can become specialized. Mediators come to be seen as experts in certain disputes and not others, and thus they tend to hear only specific kinds of disputes (Kolb, 1989). Second, individuals who are known within the system and respected for their skills take on the role of informal mediator. In both these situations, the mediator role is institutionalized on either a formal or an informal basis.

In the actionist perspective, conflict is recognized as an essential element of organization. The coalitional and fluid structures of these organizations create the conditions for mediation (Mintzberg, 1983). Indeed, it is impossible to conceive how such an organization could function without the assistance of individuals or groups who mediate on an ad hoc or even more or less permanent basis. Because these organizations are negotiated orders, they require a regulatory function to keep the process going and to build coordination and cohesion among the parts (Strauss, 1978). Mediation is such a function.

The individuals or groups who fulfill the mediation function do so because they provide a service to the organization. These organizations require

coordination and unity of purpose. Individuals who fill this need, even though they operate without formal authority, tend to gain power and influence from this role (Pfeffer and Salancik, 1978). Furthermore, in carrying out this function they also serve their own interests in the ongoing negotiations. In this way, they are neither neutral nor impartial for they have stakes in the outcomes and preferences among the parties (Faure, 1989).

In sum, it is possible to distinguish organizations on the basis of these dimensions and to predict some of the ways that negotiations will be affected. If an organization has a well-articulated structure that allows it to work proactively toward the achievement of a consistent set of goals and has an organizational culture that supports these formal activities, the negotiations that take place under its aegis will replicate these features. Organizations that are negotiated orders, exemplified by diverse cultures and goals, and whose decision making is highly politicized, will produce negotiations that are constantly in flux.

Applications of the Theory

The EC and GATT are organizations that act as conveners for negotiation and also, at times, as parties to the process. The Uruguay Round and the SEA negotiations, which occurred under their auspices, can be viewed as subprocesses within a more global system of interaction, or as subsystems that more or less reflect the characteristics of their convening organization. However, every negotiation is in some way unique unto itself as the negotiators develop their own rationale and strategy within the context of the organization. These actions in turn influence the organization in its future negotiations. Our purpose in this section is to compare the two negotiations according to the main structural, decision-making, and conflict-resolution dimensions.

Formal Structure

The EC and GATT can be differentiated along a number of structural lines. The EC has a well-articulated formal structure of roles and responsibilities and a set of formal rules and procedures that enable it, in competition with the actions of the member states, to have considerable influence in the design of negotiations. The structural dynamics are so well established that the SEA can be perceived, in its general features, to be the result of an ongoing process of constitutional adjustment: the organization develops a set of new rules in order to promote global integration in a way that is quite consistent with the aim of the SEA— to advance European union. However, parties to the process may take extra initiatives and develop increased influence. Indeed, units within the EC, particularly the European Parliament (EP), came to play pivotal roles because they were able to find ways to avoid the failures of the past, particularly the problem of national parliaments thwarting their efforts.

Each of the three major EC institutions—the Council of Ministers, the

Commission, and the EP—has a clearly defined role in the ongoing work of the EC and in major negotiations that occur. However, each part also has its own goals, agenda, and modes of operating, which influence the course of negotiations. The EP, although its formal role is marginal, came to play an active role in the SEA process and to enhance its own influence in future negotiations. It could do so because it had access to specific information from its Institutional Affairs Committee, knew the rules and procedures intimately, had a well-developed strategy of keeping itself involved, and had cultivated commitments from key actors like Italy. Because of its formal position, it knew from experience what had to be different in the SEA negotiations.

The EC also has rules and procedures in place that affect the negotiation. Most critical are the voting procedures, which push the organization to a slow but consensual approach in resolving differences. These procedures were so institutionalized that, when the Italian Council presidency tried to set them aside in the interests of moving ahead, several governments pressed to continue according to the usual practices. However, when these procedures proved cumbersome later, they were altered.

In contrast, the GATT secretariat is considerably smaller than the EC institutions and lacks a well-defined structure of roles and responsibilities. As a result, it has difficulty taking control of a process in order to move it toward a particular end. The deadlock that lasted several years on agricultural issues illustrates the relative weakness of the secretariat when facing the conflictual attitudes of the United States and the EC. In the Uruguay Round there was evidence of the fluidity of organization that marks these negotiations. Individual constituent nations have considerable discretion in forming ad hoc groups, commissions, and temporary organizations that bypass the secretariat. In marked contrast, the EC has a much more formal, institutionalized, and well-tried method of handling processes.

Culture. The existence of a shared organizational culture can aid negotiations in a number of ways. All negotiations in the EC take place against a background of a shared culture of problem solving; when members come to negotiate, others interpret their opening positions and tactics with a shared commitment to problem solving in mind. Aspects of this culture can interfere with efficient decision making by leading to lengthy deliberations in which action is deferred. In the SEA case, knowledge of the problematic aspect of this culture, the lack of an overarching European vision, led the EP to push for different kinds of voting procedures.

The dominant culture within GATT does not appear to carry many, if any, integrative values. It is not as a component of GATT that a party intervenes, but as a state exclusively concerned with its own interests. The existing structure is an arena where diverging interests confront each other rather than a place where everyone contributes to the building up of a common destiny. As a consequence the organizational culture is quite competitive.

Culture is also important in another way. Both organizations face, to some

degree, the challenge of working across diverse national cultures. Absent a shared culture, the kinds of assumptions that are critical to interpreting the actions of others are not available to negotiators. The possibility of misunderstanding and escalation is exacerbated. In GATT, the twenty, later fifty, key countries saw it as one of their challenges to try to develop a shared perspective on the issues so that productive negotiations could occur. Within the EC, half of the countries were founding members of the Common Market in 1957 and so have been developing something of a shared organization culture for quite a while. Members know how to interpret the tactics of others and develop their own approaches accordingly. Cross-cultural communications become important, however, in the relationship with the United Kingdom, which did not have this shared history. Indeed, one of the ways one can understand some of the problems in integrating the United Kingdom into the EC is by noticing that an existing cultural coalition contributed to the United Kingdom's isolation, which led to a potential threat to proceed without the British.

Goals. Both organizations have multiple constituencies and stakeholders, each of which has both shared and divergent goals. The degree to which consistency is achieved differs between the two organizations and begins to explain why one is better able to take concerted action. The EC is a goal-directed organization whose aim is to advance European integration. Within the EC, particular units have their own subgoals, specifically the EP. However, its goals to get an equal voice for itself and to enhance its influence worked to promote the achievement of the overall goal of the SEA. Furthermore, it had, based on its past experiences and knowledge of the informal organization, a lobbying strategy to do so.

In contrast, GATT has a number of goals that stem from the different functions that negotiations might serve in the international trading system. These goals include revising the international trading regime, handling a number of specific issues concerning market access and national autonomy, and keeping the process moving. There is nothing inherently inconsistent in these goals. However, inconsistency can become an issue in at least two ways. The first is that not all the players place the same value on each of the goals. As a result each player pursues a differentiated strategy that makes some of the goals more prominent to one group of players and other goals to other players. A second way inconsistency becomes an issue is when multiple parties not only pursue different objectives but, because of cultural and other differences, perceive even similar goals in different ways. What constitutes market access, for example, differs depending on whether one consults the United States or Brazil, among others. These differences mean that parties frame the issues differently and pursue similar goals that are in reality at odds with each other. In the absence of shared goals, progress often proves elusive. The picture that emerges from the Uruguay Round is one of disjointed bursts of activity but little progress.

Predicted Patterns of Negotiation. Differences in organizational structure—particularly the degree to which the organization (and its subparts) is

poised to act, has a unifying culture, and has overall subunit goals that are mutually supporting—will lead to quite different patterns of negotiation. GATT is a coalition structure with loose integrative mechanisms, a weak hierarchy, and a mosaic of cultures. It constantly struggles to find a structure to deal with its conflicts over procedure and substance. It does not operate as an autonomous organization; therefore, in the Uruguay Round individual members pursued their interests without regard for the whole. It deals with complexity by dividing tasks, assigning them to other organizations, and attending to the issues in a sequential and segmented manner. Although this information-processing approach is characteristic of many organizations, it requires elaborate integrative mechanisms in order to achieve some unity of purpose (Lawrence and Lorsch, 1967). This kind of structure tends to lead to negotiations that resemble a coalitional game in which each party (or group of parties) is out for itself. Indeed, negotiations in the Uruguay Round appeared to be largely distributive.

The EC has a formal organizational structure in which roles and responsibilities are defined. Indeed, under ordinary circumstances, the Commission would initiate negotiations. However, the SEA was the initiative of the EP, which saw an opportunity for potentially advancing its own interests while moving the overall aims of the EC ahead. An astute group can use a shared organizational culture and a well-developed informal organization to move its agenda along. Interactions within the EC are of a cooperative nature even if, for tactical reasons, one party initially adopts an oppositional attitude. Such an organization has a true propensity to generate package deals and integrative bargaining. The procedures for negotiating differences are codified and promote problem solving. Given this structure, the culture of this organization, and its goals, it was able to design a variant of traditional negotiation that suited the challenges presented by the SEA process.

Decision Making

Both organizations, GATT and the EC, have a decision-making system that aims at producing legislation. The organizational procedures designed by the EC provide ways of accelerating European integration by facilitating decision making. The principle of weighted majority voting in some instances is an example of such a procedure, but often current practice still aims at reaching consensus through negotiation. This process demonstrates the ability of the organization to reconcile two somehow conflicting goals: the common concern for taking into account the particular position of any state and the need for global efficiency. Both GATT and the EC had to manage information-processing and decision-making procedures during prenegotiations and then during the negotiations proper. In the Uruguay Round, specialized organizations, such as the Organization for Economic Cooperation and Development (OECD), the U.S.-Canada National Studies, and the Australian Bureau of Agricultural Economics, gathered information and performed technical analyses for the larger organization. This procedure had two effects. First, these organizations provided frameworks that

guided the negotiations on these issues and moved the negotiations forward. Second, the countries that initiated these efforts benefited because the frameworks enhanced the capacity of the organization to deal with complexity, a capacity it did not already have (Crozier, 1964).

Complexity arises from the number of actors, the great variety of interests at stake, the many variables involved in the negotiation process, and the number of issues. To deal with this complexity in the Uruguay Round, negotiations were conducted, by compartmentalizing the issues and by assigning them to different negotiating groups. Dividing the issues among fifteen negotiating groups not only reduced the number of interests at stake and the number of variables involved but also reduced the number of actors within each group because each country had interests in only a subset of issues and therefore could limit its participation. In the context of multilateral negotiations, managing complexity means dealing with information and issues primarily by segmenting information processing and decision making.

In the SEA negotiations, the EP directed the process even though it lacked the formal mandate to do so. Early in the process, the EP developed a strategy of cooperation that allowed it to participate. Its clear agenda to expand its role and its strategy of allying itself with Italy allowed it to influence decision making. It managed the agenda in such a way that expedient, rather than optimal, outcomes could be achieved. It easily dropped issues that lacked widespread support. Under the informal influence of the EP, decision making led, as an outcome, to a more integrative approach to negotiation than had previously existed.

From this comparison, it is clear that in any international, multilateral negotiation, organizations will have to deal with significant issues of structure and culture. The decisions that are made on this score seem to depend on how the organizations manage complexity in both a structural and an information-processing sense. Furthermore, in order to keep the process going, the rules of the game will be continually modified in either a formal or a tacit manner.

Actors in organizations manage decision making strategically for their own political ends. In the negotiation cases, for example, key players produced new information to make their goals more prominent and so get more leverage on the process. One of these activities was rumor management. The EP, which had no formal role, was an important actor in the SEA prenegotiations. It acted not solely because of its interest in the SEA process but because it saw that doing so would allow it to gain power in other dealings. The situation in GATT was different. In an effort to find some common ground, the executive director tried with the secretariat to formulate an agreement that he would issue. However, his weak position, among other factors, meant that his effort to control decision making was rebuffed.

Both GATT and the EC found that existing decision-making structures proved inadequate for the kinds of innovative negotiations that were required. The parties in the Uruguay Round made use of a number of ad hoc and secretive groups to carry out different types of work. In the face of GATT procedures and pressures from India and Brazil, it was impossible to bring up the trade issues

on services. The United States had overlapping membership in GATT and in the OECD and used this boundary role to commission the OECD to perform the technical analyses on trade in services. The OECD had the technical expertise to carry out such a task and to produce a comprehensive framework for interissue links. Likewise the Inter-Governmental Conference (IGC) was formed because existing procedures would have proved too slow and cumbersome.

The parties also went outside the existing structures to increase their leverage and position. A restricted group of twenty key countries constituted themselves a secret working group to deal with some of the political aspects they might face during the Uruguay Round. International multilateral negotiations require considerable creativity and innovation, and existing structures are generally not appropriate to meet this challenge. Thus, organizations develop new structures on either a formal or an ad hoc basis. For each party, a major part of prenegotiation seems to involve altering some of the existing coalitional relationships in order to modify the structures of power and to affect those external elements that act as a constraint on strategy.

The parties have options about the structures or settings in which to conduct the negotiations. Parties try to operate in the settings in which they think they will be most powerful. In the Uruguay Round, the United States was relatively powerless in the traditional setting because of the consensus requirement and the opposition of some influential countries such as Brazil and India. So the United States shifted the negotiations into an extraordinary meeting of the Contracting Parties. To determine the organization of such a technical meeting, an absolute majority was not required. The choice of structure for negotiation is a function, therefore, of both rational and political analyses. Parties play out their strategies within the structures and play with the structures according to their strategies.

Conflict Resolution

Managing conflict through mediation occurred in both negotiations. However, the function took on different forms in the two settings. During the Uruguay Round, mediation was more of an ad hoc function performed by different groups as they saw the need arise. Within the Cairns group, Australia mediated in order to keep the coalition together. Similarly, the de la Paix group, in addition to operating as a supercommittee, also mediated between the United States and Third World dissidents. However, in GATT, conflict management is based on widely improvised procedures that result in highly questionable efficiency if one considers, for instance, the protracted deadlock on agricultural issues.

In the context of the EC and therefore in the SEA negotiations, mediation was more institutionalized in the roles of the actors. Informal practices in past bargaining fostered mediation as a means to find consensus with the Commission traditionally playing the role of mediator. As there was more than one candidate (the Commission, Italy, the Luxembourg presidency, the Dutch presidency) to act as an honest broker in the SEA negotiations, it seems that the capacity to generate

this function truly belonged to the culture of the organization. In addition, certain individuals developed reputations that enabled them to work as mediators. James Dooge played this role during the early rounds of the SEA negotiations.

These distinctions between mediation as a function and as a role reflect differences in the structure and size of these organizations and in the requirements of negotiation. The Uruguay Round, because of its coalitional structure, required the opportunistic use of mediation to move the negotiations along. In the EC, mediation roles are more institutionalized at both the organization and individual levels. Thus, mediators were in place to help during the SEA negotiations.

Patterns of Negotiations. Contrasting patterns of negotiations lead to differences in how one judges performance. The parties to the Uruguay Round lacked organizational cohesiveness and so tended to act as individual parties. Thus, they have only their own self-interest on which to gauge the negotiations. The preference for problem solving and consensus evident in the SEA reflects the long-term commitment of the member states. Thus, although the parties judge the SEA negotiation according to the way it affected their national self-interest, they are also concerned with its impact on the long-term relationships among the parties. Given the long-term goals of the EC, every negotiation becomes an opportunity for building trust and for learning from the experience. These lessons then are incorporated into the policies and culture of the organization.

It is clear that the two organizations—GATT and the EC—conduct different types of negotiations under their aegis. But one can ask whether the patterns in the negotiation contribute to the evolution of different organizational types. One issue involved here is the nature of the interaction between the structure of the negotiations and the associated organization. Do plurilateral negotiations, such as the SEA negotiation, facilitate the development of an organizational structure that in turn, and in subsequent negotiations, leads to a problem-solving form of negotiation? By way of contrast, do multilateral negotiations, like the Uruguay Round, because of their size and cultural diversity, not contribute to the establishment of stable and efficient structures? And does this type of negotiation explain, in part, why the organizations that develop find it difficult to influence the negotiations and channel the natural coalitional tendencies into other forms? These questions, as well as other relationships between organizational structure and form and negotiation process and outcomes, certainly merit empirical inquiry.

Conclusion

Negotiation is the organization in motion. By examining the interaction between negotiation and organization, we become aware that the Uruguay Round and the SEA negotiations cannot be viewed simply as negotiation encounters. They are negotiation processes that are set and managed by organizations. As such they replicate characteristics of the mother organizations that house them. Thus, the structure of the organization, its culture, modes of decision making, and ap-

proaches to managing conflict influence each particular negotiation and in turn are affected by them.

These multiparty negotiations can be seen as organizational subsystems. As a consequence the processes they go through can be explained by concepts drawn from organization theory. In this sense organization theory can, as well, explain why the SEA negotiations resulted in agreement and why the Uruguay Round became deadlocked. It is impossible to understand these different outcomes without reference to the efforts of organizational actors to control the process.

At the same time, these interactions are dynamic—that is, what occurs in the negotiation will affect the organization throughout a process of institutionalization and learning. As parties negotiate, those strategies that prove to be effective become apart of the organization's repertoire (Zucker, 1977). Organizations need to be structured to learn from experience. The structural model suggests that knowledge can be accumulated and processes institutionalized. The actionist approach is characterized by a much looser degree of institutionalization and a weaker structure. Although individuals may learn, the very fluidity of the organization means that the actors change and so it is difficult to accumulate knowledge. For these reasons, the learning from one negotiation to another is likely to be incomplete, and information about process and substance is likely to be lost from one negotiation to another.

The organization influences the negotiation at another level. Organizations that fail to institutionalize their process and treat each negotiation *de novo* will implicitly tend to structure these proceedings as encounters. Encounters involve strangers who have a more or less fleeting relationship with each other (Goffman, 1959). Negotiations in encounters tend to follow a competitive track (Pruitt, 1981). In contrast, in integrated negotiations the parties have many strong ties that bind them together in a shared history and future relationship (Granovetter, 1973). These negotiations tend to follow a coordinative track and to be associated with those organizations that have been able to institutionalize negotiation processes and learn from round to round.

The environment in which negotiations take place also has a potentially strong impact on the process. Because negotiations tend to replicate, at least at the symbolic level, the key features of the environment, an organization needs to transform and channel the features of the environment toward productive ends. To the degree that an organization develops a structure for interaction and systems and procedures for handling routine and unexpected contingencies, and can learn from experience and institutionalize that learning, it can focus the negotiations on the tasks at hand.

When negotiations occur under the auspices of generally weak convening organizations, the process is not insulated or buffered from its environment (Thompson, 1967). In these situations, one can expect that the existing relationships and antagonisms among the parties will be acted out in the negotiations. Thus, in many multilateral negotiations the parties seem to replicate unproductive aspects of their relationship. Although substantive and procedural issues are

ostensibly being negotiated, the negotiation forum becomes an arena for open confrontation. Indeed, antagonisms may actually increase at the bargaining table because the parties feel insulated by the rules of the negotiation game from the risks of their actions. Interaction dynamics can appear as a symbolic substitute for war, where the outcome is not the destruction of the other but the maintenance of the status quo ante. When negotiations take on this kind of character, the parties do not seek a common satisfactory agreement. Rather, their aim may be to make things difficult for their adversaries, achieving their end by denying the others.

Within the EC, there seems to be a unity between negotiation at the actual and the symbolic levels. Hence, the likelihood of agreement, despite the difficulty of particular issues, will always be high. The Uruguay Round, however, does not have the same convergence. Differentiation between the actual and the symbolic levels means that negotiations can become a forum for escalating hostilities rather than for the settling of differences. Under these circumstances achieving satisfactory outcomes is unlikely, if not impossible. This kind of situation may result in a "negotiated symbolic disorder," where international multilateral negotiations become a hindrance, not a contributor, to the global order.

We have used this chapter to begin to sketch out ways in which an organizational perspective can contribute to understanding international multilateral negotiations and improving them. It is clear that this perspective calls attention to facets of negotiation that have not been the subject of much serious study. Additional attention and inquiry need to be directed at the organizations under whose auspices these negotiations are convened, for these organization have the potential to channel and direct the negotiations so that nations can put aside their other agendas and focus on the substantive tasks at hand. Organization theory has much to contribute to the kinds of structures we might consider building in order to improve the practice of multilateral negotiation.

Chapter 6

Small Group Theory
Forming Consensus Through Group Processes

Jeffrey Z. Rubin, Walter C. Swap (USA)

The following opening passage from one of the most influential book-length treatments of group dynamics (Cartwright and Zander, 1960, p. 3) captures both the ubiquity and importance of the group in human activity:

> If it were possible for the overworked hypothetical man from Mars to take a fresh view of the people of Earth, he would probably be impressed by the amount of time they spend doing things together in groups. . . . He would see that much of the work of the world is carried out by people who perform their activities in close interdependence within relatively enduring associations. . . . [He] might be puzzled why so many people spend so much time in little groups talking, planning, and being "in conference." Surely he would conclude that if he wanted to understand much about what is happening on Earth he would have to examine rather carefully the ways in which groups form, function, and dissolve.

As experimental social psychologists, we have learned that any form of social behavior—of which multilateral negotiation is surely a cardinal example—can be understood only if one takes into account the behavior of each individual in the relationship, the influence each person exerts on others, as well as the particular structural or organizational context in which the relationship is embedded.

When the relationship consists of two or more people who are interdependent in some way and who share at least a minimal sense of identity as

members of the same social arrangement, then (consistent with the definition advanced by Swap, 1984, pp. 16–17) we say that a group exists. A small group, in turn, ranges in size from three to twenty. The term *small* is used to distinguish this configuration from one (for example, the United Nations Conference on the Law of the Sea) in which there are dozens, even hundreds, of participants. Even such an arrangement, however, can work only if the dozens or hundreds of participants arrange themselves in a series of subgroups, task groups, and committees that function naturally as small groups.

The concern with groups has been central to social psychology, and research since the 1940s has resulted in a body of findings applicable to a wide range of social settings.[1] In the spirit of this book's *Rashomon*-like intellectual experiment, it is our contention that the small group perspective can be brought to bear on multilateral negotiation. Indeed, although it may be useful to consider game theory, decision theory, and leadership, organizational, and coalition approaches to multilateral negotiation, the fact remains that the actual multilateral negotiation process during the Uruguay Round of the General Agreement on Tariffs and Trade (GATT) and the negotiations on the Single European Act (SEA) in the European Communities (EC) occurred within a small group context. To understand—really understand—that process and the decisions toward which that process leads, one must grasp the essential dynamics of small group interaction.

Along with Chapter Eight in this book, on leadership (a topic that has long been an essential component of small group research), this chapter is distinctive in its emphasis on process in multilateral negotiation. As other chapters document, a structural approach may be useful in understanding how groups respond to organizational demands or the rational decision rules of game theory or decision theory. But once we acknowledge that these groups are made up of individual actors, interacting in face-to-face encounters, we have moved squarely into the domain of social psychology. Small group research can inform us about the rules governing these interactions, how the process can be facilitated, and how pathologies may emerge to subvert effective decision making. This emphasis on process is the particular strength of the small group approach.

For example, an inherent tension exists in many small groups, particularly those that are highly cohesive. On the one hand, there is a need for fresh, interesting ideas that may appear to be obstructive but that contribute to the group's ability to appraise alternatives fully. On the other hand, there is a need to reach consensus in groups, to make the decisions necessary to complete the group's work. This tension, and the way in which it is managed by the group's membership, helps determine the difference between an effective and an ineffective group process.

This chapter is organized into five parts. We begin by outlining some central concepts in small group theory, as it has been promulgated by sociologists and social psychologists since the 1940s. We then turn to a selective application of small group theory to the SEA negotiations and to the Uruguay Round; in each case we attempt to document a few of the ways in which small group theory

can be used to explain why the negotiations followed the course they did. We close the chapter by comparing the two case studies and then reflecting on several prescriptive lessons for multilateral negotiation as these build on small group theory and are informed by practice.

Some Key Ideas from Small Group Theory

Most groups come together because of some joint task that the members wish to perform; this is certainly the case for groups that engage in multilateral negotiation. As a way of summarizing work in the area, we focus first on the conditions that facilitate effective task performance in groups, then turn to the conditions that impede such work.

Conditions Facilitating Effective Task Performance

Although many conditions facilitate effective task performance, four are of particular prominence: leadership, group composition, group history, and group cohesiveness.

Leadership. As Chapter Eight indicates, leadership can make the difference between a group that works well and one that fails miserably in the completion of its chosen task. Effective leadership, however, can occur only if the group tolerates it; expressed another way, an effective leader is empowered by the group's members, even as those members are empowered by an effective leader.

Leadership can emerge from within the group, as when a particularly competent, powerful, or likable member moves up through the ranks (for example, Australia's leadership of the Cairns group); or leaders can be appointed from without (for example, the European Council presidency). Either way, research on leadership indicates that effectiveness is determined by the leader's ability to adjust his or her style to the particular task demands of the group. Years ago, Lewin, Lippitt, and White (1939) demonstrated the existence of two dramatically different leadership styles: autocratic and democratic. The autocratic leader imposes decisions on the group because of greater strength and resources: "Do what I ask of you," this leader asserts, "because I am stronger, know better than you what needs to be done, and have a right to make these demands of you." In contrast, the democratic leader consults with the group members, canvasses opinions and expertise, remains open to new ideas, and makes sure that the group does not move ahead without some measure of consensus.

Although the democratic leadership style may appear preferable to its more autocratic counterpart, research has indicated the importance of a match between leadership and the group situation (Fiedler, 1967). When the group's task is extremely simple (this will rarely be the case in multilateral negotiation), an autocratic leadership style may prove more effective; if the task is to shovel a hole in the ground as quickly as possible, the group has little to discuss. However, when the group's task requires analysis of competing alternatives and evaluation

of these in relation to some optimal decision, then a democratic style proves more effective.

In addition to understanding leadership style, it is important to understand leadership roles. Almost any group, as part of its work, is likely to require the emergence of individuals who perform rather different functions or provide different services to the group. As documented by Bales (1950), at least two kinds of leaders tend to emerge from a group: a task leader, whose self-appointed job is to keep the membership oriented toward the completion of its work; and a socioemotional leader, whose responsibility is to ensure that group members are reasonably satisfied with the process by which the group is functioning. Both roles are necessary if a group is to function effectively, and they almost always tend to emerge from within the rank-and-file of the group's membership. Only rarely does a single individual occupy both roles, and Bales considers such people to be "great leaders"—people who can accomplish the group's mission effectively while maintaining the deep affection of the led.

Group Composition. This term refers, most generally, to the identity of the members in relation to any number of attributes. Among the most important is the degree to which members may be characterized as homogeneous or heterogeneous. Social psychological research indicates that homogeneous groups (those whose members have been selected or happen to be highly similar in their background, skills, orientation) tend to perform better than more heterogeneous, diverse groups when the group task is relatively simple and straightforward; if an aspect of the GATT negotiations required analysis of plans for implementing a relatively simple economic scheme, then a group of economists might be best positioned to move this agenda forward.

If, however, the group's work requires brainstorming new and unusual ideas or the invention of options without deciding on any one of them, then membership diversity is likely to be a virtue, not a liability; to wit, a group that is stuck in a conflictual impasse and is looking for as many ideas as possible for breaking out of this deadlock and moving toward settlement of the conflict may be served best by allowing as many different viewpoints to be aired as possible. Although a group whose members are heterogeneous is less likely to reach agreement than a more homogeneous group, if and when agreement is reached, it is more likely to be persuasive to one and all, hence more likely to endure.

As we will argue subsequently in our discussion of the Uruguay Round negotiations, a number of small groups came into existence precisely because they shared some mix of similarity and diversity. Witness the Cairns group in this regard; it consisted of a heterogeneous cluster of developed and developing nations, all of whom shared a common interest in creating a certain kind of agreement. To this end, the members of the Cairns group formed a coalition whose purpose was to move toward the creation of a larger consensus (Higgott and Cooper, 1990).

Group History. Do group members know each other from prior work? Or have they been convened for the first time? Are they likely to work together again?

Groups whose members have a history of working together (and who may anticipate doing so in the future) are likely to be more effective than those that do not have such a history but only if their prior history has been one of productivity. Groups whose members have a long history of animosity and antagonism may find they are so concerned about matters of precedent (in particular, the possibility that other group members will attempt to take advantage of them because of some previous alleged offense) that they are hindered from working effectively. If the previous acquaintance and work are generally positive however, then such acquaintance should facilitate the completion of work in the present round. Furthermore, groups evolve over time, and goals may shift as alliances change or strengthen. As we shall see, in the SEA negotiations, changes in group history made it possible for crucial adjustments in voting rules to be introduced; these adjustments, in turn, resulted in important shifts in group dynamics and group effectiveness.

A corollary of group history is the possibility (witness the GATT negotiations in this regard) that the group will have begun its work in some previous incarnation, then have several important items on the agenda left incomplete. Such items carry over to future rounds of the group's work; tasks that have not yet been completed will be remembered better and will be more motivating than those already finished (the so-called Zeigarnik effect).

Group Cohesiveness. Groups whose members are united in some common purpose, or who have a strong esprit de corps, are more likely to work effectively than less cohesive groups. Group cohesiveness can spring from one or more of several sources, including a long history of positive relations among group members, and consequent mutual trust and affection; the presence of a strong leader, someone who has the personal appeal or charisma necessary to bind the group's members to a common purpose; or the existence of some sort of external threat to the survival of the group, some danger from without that leads the members to band together. The greater a group's cohesiveness, the greater its tendency to function in unison and to experience relatively little conflict, and for members to believe that they are each part of a transcendent enterprise.

One of the things that an effective leader can do to create this sense of "transcendence" is to introduce a "superordinate goal" (Sherif and Sherif, 1953), a group objective that bridges existing bases of conflict or competition in order to reach the goal of increased cooperation.[2] The deliberate introduction of such a superordinate goal increases group cohesiveness. Note that a similar effect is likely to result from the emergence of an external threat to the group's welfare or survival.

In summary, if one wishes to enhance the task effectiveness of a group, one can do so by modifying the group's leadership, membership composition, history, or cohesiveness—alone or in combination. Each factor varies in relation to the others and in relation to the particular context in which group decision making transpires.

Conditions Impairing Effective Task Performance

Obviously, the absence of any of the conditions for group effectiveness, as described above, impedes the group's ability to accomplish its objectives. In addition, three factors hinder the group's work: the existence of blocking coalitions, the presence of deviates, and pressures toward conformity.

Blocking Coalitions. As mentioned earlier, some coalitions of two or more group members may come into existence in order to help forge consensus; if three, four, eight, or ten group members can agree on the wisdom of a particular course of action, then perhaps they, in turn, can persuade others. But in addition to these consensus-building coalitions, there are also blocking coalitions, whose purpose is to unify a subset of the membership around the common objective of opposing the prevailing wisdom, blocking efforts to commit the group to a particular course of action. During the Uruguay Round, for example, India and Brazil repeatedly attempted to form a coalition whose purpose was to prevent the emerging majority from having its way. Blocking coalitions may be viewed as constructive or destructive, depending on one's goals; proponents of a stronger European Parliament (EP) rejoiced when it enlisted the support of Italy as a blocking partner.

Deviates. If two or more opponents to a particular group recommendation or action can be construed as a "social movement," then a single opponent is a "deviate." This individual refuses to go along with the group philosophy or plan of action; like the lone dissident juror portrayed by Henry Fonda in the film *Twelve Angry Men,* these individuals stand up for what they believe—and, in so doing, interfere with the group's ability to move forward. The United Kingdom played this role during the SEA negotiations. In fact, some of the decision rules in the EC were changed from unanimity to majority in order to avoid the necessity of enlisting British support.

When a deviate exists, typically the majority (as well as the group's leadership) attempts to take several sequential steps. First, the group tires to persuade the deviate to come around to the majority position, to enter the warm confines of the group, to accept the group's protective embrace (in exchange for recanting); second, if and when efforts at persuasion fail, the group moves to isolate, ostracize, or forcibly extrude the deviate: "If you won't join us, then to hell with you!"

Conformity Pressure. It was argued earlier that highly cohesive groups are often able to function more effectively than their more dissident counterparts. Offsetting this virtue is the possibility that cohesive groups will be so eager to instill uniformity of opinion and purpose that they apply undue pressure on dissidents to conform to the group's agenda (Asch, 1952). "Unless you do our bidding," the membership implies, "we will come to regard you as someone unworthy of our support and affection." Under conditions of conformity, dissent-

ing points of view are likely to be suppressed in favor of unanimity. The result, too often, is a decision based more on expediency than on wisdom.[3]

Janis (1982) has described at length a particular variation on the theme of conformity in his discussion of the phenomenon of "groupthink." Patterned after some of the ideas in George Orwell's *1984*, groupthink is a pattern of ineffective, faulty group decision making that results from excessive cohesiveness. As a result of this cohesiveness, private doubts about the wisdom or efficacy of a particular recommendation are suppressed in favor of what is believed to be the group "will." As illustrations of groupthink in action, Janis offers the 1961 decision by the U.S. government to support the invasion of Cuba at the Bay of Pigs (a decision that led to an overwhelming defeat at the hands of Fidel Castro) and the U.S. decision to move north of the 38th parallel in the Korean War (thereby bringing the Chinese into the conflict).

In summary, groups that function effectively are likely to adjust themselves to the particular task demands at hand. Simple tasks can be completed best by yielding to a common group purpose, setting aside private reservations, and simply getting on with it—perhaps under a so-called autocratic leader who indicates precisely which group member is to complete which piece of the overall task. More complex tasks, however, of the kind that most multilateral exchanges are likely to entail, requires openness to diverse viewpoints, group cohesiveness (but not at the expense of suppressing differences of opinion), and leadership that encourages heterogeneity of opinion and the development of decisions based on consensus rather than imposition of the leader's unilateral wishes.

The SEA Negotiations

The process leading to ratification of the SEA provides ample material for demonstrating the importance of small group theory for explaining complex multilateral processes (Lodge, 1986a; Sandholtz and Zysman, 1992). We begin by stating the obvious: the processes that culminated in the ratification of SEA occurred in groups of varying size, power, and complexity. Nearly a score of acronyms for various groups pepper the pages of Chapter One. These groups may be analyzed on the basis of the factors that characterize all groups: formal and emergent leadership, composition, evolution over time, cohesiveness, coalition formation, pressures toward conformity, and treatment of deviates—all central components of the small group approach. Lodge has touched on each of these factors, albeit to varying degrees, in her case history in Chapter One. We will illustrate the utility of our approach by considering several of the most significant of these factors. In so doing, we hope to shed some light on the course of events characterizing the movement toward unity.

Group Evolution: Changes in Group Identity

As any group member can attest, the reasons for joining a group are seldom identical to the reasons for remaining in it. A reading group may evolve into a

political action or personal support group. Similarly, the reasons for participating in the EC have changed over time, an these changes have been reflected in the rules governing the way its members make decisions. A voting rule requiring unanimity was essential in the early stages of the EC to assuage fears of threats to national sovereignty; it permitted each state to know with certainty that no agreement could be reached unless it gave its consent. The rule of unanimity also embodied an ideal state toward which the EC could aspire: a single community of nations in which members decide on any course of action through persuasion rather than coercion.

As any group matures, reservations about its continued viability begin to wane, and the group agenda is likely to shift accordingly. Again, witness the SEA talks. As the deadline of 1992, once comfortably in the future, began to loom large, and as general concerns about sovereignty were reduced to the opposition of one or two key dissenters, it became necessary to reconsider the way in which decisions were made. The original system, as described by Lodge, for example, included avoidance of divisive behavior that led to Council presidents' avoiding putting proposals to the vote. The effect was nondecision and procrastination. It was not unusual for several years to elapse before a proposal got adopted. Eventually, unanimity was selectively replaced by majority rule; for example, in the arena of environmental issues, unanimity is still required in defining aims and principles, while majority rule applies to the implementation of specific environmental measures.

Pressures from various sources to change the voting rules from unanimity to majority would not have been possible, much less successful, had there not been accompanying changes in group identity. The passage of time no doubt assured many member states that although national sovereignty remains important, identification with the concept of a single European community is also crucial. As described by Lodge, pro-European Union stands have come to represent the high ground, with stronger moral justification than "mere" nationalism. Indeed, the idea of a unified Europe has begun to attain the status of a superordinate goal, one that can be used to heighten group cohesiveness and provide leverage for group leaders to attain their goals. The initial failure of Denmark to ratify the Maastricht Treaty, coupled with continuing British ambivalence and the marginal ratification by France, points again to the tension between pressures toward consensus and tolerance of differences. Clearly, the identity of the EC continues to change in response to this most recent challenge to its very survival.

Treatment of Deviates

Once group members began considering the move from unanimity, policy dissenters could be dealt with much more effectively than was possible before. One of the best documented findings in small group research is that when unanimity is required, the group's undivided attention becomes focused on the deviate in an effort to bring this individual around to the prevailing point of view. With

majority voting schemes, however, the attention enjoyed by a deviate is short-lived. A recalcitrant member is soon ignored or, if necessary, threatened with expulsion.

This threat of "go along or go alone" was implicit in the European Council's deliberations: "a carefully managed strategy evolved of allowing states to isolate themselves from the wishes of the majority at their peril" (Chapter One). The United Kingdom was a frequent target of this threat; Lodge describes Britain's frequent opposition as "irrelevant," and the threat of isolation served to push the country, kicking and screaming, toward the new venture. Denmark is the latest target. Of course, such pressures toward consensus, borne of general adherence to a superordinate goal, may deter the group from thoughtfully considering legitimate, constructive objections raised by deviates.

Strategies of Empowerment

One of the surprising actors in the drive toward union was the EP. The actions of the EP offer a classic illustration of a successful low-power influence strategy at work; the EP evolved from a body to be "consulted" to a group that could push hard for a central role in the adoption of reforms. Groups or individuals with high vested power are able to accomplish their goals through more or less straightforward social influence tactics such as threats and promises. Those lacking power must navigate a far less direct route; essentially, they must persuade their more powerful counterparts that their cause is just and merits a change in rules. Such appeals must be nonrancorous (to avoid alienating other parties), must be based on a deep knowledge of other parties in the process, and generally must appeal to norms of fairness and legitimacy.

The process by which the EP attempted to attain power forms a centerpiece of the case presented in Chapter One. The EP appear to have had strong, savvy, innovative leadership. Pierre Pflimlin and Altiero Spinelli understood the political process (including engaging Italy in a blocking coalition), realized the importance of involving François Mitterrand, lobbied effectively (with, for example, labor and business elites, governments, and opinion leaders), and were able to represent the ideal of unity from the perspective of a large, representative, transnational body. This combination of political skill, an image of legitimacy, and espousal of the superordinate, transnational goal of unity was successful in gaining a number of significant concessions (although by no means all that had been sought).

Emergence of Different Group Roles

Throughout the SEA talks, groups were propelled by leadership, both assigned and seized. The exercise of leadership makes it possible for groups to go forward; and, as described in the case study, there were ample opportunities for such leadership to emerge. The Council presidency provided a formal opportunity for the exercise of influence. One particularly theatrical moment must have occurred

when the Italian Council president decided to take an unprecedented vote on convening the Inter-Governmental Conference (IGC), much to the chagrin of the United Kingdom ("There was an uproar," Lodge reports.) This innovative tactic subsequently served to warn other states that movement toward agreement would not be halted by obstructionist tactics.

From Lodge's account, it appears that the two task leaders during the SEA talks were France and Germany. At least one of them had to advocate a particular position or policy—while neither could be actively opposed—if agreements were to be reached. For example, we are told that Germany and France were essential in EC bargaining—not so much that each had to support a particular initiative, but rather that neither could actively oppose it. The third member of the big four, Great Britain, did little to build an effective leadership role for itself and was frequently dismissed out of hand.

Although Germany and France may have been the acknowledged task leaders, the role of the remaining member of the big four, Italy, was more complex. As "honest broker and coalition cementer" (Chapter One), Italy managed to keep integrationist sentiments alive when the venture was threatened in 1985. Consistently pro-Union and proactive, Italy was able to perform essential tasks while avoiding alienating other states. The Italians went beyond Bales's notion of "socioemotional" leader to be a "great leader." That Spinelli is referred to as a "father of European integration" (Chapter One) is testimony to the appropriateness of that label.

Effect of a Deviate's Departure on Group Functioning

The United Kingdom's role in the SEA process has been characterized by some as obstructionist and anti-integrationist, with Prime Minister Margaret Thatcher epitomizing British arrogance. No doubt her actions contributed to the frequent isolation of Britain in the SEA negotiation process. But with the replacement of Thatcher by John Major, an important dynamic change occurred. No longer do the other eleven member nations have a common external threat to unite against and to promote group cohesion.[4] With the more phlegmatic, less obstructionist Major at the helm, internal disagreements that had been suppressed reappeared. Specifically, France and Germany are increasingly antagonistic, as Bonn is urging delays in creating the regional central bank. At the same time, Britain is enjoying something it had not had in Europe in some time—negotiating power.

In summary, the SEA negotiations offer a good illustration of small group process at work. Through dynamics both at the table and away from it, the SEA group evolved an identity, a set of decision-making rules and procedures, and a means for addressing the problem of obstructionism that allowed it (at least for a moment) to move forward with great effectiveness.[5]

The Uruguay Round of GATT

If the SEA negotiations included a relatively small number of players representing each of the twelve European nations involved, then the Uruguay Round of

GATT tells a very different story. The Uruguay Round appears to be far more complex than its European counterpart because it consisted of 100 different nations, extended back to 1947, when the first GATT meetings took place; and focused on a great many different, highly complex issues. Indeed, in Chapter Two Sjöstedt has even dignified this distinction by referring to plurilateral versus multilateral negotiations, where the SEA case would appear to be plurilateral (involving relatively few players) and the GATT case, multilateral (involving many). By implication, the key element differentiating plurilateral from multilateral negotiations is complexity. Multilateral negotiations are more complex because of the greater number of parties, issues, and perhaps a longer time frame as well. Although we agree that increasing the number of parties to a negotiation (from 12 to 100, for example) does lead to increased complexity, the underlying processes are fundamentally alike. As small group theorists, we believe that any social arrangement, no matter how large, quite naturally breaks down into smaller groupings that allow work to be accomplished. Had all 150 or so nations represented at the Law of the SEA negotiations insisted on meeting exclusively in plenary session, virtually nothing would have been accomplished.

When large, variegated organizations are reduced to smaller groups (called task forces, committees, working groups) the real work of negotiation takes place in these far more compact and intimate gatherings. Although Sjöstedt tells us that the Uruguay negotiations were characterized by the "extensiveness and complexity of the agenda as a whole," he goes on to enumerate the several dozen negotiating groups that either were appointed during the Uruguay Round or evolved because of member wishes to move (or block) a portion of the agenda. Because of this natural tendency for large negotiations to devolve into smaller negotiating groups, we believe that small groups formed the building blocks of the Uruguay Round. In keeping with this view, we believe that the GATT process was influenced—among other things—by four considerations: group history, external threats, conformity pressures, and the success of the Cairns coalition.

Importance of Group History

GATT was founded in Geneva in 1947. Since then the membership was widened and issues have proliferated, as one round of negotiations has followed another. Each negotiating round has left unfinished items of business on the table, and these, in turn, have had the effect of motivating the initiation of a successive round. For example, Sjöstedt points out that the Tokyo Round (1973–1979) included agreed-upon procedures for continued postnegotiation deliberations. In addition, he points to the many "backlog issues" that the Tokyo Round left behind. These unresolved issues, when analyzed on the basis of group research and analysis, would be expected to be more motivating (recall the Zeigarnik effect, described earlier in this chapter) in shaping a subsequent agenda than those issues that were addressed successfully and completely—or those that had not previously been considered (for example, intellectual property rights).

Also noteworthy in this case is the generally hostile and contentious cli-

mate that seems to have characterized much of the work in previous negotiating rounds. As alluded to earlier, social psychological research indicates that groups with a history of successful, collaborative work are more likely to adopt such a style and to function effectively in the present than are groups with a history of acrimony. A group culture of consensus-seeking develops and motivates future behavior. The fact that the Uruguay Round (as of this writing) had not come to a successful conclusion can be understood, in part, as a result of the influence of a negative group history on subsequent behavior.

Motivating Effects of External Threat

After a careful reading of Chapter Two, as well as other documents on the Uruguay Round (for example, Higgott and Cooper, 1990; Prestowitz, Tonelson, and Jerome, 1991; Winham, 1989; Winham and Kizer, 1990), one forms the impression that a large group of national representatives, replete with conflicting interests and agendas, many of whom (for example, India and Brazil) were quite reluctant even to convene another GATT negotiation, were nevertheless thrown together into the Uruguay Round. It is not so much that negotiators wanted to come together or that they had a history of successful work together; rather, they were impelled to meet.

Part of the reason for reconvening may derive from the motivating effect of unfinished group work. In addition, negotiators at the Uruguay Round may have been motivated by two forms of external threat. In explaining the decision to convene the Consultative Group of 18 in June 1981, in order to plan a GATT ministerial meeting, Sjöstedt points to the key role of neoprotectionism. In the face of this threat, a relative consensus emerged that the necessary defense of the open, multilateral trading system required a strong manifestation in GATT at the highest political level.

Time pressure constituted a second external threat with motivating properties. In describing the ministerial meeting at Punta del Este in September 1986, Sjöstedt points out that, although the meeting had gone on for the better part of a week, no agreement appeared to be on the horizon. Only at the very last moment, and only after a last round of hard bargaining, could agreement be reached.

Positive Benefits of Conformity Pressures

Earlier, we characterized conformity as a force impeding effective group work; group members reach agreement not because it is sensible but because they wish to garner group approval and avoid group censure. In the often chaotic environment of the Uruguay Round discussion, however, it can be argued that anything that contributed to conformity may have also increased the chances of joint decision making and goal attainment. Given the disarray and disagreement among so many GATT members, it seems reasonable to inquire what factors contributed to conformity with an emerging point of view.

First, recall the so-called bicycle theory of trade negotiation (Chapter

Two). Just as a cyclist can stay upright only by continuing to pedal along, international trade negotiations can continue only so long as the parties to the discussions try to maintain their momentum through ongoing exchange. Unless ways can be found to keep the conversation going, this position argues, international trade negotiations are in danger of sliding into protectionism. So, any passing reference (by the GATT secretariat or anyone else) to the invidious bicycle theory could have had the effect of increasing pressures to conform with plans to negotiate a new GATT in Uruguay.

Second, the decision to build into the Uruguay Round an opportunity for midterm review, for the ostensible purpose of stocktaking and midterm adjustment, may have had the beneficial effect of building greater commitment to GATT. The mere act of convening the ministerial-level meeting in Montreal, in December 1989, provided participating group members with the sense that their opinions mattered, that their points of view had to be taken into account if the process was to be an effective one. As social psychological research on motivation in work settings has demonstrated (through the Hawthorne effect), group members who believe their views are of interest and concern to the leadership are more motivated and more productive than those who are not the beneficiaries of such an approach. In general, the way to build commitment to a group process or product is to first get one's foot in the door (Freedman and Fraser, 1966), then extract a series of small, incremental decisions in support of the regime advocated, and finally (using the psychology of "entrapment" among other things—see Brockner and Rubin, 1985) persuade group members that they have too much invested in keeping the bicycle upright to quit.

A Successful Coalition at Work

It is interesting to compare the unsuccessful efforts of the United Kingdom, Denmark, and Greece to block efforts to move toward the SEA with the strikingly effective work of the Cairns group during GATT. Why was one coalition so ineffectual, while another worked so much better? Several differences are striking in this regard. First, the Cairns group, consisting of fourteen nations, was significantly larger than the three-nation potential blocking coalition of the SEA talks. Although a larger group is a harder group to coordinate and manage, it is also one in which more ideas and approaches are likely to be advanced. Second, the Cairns group generated a great many proposals and alternatives, all pivoting on issues of agriculture, whereas the SEA coalition was largely a "Johnny One Note" group that perhaps came together solely for the purpose of blocking efforts to create European unity.

Third, whereas the SEA coalition existed solely to block, the Cairns group was oriented toward advocacy. Indeed, the Cairns group emerged to help bridge the rift between the EC and the United States. Functioning as a go-between and mediator of sorts, the Cairns group managed to place many ideas and approaches on the table; in doing so, it helped to move the GATT talks forward, even if there is as yet no conclusive agreement to report.

Finally, note should be made of the effective leadership exercised by Australia. Stepping into the large shoes of its coalition partner, Canada, Australia revitalized the work of the Cairns group. Although we have no data to base this guess on, we surmise that the three-nation blocking coalition at the SEA negotiations had no such clear and effective leadership. Prime Minister Thatcher, the obvious choice as leader of this little band of rebels, had already besmirched her image through her rough treatment of colleagues in countless meetings. She thus probably had little credibility as a leader, and it was not clear who could step in to take her place.

A Comparison

There is little doubt that the SEA negotiations resulted in greater progress than the GATT talks, as of this writing. Our analysis of the two cases suggests two reasons for their differential success. First, in GATT the participants appear to have been granted little autonomy; instead they were constrained by tight governmental instruction; witness Chapter Three in this regard, where actors are typically identified by the country they represented rather than by name. Under these conditions, many of the principles of group dynamics outlined in this chapter are vitiated. Indeed, it is questionable whether we can speak of a group at all when the participants are functioning as agents, marionettes whose strings are pulled by players away from the table. The SEA negotiators, in contrast, were often heads of state or, more commonly, close associates with wide-ranging power to negotiate. It is in such face-to-face exchanges that group dynamics will likely play a powerful, consensus-creating role.

Second, the SEA negotiations appear to have been characterized by the presence of a clear superordinate goal that was simply not present during the GATT talks. Representatives to the SEA talks were motivated either by the desire for European economic union or by the fear of exclusion from such an arrangement. In contrast, representatives to the Uruguay Round shared no such overarching concern; nor was fear of exclusion from an agreement sufficiently powerful to drive the parties toward consensus.

Prescriptive Lessons for Multilateral Negotiation

In concluding this brief sojourn through the world of small group theory and its relevance for multilateral negotiation, it may be useful to summarize our analysis by indicating briefly some prescriptive lessons. We direct the following advice to would-be organizers of a multilateral conference, regardless of its size and agenda.

Remember to focus on process, not outcome. It is tempting to measure the effectiveness of group work by looking at the products made or results achieved. What small group theory, the two cases in this book, and other illustrations of

international negotiation (see McDonald, 1990) make clear is that satisfactory outcomes can result only if the underlying process is effective.

If process is as important as we believe, then it is essential that ways be found to develop a group climate that encourages the open expression of ideas. Early in the life of a group it is important that conflicting, dissenting points of view be encouraged; to that end, we recommend forming groups that are heterogeneous, thereby making it likely that many different ideas will be put on the table. At some point, however, it becomes necessary to move beyond the creative work of the group to a decision. At this time, a homogeneous group is more effective than a heterogeneous group.

This move toward greater homogeneity is demonstrated by the group's treatment of deviates. As illustrated by the two cases, deviates can be important contributors to the work of a group. As outsiders, they contribute a different perspective (making it less likely that groupthink will result); and as developments in the GATT negotiations make clear, they also offer a common focus for the group's attention—at least temporarily increasing the sense of group solidarity as a result. At some point, however, a deviate becomes a nuisance, even a menace, to effective group work. If the deviate cannot be persuaded to come around to the prevailing viewpoint, he or she may have to be excluded—or, as in the SEA talks, decision rules may have to be changed in order to "legislate" a conducive environment.

Develop a strategy for creating group cohesiveness. Group cohesiveness is an important ingredient of effective group functioning, and it can be achieved in several ways. One is by introducing dynamic, charismatic leadership—easier said than done, we suspect. A second route, more open to intervention by the innovative conference planner, entails identifying possible superordinate goals. Such a superordinate goal already existed in the SEA case, in the form of allegiance (more or less) to the concept of a European union that transcends national identity. In the Uruguay Round, however, which was fraught with dissension, it appears that superordinate goals were few and far between. If ways could have been found to encourage more of a global—rather than a strictly national—point of view (as seemed to happen at the Law of the Sea Conference), perhaps more group cohesiveness would have been the result. Depletion of the ozone layer is a problem (an external threat, if you will) that confronts each and every one of us, as is the threat of worldwide recession in the absence of thoughtful trade policies. Attention to such issues and countless others could have had the beneficial effect of enhancing group cohesiveness.

If the group is to reach closure at some point, ways have to be found to help move that process along. As described in this chapter, several techniques may be helpful in this regard: extracting a small commitment from group members, thereby getting one's foot in the door; using the psychology of entrapment to engender the sense that one has too much committed to the group's work to quit; and introducing stopping points along the way (witness the midterm review of the GATT Uruguay Round) to encourage group members to take increased ownership of the group's work.

Finally, remember that most of the work in multilateral exchanges does not involve negotiation at all. A small group approach can go a long way toward explaining what transpires during multilateral exchanges. Although the stated focus of this book is multilateral negotiation, we have been struck in our reading of the two cases by the surprising paucity of evidence of negotiation per se. The SEA and GATT talks seem to have been driven not by negotiation but by group process. It is not the staking out of positions, from which concessions are subsequently made, that best characterizes the work that takes place in multilateral encounters. Building group consensus, through the dynamics of group process, is the key feature.

Notes

1. Surprisingly little of this work has lent itself to a direct application of small group research to international negotiation. For an important exception, see Galtung (1968), and see Druckman (1990) for an excellent review of the relevant literature that does exist.

2. In their research on intergroup conflict, the Sherifs describe the following innovation used by them to create cooperation between cabins of adolescent summer campers who had been caught in the throes of an intense rivalry. They arranged for a vehicle that was to take the two warring cabins of adolescent boys on a trip to run out of gasoline. Only by working together and jointly hauling the truck to a filling station (with a rope that had previously been used only for tug-of-war) were the boys able to get the truck filled with gas and reach their destination; because neither group of boys alone had the strength and numbers to do the job, they had to work together.

3. The twin concepts of cohesiveness and conformity bring into focus an essential conflict in group functioning: although the members of a cohesive group feel free to generate fresh and innovative ideas, such groups also tend to be driven by the need to reach consensus before such ideas can be aired thoroughly.

4. Actually, in light of Denmark's initial refusal to ratify Maastricht, this is not strictly true. An external threat to the group's survival is alive and well!

5. In regard to dynamics outside the negotiations, witness the deliberate spreading of rumor alluded to in Chapter One.

Chapter 7

Coalition Theory
Using Power to Build Cooperation

Christophe Dupont (France)

For many authors and researchers in political, organizational, and social sciences the concept of coalition has "wide intuitive and scientific appeal" (Stevenson, Pearce, and Porter, 1985). Coalitions and alliances are fundamental and universal aspects of international relations and politics and therefore have long been at the center of concern in these fields; social psychology has been interested in coalitions as part of the exploration of group behavior; and the organizational literature has increasingly used the concept in connection with such issues as organizational processes, cooperation and conflicts, constraints, and goals. Many efforts have been made to develop testable and relevant models to describe accurately, explain convincingly, or predict probabilistically key developments in the field. Indeed, several of the previous chapters have incorporated coalition into their explanations.

Although there are different definitions of the concept, *coalitions* may be defined as cooperative efforts for the attainment of short-range, issue-specific objectives. In this sense coalitions are distinguished from formal alliances ("cooperative effort[s] in which the rights and duties of each member are codified in a treaty"), informal alignments ("learned expectations [on the part of nations] as to how much cooperation might be expected from other nations"), and behavioral alignments ("actual efforts [of nations] to coordinate their behavior in a similar manner with respect to common objects") (Sullivan, 1974, p. 101). Another widely used definition from an organizational perspective posits five characteristics that "must be present for a group to be considered a coalition": it must be an "interacting group, deliberately constructed, independent of the

formal structure, lacking its external goal (or goals) and requiring concerted member action" (Stevenson, Pearce, and Porter, 1985, p. 261).

If coalitions are an ever-present possibility and most often an observed reality in groups—whatever their form, structure, or purpose—it is not surprising that they may be expected to play a role in conference diplomacy, a not entirely new but increasingly observable form of international relations (Kaufmann, 1989a). Examples of conference diplomacy are the plurilateral negotiations that took place to elaborate the Single European Act (SEA) in 1985 among the twelve members of the European Communities (EC) and the multilateral negotiations between 1986 and 1993 in the Uruguay Round of trade negotiations. These two cases show evidence of coalition emergence and attempts to use collective influence to fulfill certain goals. This chapter analyzes these two negotiations from the viewpoint of coalition theories. The first section gives an overview of these theories; the second section examines their relevance to negotiation theory; and the third applies the analysis to the SEA and Uruguay Round negotiations.

In this chapter I attempt initially to identify the number and types of coalitions that could be observed in the two cases studied. Based on this descriptive approach, I then tackle the difficult issue of coalition effectiveness. This more exacting purpose (which could possibly lead either to predicting certain negotiation processes and outcomes or to testing certain propositions of coalition theories) has been inspired more deductively by operational taxonomy than by detailed and inductive analysis—a taxonomy (for example, coding criteria) that rests essentially (although not entirely) on the two cases in question.

On balance, the purpose of the chapter is to complement the concurrent approaches to multilateral negotiations. If one of the main conclusions is relatively unsurprising (that coalition formation and behaviors were important factors in the two cases, a statement that can be generalized to almost all multilateral negotiations), another—more basic—result is that negotiators in multilateral encounters would be well advised to include in their thinking about prenegotiations and formal negotiations the appropriateness of forming (or being part of) coalitions and the contribution this behavior may—or may not—make to the fulfillment of their individual goals and their eventual reconciliation with the shared goal of making the multilateral conference a joint success.

Coalition Theories: Approaches and Issues

Coalition theories—whether applied to political entities, groups, or organizations—are attempts to construct models of an explanatory or predictive nature (or both). The main areas that are addressed fall into roughly three categories: formation, stability and duration, and impact and outcomes.

Formation

Discussion of coalition formation can be subdivided into three subsets: rationale (motivation), goals, and prerequisites (a problem of mobilization). Political mod-

els place ideological variables at the center of the process; social psychology and game-theoretical models—although with different approaches—assume the need for a joint payoff not attainable through individual action alone. Motivations and goals for a coalition have been apprehended differently by the various theories. The first theories using power (Caplow, 1956), minimum resources (Gamson, 1961a, 1961b), and even bargaining (Chertkoff, 1970) emphasize the payoff dimension. In these theories, coalitions are formed on a utilitarian basis—for example, coalescing to gain a reward (benefit, payoff) that individual action alone would not permit. The motivation may be power maximization within and outside the coalition (Caplow, 1956), payoff maximization based on "equity" (Gamson, 1961b), or some compromise between "equity" and "equality" (Chertkoff, 1970; Komorita and Chertkoff, 1973). In these models, variables are the comparative assessment of resources among members of the group, and the most important issues are the definition and identification of resources, which results in comparison of the resources obtainable through alternative coalition opportunities. The number of alternatives available to members of a coalition has also been used as a variable in the so-called weighted probability model (Komorita, 1974).

The models develop predictions of the number and composition of winning coalitions, although they do not always agree on the results. These approaches have been criticized (see, for example, Bacharach and Lawler, 1980) because they assume divisible payoffs; exclude some variables that play a role in actual settings—for example, ideological factors; do not treat the dynamics of coalitions over time; and do not deal with size. Political and "ideological distance" models have emphasized the role of ideological proximities and distances as an important factor in coalition formation as well as the role of size (for example, Riker, 1962; Lawler and Young, 1975; Murnigham, 1978). Organization theories have attempted to combine the contributions of social psychology and political science. Bacharach and Lawler (1980), for instance, have proposed a "bargaining-and-power" theory of coalition that emphasizes, in particular, dependence dimensions.

Stability and Duration

Another important area in coalition theories has been the attempt to explain and predict the resilience of coalitions over time—in other words, their stability and duration. The dynamics dimension takes on increased importance as soon as some of the scope conditions of the theories have been loosened or enlarged. Thus the introduction of such concepts as minority coalitions, nonwinning coalitions, interest groups, influence versus power, countercoalitions and retaliatory actions, constant intracoalition bargaining, and never-ending reshuffling makes it possible to explore the preconditions necessary for a coalition to maintain or to increase its role. Propositions to this effect have been offered, most of them qualitative in nature and not yet fully empirically tested (see again, for instance, Bacharach and Lawler, 1980, or Stevenson, Pearce, and Porter, 1985, on a process model of development).

Political scientists have also proposed models in which they attempt to identify stability/instability variables of alliances and coalitions—for example, by making an inventory of causes of stresses and strains that eventually lead to the disbanding of the group. For instance, in political/military alliances, a number of cultural, military, economic, environmental, and structural factors have been identified (see, for instance, Sullivan, 1974). Some of these approaches have been qualitative as well as quantitative, two relevant illustrations being Haas (1974) and Attali (1972).

Some general models—mostly inspired by game theory—have provided an increased understanding of the process and conditions of stability. Prominent among these has been the Shapley (1953) model, which has been complemented by several subsequent contributions, as noted in Chapter Four. Shapley developed mathematical tools and concepts that apply to coalition formation and stability over time. The Shapley value, according to this theory, is a predictor of coalition stability; shifts in coalitions are explained by the interplay of actors constantly comparing the actual benefits they derive from present membership in a coalition to what they could obtain in alternative opportunities. This value is subsumed in an average value that takes into account actors' marginal contributions in the large number of potential 2^n-1 coalitions (which is made additionally complex by the order of appearance of the member concerned in the various coalition alternatives).

Research (mostly of a descriptive nature) has also examined the main organizational dimensions of coalitions. These include, *inter alia*, the degree of size, formalism, leadership, commitments, decision-making mechanisms, power-and-influence structure, relationships within and outside the group, and constituencies. Links with related fields in the literature (for example, organizational, social psychological, or political science) have proved useful regarding the organizational, behavioral, and operational variables of coalitions as well as their potential transformations and changes.

Impact and Outcomes

Questions concerning impact and outcome are obviously of the greatest importance to both researchers and practitioners. Do coalitions, the networks that they organize and rely on, the power struggle they initiate or are confronted with (within and among themselves), the conflictual/cooperative moves and tactics that they resort to have any influence on the patterns of events in the whole group, the organization, the political entity, or the "conference" in which they are created and where they develop, gain or lose strength, are countered, and are reshuffled or disappear? Thus the relevant questions are: What degree of influence do coalitions have on processes and end results of the group—(its purposes, goals, outcomes, and aftermath)? Through which mechanisms does that influence develop? What kind of changes (both internal and external) do they bring about, and are such changes of a durable nature? To what extent can a coalition be appraised as successful?

Unfortunately theories have not been able to give unified and convincing results. We do, however, have a set of testable propositions, most couched in an "if-then" sequence in a probabilistic mold or in the typical social science proposition: "the greater or the lower characteristic A or condition B, the more or the lesser the probability of outcome characteristic X or variable Y." In the organizational field propositions of this kind have been developed in some details, mostly on the problematics of change. To take a few examples, Bacharach and Lawler (1980), Stevenson, Pearce, and Porter (1985), and Mahon and Bigelow (1990) have been able to list propositions linking outcome (dependent) variables to various organizational (independent) variables. Mahon and Bigelow, for instance, adapting a typology borrowed from Eccles (1983), show that outcome is a function of the type of coalition (policy- or resource-oriented, internal or external).

Using Coalition Theories to Explain Multilateral Negotiations

Coalitions are often presented as a specific bargaining problem; conversely, in multilateral negotiations bargaining has a lot to do with building and working with coalitions. Furthermore, a coalition emerges as soon as there are more than two actors (although the coalition may even emerge in a dyad if external actors and constituencies are included). In this section the focus is on the relevance of the coalition conceptual and methodological framework to multilateral negotiations (as distinguished from bilateral ones). The gist of the argument is that coalition analysis is a key to explaining the processes and outcomes of multilateral negotiations.

Aspirations, Purposes, and Goals of Multilateral Actors

Multilateral negotiations take many forms, among which conference diplomacy is the most prominent. As defined by Kaufmann (1989a), negotiations in conference diplomacy are the sum total of talks and contacts intended to solve conflicts or to work toward the common objectives of a conference. Conferences may have many different objectives. Kaufmann distinguishes eight different categories, one of which is to "negotiate and draft a treaty or other formal instrument" (p. 8). The following analysis applies to this category, although most of it is also relevant in general. Kaufmann's definition includes the "mixed motive" characteristic of conferences. Negotiators—representing states—are inspired by two often opposite motives: on the one hand, they (normally) share the common objective of the conference (to solve a specific conflict or work toward a given objective such as drafting a treaty); on the other, if not always by personal conviction, at least by mission and duty, they have to present and defend the self-interests of the nation they represent. This dual motivation is never ignored in the political or diplomatic literature. Because of mixed motives members of a conference look for ways to make reconciliation possible. The principal way is through coalition, which has several consequences.

In multilateral negotiations, coalitions form and act according to the amount of congruence in the aspirations, goals, and purposes of the actors concerned. The more congruent these factors, the greater the coalition's activity and

stability. If subsets of members share congruence, there will be competing coalitions. These ideas about congruence are roughly in line with coalition theory, although they raise the question of size: does a coalition—in a conference setting with the objective to draft a treaty—seek to increase its influence and work toward its goals by gaining the largest membership or by restricting it to the minimum efficient size?

Existing theories help explain, if not always predict, the emergence and the composition of coalitions. Concepts like conditions to gain control, alternative opportunities, and above all ideological distances are certainly applicable. Some of the sophisticated concepts may not apply as well or as easily. One major issue is divisibility, a concept linked to a measure of resources. However, in treaty drafting, concessions on content or formulation of clauses constitute a form of divisibility. The concept of resources, basic to many theories of coalitions, is at best fuzzy in conference settings. With these reservations, which call for adjustments in order for coalition theories to be applicable to negotiations, there is a large area in which coalition theories in general are relevant to multilateral negotiations.

In a conference setting the dominance of a "winning" coalition does not necessarily mean "success." Success depends on a decision rule that involves a no-veto (or no–quasi-veto) mechanism, or else even a winning coalition could be blocked. The coalition framework distinguishes formal success (formal achievement of aspirations, goals, and purposes) from inferior—yet potentially substantial—results. For example, some coalition theories, by repudiating the winning-coalition concept, have shown that minority coalitions may form simply to gain influence or to attain some intermediate objectives (exerting pressure, gaining recognition). Inverting this idea, one can see how a majority coalition may be formed—even though members are aware that formal success is not achievable at this point of time—simply because such an important body of congruent interests may create background preconditions for future "success." One may also take the view that minority (defensive) coalitions are built to protect themselves from this time-oriented design.

The coalition framework has developed normative concepts (equity, equality), that are often present in conference settings; they range from principles considered shared by the whole group to the different and more difficult concept of universal normativity ("what is good for my coalition is good for all"; "what we believe to be the 'best' rules, regimes, or systems is 'necessarily' the best for all"). This culturally ethnocentric orientation obviously is a key issue: in coalition analysis ideological variables therefore appear crucial.

Coalition theories have sometimes made use of the concept of *linkages:* coalitions develop because there may exist complementary self-interests, attainment of which is helped by some potential linkage or trade-offs among members of the coalition. These issue-linked coalitions are often observed more in small groups, in which identification of potentially promising issues and potential benefit measurement are easier, than in large groups, where complexity makes it more difficult to create joint issue-linked platforms.

Finally, coalition theories suggest some methodological devices; their use can contribute to better organization and deeper analysis than are otherwise possible. Thus it may be of interest to build "congruence" matrices and attitudinal (policy or issue preference) scales, as Chapter Three discusses.

In summary, in a conference-setting coalition, formation, composition, behavior, and success depend on such qualitative variables as degree of congruence, decision-making variables, criteria, stakes, and potential for issue links and trade-offs. These seem to be the primary, but not the exclusive, variables. For instance, external and time-contingent factors, the duration of past relationships, past experience with coalitions or alliances, adroitness in or proneness to coalescing, the role of secretariats and presiding officers, and, above all, the capacity to reward or punish should also be included in this inventory.

Decision Making, Power, and Influence

Among the factors that determine coalition behavior and outcomes in multilateral negotiations, two important variables are the decision-making mechanism and interacting power and influence patterns.

Decision-Making Mechanism. Procedures and rules have a bearing on coalition behavior. For instance, organization theories admit that variables relating to authority structure (degree of centralization, degree of organizational formality, communication lines) play a role in coalition formation and behavior (see, for example, Bacharach and Lawler, 1980). The rule structure leads parties to consider coalescing in order to change or (in the case of a "dominant" coalition in the organization-theory sense) to reinforce or adapt the rule patterns, and to behave accordingly. Although some of this analysis may be transferred to multilateral negotiations (for example, parties may coalesce in order to change the rules of the game, such as reinforcing or loosening the scope of the rules or modifying procedures of admission), multilateral negotiations may exhibit a major difference, voting and veto procedures.

The problem of power has formal as well as informal aspects. The formal aspects focus on the problem of voting. Voting rules condition member behavior (for example, rallying members in a sufficient number to gain a simple or qualified majority). More important, they define constraints to action. If decisions (be they resolutions, binding commitments, or final declarations) are based on "legal" or de facto unanimity, potential veto power exists. Veto power exists also under nonunanimity procedures. Veto power constrains strategies of coalitions to resolve the problem, to obtain (by whatever means and tactics available) immediate backing or at least abstention (an interesting illustration is given in Kaufmann, 1989a, p. 28, on an agreement in the United Nations Special Committee on Principles of International Law in 1966), or to build long-term influence to gain support later or to change the rules of the game.

As a concept, voting has been embodied in some of the important works on coalitions. The rationale behind the Shapley value is that the real foundation of the power of a member in a group/organization/assembly is his or her capacity

to be indispensable for the success of any coalition. The *pivotal member* is the one whose inclusion in the coalition is necessary for the coalition "to win." This approach is of interest in legislative or quasi-legislative (such as a treaty-drafting conference) settings because it makes use of such concepts as power indices and indices expressing the capacity to block, blunt, or defer decisions. Although these indices have not always shown convincing results, they are conceptually helpful for understanding coalition behavior in the context of constraints related to voting (Attali, 1972, p. 109).

They can also explain certain institutional arrangements (or at least give an ex post rationale to what are generally intuitive political decisions). Examples borrowed, for instance, from the French coalition literature show some applications of interest, the most intriguing and convincing being the analysis by Ponssard (1977) of the changes in the voting rights in the European Parliament (then the European Parliamentary Assembly) in July 1976 after EC membership had been increased from the original six to nine countries and the number of votes correspondingly adjusted from 198 to 410. The new partition of votes (which conforms to certain formulas of coalition theory, notably the Shapley value and indices of power) shows an elaborate construction of subtle power balances among the "larger," the "medium-sized," and the "smaller" countries. An interesting aspect of this construction is the de facto "right to veto" given certain combinations of these various groups, which are also examined in Chapter Three.

However, it would be inaccurate to emphasize only veto power in conferences and similar entities. Many institutions are precisely built or organized to achieve a common objective, and this objective may be attained only if veto power does not exist or, if it exists, is not exerted. Veto power is often a protective mechanism rather than a major strategy. In this respect a major difference exists with bilateral negotiations. Strictly speaking, in any such negotiation each party disposes, at will, of its veto power by refusing the terms and conditions of the agreement. Refusing a negotiated settlement may not be in the final or long-term interest of the party (for instance, because this decision is objectively not efficient), but it may be due to misunderstandings or judgmental or behavioral errors of the party or its opponent or both of them. Whatever the motivations and causes, the capacity to withdraw from the relationship is equivalent to a veto power.

Such is not the situation in multilateral negotiations because the decision-making mechanism is not the same. There is not necessarily a veto power (for example, if an agreement is binding subject to the extremely constraining rule of 99 votes out of 100, the 100th member may not be able to make its theoretical veto power effective); but if veto power can be exerted, there are also other factors at play (for example, moral suasion or pressure). These moves are not of the same nature as those in bilateral negotiations. Thus one may regard the difference between bilateral and multilateral negotiations as a difference between veto and contiguity.

Power and Influence Patterns. Typologies in coalition theories have distinguished "formal" and "informal" coalition (Eccles, 1983) and "explicit" and

"tacit" modes of bargaining (Druckman, 1977) within or across coalitions. These two dimensions find applications in multilateral negotiations, shedding light on the often subtle way in which actors (within and outside coalitions) try to gain control. The first distinction invites researchers to look not only at formal groups (the degree of formality varying from a weak structure to official status, leading even in some cases to the granting of specific rights) but also at less visible ones (the looser form being interest groups or lobbies). Theory has shown that strategies and tactics are often different in both cases.

These differences are the main focus of the second distinction. Coalitions may use explicit behavior—for instance, demands, proposals, offers, and counteroffers—or they may have recourse to tacit behavior, which handles information and issues in a more ambiguous way. Organization theories have made attempts to link these dimensions to other variables (internal/external, integrative/distributive nature of relationships), in order to submit propositions about specific behaviors and outcomes.

Tactics constitute a vast domain in which there is clearly a close correspondence between coalition and multilateral negotiations analysis. Coalition theorists have conducted numerous studies on the use of tactics for making threats (one of the main topics in most coalition theories), for manipulating information (part of the more general subject of communication), for blunting and blocking moves, for retaliation, and for coercion. Whereas these tactical moves are clearly distributive in nature (corresponding to coalitions designed to combat rival or minority adversarial groups), another part of the theory has rightly emphasized cooperative moves aimed at influence rather than at power and based on nonadversarial tactics such as persuasion, trade-offs, compensations and rewards, concessions, creative new solutions, enlargement, openness and frankness in communication, "principles" (including superordinate goals), loyalties and legitimacy of solutions, and small group cooperation.

A final domain in which coalition theories contribute to an understanding of multilateral negotiation is the source and role of power. For example, Bacharach and Lawler (1980) have presented a theory of coalitions based on "power and politics," power being analyzed as a form of dependence of one party (coalition) on another. This framework can be applied in the study of multilateral negotiations.

Coalition Approaches: The SEA and Uruguay Round Negotiations

The previous sections provide the theoretical framework for decoding concrete cases such as the two negotiations under review. Such an effort can be subdivided into several interconnected parts (Kremenyuk, 1991):

- *Actors:* Can we observe the actual emergence of coalitions as actors in these two events? What kind of coalition patterns can be identified and decoded in a relevant taxonomy?
- *Strategies:* To what extent did observed coalitions develop distinctive behavioral roles and strategies?

- *Outcome:* To what extent did the coalitions prove effective in making significant contributions to outcomes and in ensuring their own durability?

Descriptive Analysis

Coalitions in the two negotiations can be depicted through the use of several instruments. For example, one could use diagrams such as Likert-type scales or mapping representations in order to identify similarity of positions (Figure 7.1) or interconnected networks (Figure 7.2). By aggregating these itemized represen-

Figure 7.1. Initial Positioning of Countries on the Definition of Internal Market: Proximity to Commission Proposals (Issue C-1).

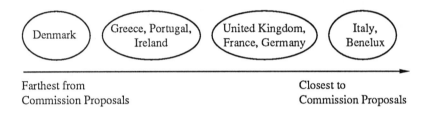

Farthest from
Commission Proposals

Closest to
Commission Proposals

Figure 7.2. Mapping (Networks) of Actors and Coalitions in Regard to the Definition of the Future of the European Community Structure.

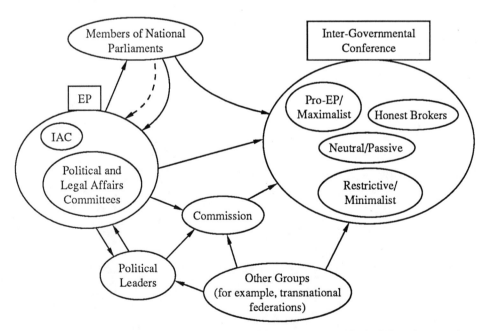

Note: The arrows denote influence strategies of the groups; the dashed line denotes that members of national parliaments belonged to the EP committees indicated.

Table 7.1A. Coalitions in the SEA Prenegotiations (February 1984 to June 1985).

Issues	Type of Lineup	Purpose/Objectives of Grouping	Key Features and Outcomes
(A) Need for a "qualitative leap forward" (Dooge phase 2)	—Italy, France: maximalists —Germany, smaller states: maximalists —Denmark, Greece: minimalists —United Kingdom: minimalist Lineups are approximately ranged vertically by proximity to maximalist positions as defined, in particular, by attitudes toward federalism and adhesion to a European Union Treat (EUT).	Calling an intergovernmental conference on exploring ground for an agreement and ambitions (EUT?)	Maximalists (pro-communitarian coalition) are driven by outsiders (nonstate actors: IAC, Spinelli, Pflimlin, etc.). Numerous meetings, mixed diplomacy, informal working links. Apply pressure through threats (and occasional use of majority voting). Minimalists obtain redrafts of initial proposals, work also through reservations, footnotes to proposed texts. These two "hard-core" lineups did not always find themselves united on matters of substance; see (B). Outcomes: Dooge report and passing of SEA but short of EP's ambitions and maximalist preferences.
(B) Subissues		Defining contents	
B-1 Economic convergence and solidarity	—Germany, Benelux —"Other six" and United Kingdom (a) —Ireland, Greece, Denmark (b)	Subgroups differ on relative importance given to convergence and solidarity, also on external identity	The Dooge report mentions the differences but calls for an intergovernmental conference to solve the issue (also for B-2, which group (b) contested).
B-2 Convergence and solidarity: means and methods	Same as for B-1 except the United Kingdom joined group (b) on the question of nominating process (Commission) and Germany on the question of size of the Commission.	Defining the decision-making process (bicameral legislature?)	Same as B-1

B-3 Court of justice	Consensus	Consolidating the court	
B-4 Voting practices	—France, Italy (a) —Ireland and "other six" (b) —Denmark, Greece, United Kingdom (c)	Defining voting status in EC institutions, mainly ministerial councils	Disagreements occurred among the three groups (a), (b), and (c). Reservations took the form of footnotes to proposed text.
B-5 Voting to pass ICCT	—All except France, United Kingdom —France agrees but emphasizes that this is not a precedent —United Kingdom	Recourse to two-thirds majority voting	Majority voting procedure was unusual in EC matters at that time. The EP was in favor of this procedure in this case, although not satisfied with reference to conference ("Pflimlin letter").
B-6 EUT-type treaty or SEA? EP's association with IGC	Roughly same as on issue (A) but less clear-cut	Defining the legal form of future "treaty," defining rights of involvement of EP	EP was given certain "rights" (mainly information) but no strong association, which the maximalists would have supported. Italy was closely allied to EP.
B-7 Scope of IGC: enlargement of Treaty of Rome	See (A); some countries (e.g., Italy) and some "outsiders" (national parliaments, political parties, and groups) acted as honest brokers to bridge the differences between the two main groups	Defining the level of integration and the extent to which the Treaty of Rome would be modified (e.g., voting, EP powers, internal market, EMU, new fields of activity)	Intense maneuvering took place permitting delegations to adjust their initial positions and develop coalition policies.

Source: Information from Chapter One in this book and reports from the specialized press (*Agence Europe*, etc.).

tations, it is possible to gain an overview of the various groupings that could have emerged or did emerge from the negotiations.

Another method is to scrutinize the descriptive material and reorganize the information following a taxonomical approach. Table 7.1 starts with the identification of the various issues (for example, the need for a "qualitative leap forward" in pre-SEA negotiations or the extent to which negotiating parties were ready to call a conference to explore the ground for an ambitious program of intensive European integration). As seen from the length of the table, the number of comprehensive key issues at stake was large: eight broad categories with regard to pre-SEA—including the general topic of the leap forward—and nine in the 1985–1987 negotiations proper. Table 7.1 provides the lineup on each broad issue and then gives a description of the purpose and objectives of the various groupings, their key features, and the outcome. The same preliminary (descriptive) analysis would be much more complex in the case of the Uruguay Round because the number of issues (in each of the fifteen broad categories) was large and the lineups more sophisticated (as seen in the following paragraphs). Table 7.2 presents a description of the various coalitions of the Uruguay Round negotiations. This table has a descriptive quality but does not form the basis of a taxonomy. Table 7.3 is another way to present the various positions of parties at the pre-SEA and SEA negotiations. It clearly shows that the emergence of coalitions was almost inevitable; a neat picture of convergences and divergences among negotiating parties stands out.

These three tables constitute the raw material out of which a taxonomy of multilateral negotiations can be built: this is the purpose of Table 7.4, which combines concepts drawn from theory (as presented in the first and second sections of this chapter) and their application and relevance to the two cases. The table suggests that these negotiations entailed different forms of coalitions, namely:

- Type I: Groups that were broad-based, hard-core, and close on key issues; for example, the Six in the SEA negotiations.
- Type II: Intrabloc groupings; for example, the Nordic countries in the General Agreement on Tariffs and Trade (GATT) negotiations.
- Type III: Issue-specific (single-issue) coalitions; the Cairns group in the Uruguay Round negotiations.
- Type IV: Opportunistic alignments and tactical alliances.
- Type V: Groups of external actors; the GATT secretariat in the Uruguay Round.

The rationale behind this taxonomy—which seems validated by the specific references to the two cases—is threefold: visibility, cohesion or foundation (the type of links that cements the group), and role (behavior and strategies). Creating such a taxonomy is a first step in decoding the emergence of coalitions in multilateral negotiations. It clarifies a particularly complex set of interactions such as multilateral negotiations, but it is not explanatory. Explanatory analysis

Table 7.1B. Coalitions in the SEA Negotiations (June 1985 to July 1987).

Issues	Type of Lineup	Purpose/Objectives of Grouping	Key Features and Outcomes
C-1 Internal market C.1.1. Definition	—Italy, Benelux (a) —United Kingdom, France, Germany (b) —Greece, Portugal, Ireland (c) —Denmark (d) Rankings are made according to proximity to Commission proposals. Group (b) found the definition too broad. Groups (c) and (d) were opposed on certain issues (as were United Kingdom and Ireland on health regulations).	Defining the contents of the internal market ("the four freedoms")	Initial Commission proposals were revised, group (c) finding that the internal market scope became more limited.
C.1.2. Voting	—All except Denmark, Greece (a) —Denmark, Greece (b) Group (b) was opposed to majority voting.	Defining voting procedure (majority voting)	A somewhat diluted version was agreed on (majority voting except for fiscal policy, movement of persons, and employee rights).
C.1.3. Tax matters	—All except (b) (a) —United Kingdom, Germany, Ireland, Netherlands (b) Group (b) presented qualified objections	Defining content and voting procedures	See C.1.2.
C.1.4. Banking and insurance	Ireland was opposed to Commission proposals	Same as above	

Table 7.1B. Coalitions in the SEA Negotiations (June 1985 to July 1987), Cont'd.

Issues	Type of Lineup	Purpose/Objectives of Grouping	Key Features and Outcomes
C.1.5. Social security	—All except (b) and (c) (a) —Denmark, Germany (b) —Greece, Ireland, Portugal (c) Groups (b) and (c) were opposed for opposite reasons (rich/poor issue).	Same as above	Reservations of groups (b) and (c) were dealt with by declarations in act.
C-2 Monetary capacity (as part of treaty)	—All except (b) and (c)(a) —Germany, Netherlands (b) —United Kingdom (c) Group (b) objected to EMU as part of treaty; (c) was opposed	Defining the EMU	Issue was not dropped entirely from agenda, was treated in a "declaration."
C-3 Economic and social cohesion	—Greece (a) —United Kingdom, Netherlands, France (b) —Germany (c) These groupings were "fluid" according to different subissues (e.g.,Ireland opposed revision of social funds).	Defining roles and amounts of special funds and EC loans	Compromise solutions were found as a result of Commission acting as honest broker.
C-4 Environment	—Denmark (a) —Greece, Netherlands (b) —United Kingdom, Ireland, Greece (c)	Defining EC role and policies in this field	Bilateral trade-offs and diplomacy were important in this area. Initial proposals were "diluted" to accommodate group (c).

Issue			
C-5 Technology	—France (a) —Others except (c)(b) —Germany (c) German opposition related to fear of being main contributor.	Same as above	Same as above with Luxembourg presidency acting as honest broker.
C-6 Social policy	—Denmark (a) —Others except (c)(b) —United Kingdom (c)	Same as above	Introduction of this issue was an agenda-adjustment and sidestepping tactic.
C-7 Political cooperation	—France, Germany (a) —Benelux, Italy (b) —Ireland (c) —Denmark, Greece (d)	—Same as above (including voting) —Defining boundaries with other forums (e.g., NATO, WEU)	Alliances mainly between "larger" and "smaller" states.
C-8 Institutional decision making	—Italy, France, Germany (a) —Ireland, Netherlands, Belgium (b) —Denmark (c) —United Kingdom (d)	—Voting —Role of Commission and EP and their powers	Biggest arena for division; the issues were dealt with in agenda adjustment.
C-9 Ratification	—All except (b) and (c)(a) —Italy (b) —Denmark, Ireland, Greece (c) Italy's position was due to attitude toward EP. Group (c) had constitutional difficulties.	Implement act	All states finally ratified the SEA after intense diplomatic pressure from the others.

Source: Information from Chapter One in this volume and reports from the specialized press (*Agence Europe,* etc.).

Table 7.2. Coalitions in the Prenegotiations and Negotiations of the Uruguay Round (1985 to September 1986).

Actors	Traditional Coalitions	Cairns Group	De la Paix Group	Textiles	Services; Intellectual Property Rights	Safeguards
Industrialized Countries						
United States	(a)			(g)	(k)	(o)
Canada	(a)	X	X		(m)f	(p)
Japan	(a)				(l)	(p)
EC	(b)			(h)	(m)f	(q)
Nordic countries	(c), (e)		Xᵇ		(m)f	
Switzerland	(e)		X			
Other EFTA countries	(e)					
Australia	(d)	X	X			(q)
New Zealand	(d)	X	X			(q)
Developing Countries						
Newly industrialized countries	(u), (v)			(i)	(n)e	(r)
Brazil	(v)	X				
Other Latin American countries			X			
Colombia		X				
Chile		X	X			
Uruguay		X				
Argentina		X				
India	(u), (w)			(j)		
Pakistan	(w)	Xᵃ	Xᶜ	(j)	(n)e	
Other Asian countries	(w)			(j)	(m)f	

Unclassified

Hungary		X	
Others			X[d]

Notes:

1. Letters (a, b, . . . , w) identify a coalition: for example, the United States, Canada, and Japan were part of a traditional coalition (a); the Nordic countries, Switzerland, and other EFTA countries were part of another coalition (e).

2. The table does not include several groupings that were active in the negotiating process. These include principally:

- G40: a group that submitted a text prior to the opening of the conference. It comprised most industrialized countries but also some developing countries (hence its colloquial name, the café au lait group). Another group, the G10, led by Brazil, Egypt, and India, submitted an alternative proposal to the G40 proposal.

- GATT Consultative Group of 18: a semi-institutionalized structure of GATT that was instrumental in channeling discussions toward a new round of negotiations.

- Heads-of-delegations group and selected restricted group: comprised top-level delegates; these groupings were active at Punta del Este.

- G9: a constellation of free traders (mainly middle powers) active at Punta del Este.

- French-speaking African group: active in the negotiating committee on tropical products.

- Tiger group: active in the negotiating committee on safeguards.

[a] Includes Malaysia, Thailand, Indonesia, the Philippines, and sometimes Fiji.

[b] Actually Sweden representing the Nordic countries.

[c] Includes Malaysia, Thailand, the Philippines, Singapore, and South Korea.

[d] Includes Zaire.

[e] India finally adopted a conciliating position on the intellectual-property-rights issue, which led to a breakdown of the (n) coalition.

[f] The letter (m) indicates a coalition that tried to break the stalemate resulting from the opposition between the United States and most developing countries. Another effort was made by a group composed of Switzerland, India, and the Quad group (the United States, the EC, Canada, and Japan). Finally, five countries (Switzerland, Japan, Hong Kong, the United States, and Canada) coalesced to produce a text, which also failed.

Table 7.3. Convergences or Divergences in Positions on Pre-SEA Issues, Single Market, and the New Domains in SEA Negotiations (excluding Spain and Portugal).

	Belgium	Germany	Denmark	Ireland	France	United Kingdom	Greece	Italy	Luxembourg	Netherlands
I. Pre-SEA										
Overall support for institutional reform (especially EP) and federalism	■	■	▶	■/○	■	▶	▶	■	■	■
External identity	■	■	▶ ■		■	■	▶ ■	■	■	■ ○
Solidarity	○	○		○						
Commission (composition, nominations)		▶ ■ ■			■	▶ ■ ■	■ ■		■ ■	■ ■
Court of Justice	■ ■	■	■ ▶	■ ■/○	■ ■	■ ▶	■ ▶	■	■	
Voting										
II. Single Market [a]	■	■/□/○	■/○	■/○	■/○	■/○	■/○	■	■	■/○
III. New Domains										
Monetary capacity and EMU	■	○→■	□/○	▶→○	■	○	□/○	■	■	○→■
Convergence/solidarity [b]		▶	○	□/○ ▶	□/○	▶	□/○ ▶	□/○		○
Environment		■ →■	■		■	▶	▶	■	■	○
Workers' rights	○	■		■	■	▶	○			○
Political cooperation	○→	○→	□→			■	○→		○	○
Technology and research	□ ■	□ ■	■				□ ■			■

Source: Information from Chapter One in this book.

Notes:
Symbols indicate relative support for Dooge report or Commission proposals:

■ Full support (maximalist position)   ○ Moderate disagreement
□ Support with reservations   ▶ Strongly against (minimalist position)

[a] Differences appear according to issues (e.g., definition of fiscal and banking policy).
[b] Mixed positions are due to differences concerning subissues.

**Table 7.4. Application of Coalition Typologies
to SEA and Uruguay Round Negotiations.**

Types of Coalitions and Criteria[a]	SEA (the Six)	Uruguay Round (Industrialized Countries and Developing Countries)
Type I Broad-based, hard core, proximity on main issues V: preexisting groups explicit (quasi-institutionalized); relative size important (number of conference members); ability to create majority status (selectively, on certain issues, or globally) F: large degree of cohesion on hard-core issues; shared interests; political will to cooperate and unite forces toward action (either toward movement or defensively); potential ability to attract neutrals or block rival coalitions; large degree of stability and duration; behavior sensitive to "codes" (often unwritten or informal) R: driving (acting as leaders or initiators), blocking (preventing other coalitions or entities from moving), or modifying (bridging differences between groups or acting as mediators or honest brokers)	Table 7.1 provides several illustrations of the driving role of the Six. However, this role had to be supplemented by one or several individual coalition members acting as leaders (e.g., Italy) and in some instances by support of parties external to the coalition (e.g., IAC/EP). In some instances the smaller members of the coalition (e.g., the Benelux countries) acted also as mediators or honest brokers. These coalitions broke down into subgroups on certain issues (especially the substance of the Single Market, see Table 7.2).	The role of ICs was in general driving, especially in the first rounds of negotiations. But this role was thwarted by disunity on sectorial issues. DCs were rather defensive at the start of the conference but gradually attempted to play a modifying role as impasses (especially agriculture) began to block balanced progress.
Type II Intrabloc groupings V: may be apparent in preexisting structures (e.g., Benelux in EC) or result from observed coordinated action (e.g., France and Germany in SEA); may form on selective issues as well as globally (a difference with type I coalitions) F: more varied than type I; may be based on tactics and therefore may be either durable (as in type I) or less stable	Some groupings operated with consistency and solidarity (e.g., the Benelux countries). Role was either driving (to relaunch momentum) or modifying (e.g., the Benelux countries; later in Maastricht, 1991, to prevent isolation of United Kingdom).	The EC or the Nordic countries can be considered an intrabloc coalition within the type I coalition: similarly, proximate geography or ideological leanings brought forth intrabloc coalitions within DCs (e.g., the Latin American group, the French-speaking African group). Role was driving on selected issues and mostly modifying. However, on one special occasion the Latin American group

**Table 7.4. Application of Coalition Typologies
to SEA and Uruguay Round Negotiations, Cont'd.**

Types of Coalitions and Criteria[a]	SEA (the Six)	Uruguay Round (Industrialized Countries and Developing Countries)
R: may be based on issues, timing, and special circumstances		forced blocking in order to put pressure on breaking the deadlock on agriculture.
Type III **Issue-specific** Compared with type II these coalitions are formed exclusively on a specific issue: only specific interests are shared, and coalition membership does not necessarily extend to other interests, nor does it prevent parallel membership in other coalitions for other issues. Hence: V: occasional, constrained, and shifting F: opportunistic R: adapted to the particular strategies of rival coalitions These coalitions may be more or less cohesive; they may—or may not—develop into stronger, broader ties as those in type I or II. These coalitions may also be de facto alliances of parties (generally smaller states) that see their role as semipermanent mediators or honest brokers and consistently act in this capacity; they may belong to otherwise rival type I or II coalitions.		Chapter Two provides many illustrations of such coalitions. Perhaps the clearest examples were the Cairns group and the de la Paix group, whose purposes and objectives were precise and limited to achieving a specific goal. These groups saw their role as essentially modifying.
Type IV **Opportunistic alignments** One should not consider these coalitions except in a loose sense. There is no specific coordination. There are major differences with type III; opportunistic alignments are based on chance encounters of similar	Such coalitions were typical of the minority group (the United Kingdom, Greece, Denmark). But the United Kingdom joined the majority type I coalition on the problem of political cooperation; similarly certain members of the majority occasionally coalesced with the minor-	

**Table 7.4. Application of Coalition Typologies
to SEA and Uruguay Round Negotiations, Cont'd.**

Types of Coalitions and Criteria[a]	SEA (the Six)	Uruguay Round (Industrialized Countries and Developing Countries)
positions or temporary tactical opportunities.	ity group on certain issues (see Table 7.2).	
All multilateral negotiations involve such alignments occasionally. Generally these can be depicted only by detailed review of the records.		
Type V External actors Individual actors (e.g., personalities or entities) may coalesce to bring pressure on negotiators. Constellations of personalities—operating in an active network—may temporarily or more durably form to cumulate their individual influence (political clout, charisma, media coverage, etc.) in order to change the course of events. To some extent one can also often observe secretariats of international organizations and presidents in conferences entering into this pattern of largely informal groups that operate as de facto relation-based, often behind-the-scene coalitions.	The role of such groups of personalities was important (e.g., the "crocodile" initiative, the pro-EP network of domestic politicians).	The GATT secretariat, its president, and at times the presiding officers of the conference were instrumental in helping to constitute these networks.

[a]V: visibility; F: foundation; R: roles.

must therefore be based on the study of concrete cases, which is the purpose of the next subsection.

Explanatory Analysis

A number of crucial dimensions have to be examined to explain the process and outcomes of the negotiations form the perspective of coalition theories. These dimensions may be divided into three main, previously noted categories: emer-

gence of coalitions as actors, behavioral roles and strategies, and effectiveness and outcomes.

Coalition Formation. Several factors appear to be crucial to the formation of a coalition in multilateral negotiations. We can list as the most important the appropriateness and maturity of the context, the nature of the issues, and the role of initiators or leaders. The SEA negotiation exhibits a series of contextual factors or developments that seem to have been important in the formation of the two main coalitions (maximalist and minimalist) observed (see Tables 7.1 and 7.3). The first major factor was the presence of preexisting commonalities and tolerated discrepancies regarding the "future of Europe." These shared views led to the formation of the two groups, which engaged in the negotiations with different—and almost opposite—goals and ambitions.

For the majority, the negotiations were designed minimally to permit continuation and maximally to permit reinforcement of the enterprise that began some thirty years before—including, in the institutional field, the need to give the European Parliament (EP) legitimacy and the EC a democratic foundation. Hence a shared spirit of having to do something to prevent stagnation and provide renewed momentum was a sufficient common denominator or condition to coalesce in order (ideally) to finish the job previously undertaken in Paris (1950) and Rome (1957). Conversely, doubts about the radical transformation of existing arrangements (and the fact that adhering to the EC had been at least partially opportunistic) were enough to unite (albeit with some heterogeneity) the minority. Thus members (including the institutional actors) were already part of preexistent alliances whose composition and goals were well known and could be anticipated. Under these conditions there was hardly a need for special circumstances or events to trigger the formation of coalitions.

These separate and opposite views on policy and choices (and to some extent ideological leanings) were sufficient conditions to coalesce two main groups but were in themselves not enough to produce or block initial movement. They had to be supplemented by the actions of initiators or leaders—either institutions (for example, the EP), certain member states (Italy, France), or even individuals—at least as regards the majority group (the minority, the United Kingdom, can be seen as the initiator/leader acting mainly through counterproposals and rallying reluctant neutrals or doubters). There was in addition the "negative constraint" of the de facto need to obtain French and German agreement to create momentum (Chapter One). Furthermore, movement depended on appropriate timing, which proved crucial at several key moments.

Proximity in motivation and purposes, tempered by the need to satisfy members' sectorial or strategic self-interests (a good example being the mixed feeling of the Commission to grant the EP broad decisions powers), proved to be an accurate predictor of coalition formation. The coalescing of positions is confirmed in Table 7.3 for selected issues relating to the internal market and for the new domains such as the environment and political cooperation. In the pre-SEA negotiations a clear pattern emerged (distinguishing pro- and anticommunitar-

ian groups); the pattern is also visible in regard to the Single Market (with however a few divergences within coalitions); and the pattern holds again (but with more divergences) for the new domains.

Although the context, the nature of the issue (the importance given by the various participants to the problem of the future of European integration), and the role of initiators go far to explain the coalition pattern that developed in the SEA negotiations, we may also note three important developments:

- The dispute throughout the negotiations between a de facto, rather cohesive dominant coalition and a more divided minority
- The fact that coalitions crossed pro-Union cleavages on matters of substance
- The de facto alliance of institutional (nonstate) actors—the EP and subunits (such as the Committee on Institutional Affairs), the Commission, and to some extent national parliaments and diverse lobbies—and member states

The formation of coalitions in the Uruguay Round negotiations could be analyzed in the same way: context, issues, and initiators/leaders. But the analysis of these negotiations is much more complex because, as Table 7.2 amply demonstrates, the Uruguay Round negotiations had several complex networks of cross-cutting coalitions (several countries being part of several—at times contradictory—groupings). For most of these groupings it is possible to depict the role of context, issues, and initiators. To illustrate coalition formation selectively, we can base our analysis on the Cairns group, a case that has been analyzed in depth by Higgot and Cooper (1990). In their analysis they show how crucial these three factors were. The role of context is clearly illustrated by the circumstances in which many food exporters found themselves during the early 1980s and by their analysis of shifts in the world power structure. The context was thus favorable to unite a number of heterogeneous countries ("a profile of strange bedfellows")—from Australia and Canada to Hungary and Fiji—to respond to the rallying cry of Australia: the mission was to redress a situation in which these countries felt themselves to be victims of protectionism on food products but also (for example, Latin America) of the debt burden. The context was favorable; the issue could be isolated in a joint platform (producing a single-issue coalition); there were (at least in the beginning) two strong motivated leaders (Australia and Canada); and there was a clear focus on goals. Altogether the preconditions were ripe for the formation of a coalition (which was created at Cairns, Australia, in August 1986).

Behavioral Strategies. The role of coalitions in multilateral negotiations may be very different because goals vary greatly and because leadership and power are exerted in a number of ways and are of different strengths. In the SEA negotiations a majority coalition defined its role as proactive and determined (to see a breakthrough toward European integration), and a minority coalition saw its role as containing "progress" within well-defined limits. Therefore, differing goals led one coalition to press toward moving on the agenda, to expect a rapid

procedural pace, to set precedents, and so on, while the other group saw fit to proceed more slowly and pragmatically. In this manner roles were dependent on goals. They were also dependent on leadership (France and Germany, on the one hand, the United Kingdom, on the other) and relative strength (the numbers were simply in favor of one group).

Turning to the Uruguay Round one again may well refer to the Cairns analysis. The group saw its role as a balancing act between three (sometimes contradictory) tendencies: promoting its specific purpose of changing the rules of the game with respect to world trade of food products, being a mediator/bridge between conflicting parties (especially between the main players: the United States and the EC), and promoting (alternately with showing restraint toward) a multilateral agreement. Part of the role was inducing confidence among actors and searching for middle-ground formulas, transparency, and step-by-step approaches. This role was defined and aptly implemented by the two leaders of the group (although tensions arose subsequently). In the end Australia became the driving force as Canada and some Latin America members found it necessary to defend their own separate positions on certain issues (such as domestic support measures as opposed to export support measures, services, and intellectual property). As a leader Australia contributed resources, was the chief architect and organizer, and succeeded in providing intellectual dominance and innovativeness.

Coalition strategies are generally classified using several complementary criteria such as proactive/reactive, "hard"/"soft," and driving/modifying/blocking. The two cases provide many illustrations of these different options. As in every negotiation there may be a dominant strategy (for example, predominantly cooperative or predominantly competing), but many shifts may occur (for example, combining "hard" and "soft" devices).

Illustrations of such options may be found in the SEA and the GATT negotiations. The pro-Community coalition in the EC had as its main objective to make a substantial advance toward a fully integrated market and to build the foundations of an economic, monetary, and political union. In its maximalist form this objective would have led to a treaty close to the proposed European Union Treaty (EUT). In order to reach that goal several strategies were available to the dominant coalition, but these strategies were also constrained by a major problem. The strategies were rather traditional (see Chapter One), although they also involved a number of special devices:

- Setting a December 31, 1992, deadline for implementation.
- Using precedents, even if not implemented (for example, the EUT) and legislative bases (such as referring to Article 236).
- Using the large initiative powers of presidents who happened to be at that particular time favorable to the "leap forward" (mainly France and Italy, and in a more indirect way Ireland and Luxembourg).
- Letting the EP and its nonmember-state allies be at the forefront of the institutional debate, which raised sensitive questions about adopting "more real-

istic" positions in the negotiations (making it easier to reach a coalition consensus).

- Concentrating efforts on reaching the overarching goal of attaining at least a minimalist result: establishment of the Single Market and the first elements of a monetary, economic, and political union. As long as progress was visible toward that goal, tactical flexibility was permitted; also impasse or partial failure on one issue was not allowed to block the global advance (a strikingly different development compared with the situation in the Uruguay Round); similarly, partial progress on one issue was used to create momentum toward progress on other issues.

These strategies met generally with success, but a major problem arose: the strong resistance of the minority coalition against the project, which raised the fundamental question of the substance and composition of the proposed union. First, individual members of the dominant coalition did not share the same views on how to deal with the minority resistance; the coalition then resorted to a kind of middle-of-the-road strategy (as formulated most clearly by the Benelux countries), which led to the combination of several positions—for example, on majority voting after the Inter-Governmental Conference (IGC). Second, pressure was softened by agreement that only in extreme circumstances would full isolation of the United Kingdom be the sanction. Rather it was felt that the participation of the United Kingdom was a positive element in European integration and that consequently a "two-speed" Europe should be avoided, if not at all costs at least as long as the entire project would not be deprived of its minimal substance. The important strategy was agenda adjustment as well the inclusion of declarations or statements in the preambles and texts of the final act (the SEA). The opting-out clauses were thus a forerunner of the subsequent developments at Maastricht (1991). Third, the debate was refocused more on economics than on politics and, within the economic sphere, more on free trade and services (an orientation of the United Kingdom and Denmark, for instance) than on the future European Monetary Union (EMU) (for which only broad lines were defined).

Strategies of the minority group showed a skillful adaptation to the strategies of the rival coalition. Attempts to change the course of the negotiations could not be realistically envisaged. Introducing counterproposals had a limited chance of success. Most promising were repeated and, on the whole, successful initiatives to modify and soften the commitments that were gradually being spelled out in the negotiations. As a last line of defense, the opt-out device could conceal and temporarily reconcile differences on the most sensitive issues; in this manner the coalition avoided a showdown that could have had grave consequences.

Strategies in the Uruguay Round negotiations were extremely complex because of two developments. The first was the breakdown of one of the two leading coalitions on the issue of agriculture. In terms of the previous (typological) analysis, a traditional type I coalition thus broke down into type II subcoalitions, which showed a large measure of inflexibility and mutual mistrust. In-depth analyses of the structural and conjunctural elements behind this lack of

understanding and flexibility (each side being able to show impressive sectorial arguments to legitimate its position)—along with intrabloc bargaining—should be topics of interest for future research. Interestingly the first phase of the negotiations (the prenegotiations leading to Punta del Este) evidenced the traditional strength and cohesion of the type I coalition consisting of the industrialized countries (ICs), which was united and effective in gaining agreement—although reluctantly—from the coalition of developing countries (DCs). An interesting feature was the role of leaders: traditional strong leadership by the United States, on the one hand, and an emerging strong leadership from the Cairns group and Brazil and India, on the other hand. Subsequently developments showed, however, a weakening of these smaller coalitions (see Chapter Eight).

The second development was the appearance in the negotiations proper of many type II and type III coalitions, which gradually gained visibility and status, and implemented their own strategies. These strategies were based mainly on a modifying role (with accidental use of more coercive actions such as blocking the negotiation as long as the agriculture issues were not solved). However, these intermediate coalitions lacked power and influence and could not be effective enough to produce acceptable solutions for the disputants.

Coalition Effectiveness and Outcomes. Coalition effectiveness can be measured along several dimensions. To what extent have coalitions helped members reach their joint and individual goals? To what extent have coalitions succeeded in maintaining their cohesion and stability over time?

A summary view of the SEA negotiations leads to the following conclusions. Processes were highlighted by the gradual step-by-step advances of the majority group, which capitalized on each opportunity (notably summit conferences and EP meetings) to get closer to the objective of creating a new dynamics in European integration; however, in view of the declared reluctance of the minority, the majority had to make successive retrenchments from the ambitious proposals. The semiconsensual approach led to the signing of the SEA—very close to an EUT and very far from the 1957 Treaty of Rome. In this sense the outcome was more joint than unilateral.

In the case of the Uruguay Round, the process, especially after the midterm review, was more erratic and the outcome less predictable. An important factor was the mutual undervaluation of the degree of flexibility that underlying economic interests and ideological political forces left to the negotiators. Given this limiting factor and the enormous complexity of the issues at stake, the more powerful actors in the negotiations sought to tackle the problems on a fragmented basis. This strategy could have produced global trade-offs but did not in this case. Each compartmentalized issue proved to be a huge negotiating block fraught with intricate technical difficulties and real clashes of contradictory "bonafide" perceptions and "legitimate" interests. It is not enough to analyze the process and its present, if temporary, failure in terms of lack of political will. A more balanced assessment would emphasize the fact that issues were not yet mature enough for details to be worked out; there was not even a clear idea of

what the formula could be. Hence the paradox is that, despite the length of the negotiations, time did not play in favor of narrowing differences, and time limits and ultimatums had little impact in this respect.

A point of interest in coalition analysis is the degree of group strength and the capacity of a group to maintain cohesion and stability. Subsequent events regarding the SEA (notably events linked to the Maastricht Treaty) point to the relative stability of the groupings as depicted in the previous analysis. The majority coalition had elements of strength at the time of the negotiations, but one may well question whether these elements (such as ideological cohesion, parallel interests, and economic circumstances) have proved durable over time. The majority coalition is still powerful, but its strength is probably less now than it was during the SEA negotiations (as the Maastricht negotiations and developments subsequently showed).

In the case of the Uruguay Round negotiations, the relative strength of the various coalitions did not lead to full effectiveness. Many of the groupings had to make difficult compromises and goal reformulations because they were often confronted with differences in the options and priorities of their members. Even if a group had strong leadership (such as the Cairns group), it proved difficult to avoid internal tensions and rifts. For this difficulty several explanations may be found: first is issue complexity; second, the number of participants; third, the ever-present competition between existing groupings; fourth, the uncertainty of outcomes; and, fifth, changes in the environment (internal and external), which became increasingly important as the negotiations extended over several years. The variety of ideologies and national idiosyncrasies regarding the rules of the game (for example: To what extent do we want free trade? To what extent does a gap exist between rhetoric and acts?) made it difficult to attain a shared platform. The job in this respect was easier for SEA negotiators than for the Uruguay Round negotiators.

Higgot and Cooper (1990) offer an analysis of the strengths and weaknesses of the Cairns group. The strengths were, according to these authors, a strong identification with a common single issue, the capacity and will of leaders to make solidarity (relative to the key question of new rules) predominate over conflict on other issues, the acceptance of compromises when needed, strong and imaginative leadership (which, however, subsequently became less so), international credibility, an adequate power base (for example, the large market share of the combined countries in certain exports), and balanced strategies, which successfully raised the debates from technical/bureaucratic to political/decision-making levels. Following Young's (1989b) approach, they see the strength of the group as combining the three dimensions of a coalition (structural, technical, and entrepreneurial). But these strengths were more useful in attaining success in procedures than in substance. External factors were of course preponderant in this development: the United States and the EC stuck to their positions with only minor adjustments (and subsequently even the Cairns group's aligning opportunistically with the United States to pressure the EC was not successful). In addition, the Cairns group had to face a countercoalition of food importers.

Furthermore, internal weaknesses also developed in the group: heterogeneity caused some members to detach themselves or to act as free riders, and some key members of the coalition felt isolated as tensions arose about certain issues and on the appropriate strategies to counter U.S. and EC resistance (for example, blocking the negotiations on all issues as long as the agricultural deadlock was not resolved or taking specific types of diplomatic actions). Thus strengths and weaknesses somewhat offset each other, allowing for some impact on the outcomes but not all that was hoped for.

Concluding Remarks

Coalition formation and behaviors were important factors in determining the outcomes of the SEA and Uruguay Round negotiations. In both cases most coalitions were predictable, although this outcome is clearer in the SEA negotiations than in the Uruguay Round. Proximity—a concept developed by certain coalition theorists—proves to be a useful analytical tool. Similarly, differentiation helps characterize the various groupings that could be observed. Together these two concepts give interesting clues to coalition building, role, behaviors, and strategies.

As regards process and outcome, it may be objected that coalition theories perform well in an ex post perspective but that their explanatory power is far less evident from an ex ante, predictive viewpoint. Whereas the performance in this respect seems rather good in the SEA negotiations, it is far from satisfactory in the GATT negotiations. The mixed outcome of these negotiations (limited agreement at Punta del Este, uncertainties at and since Geneva) could not be predicted accurately in advance; internal and external bargaining proved to be more involved and uncertain than could have been expected; the occurrence of new (smaller and more composite) coalitions, their role in the process, and their strategies were far from predictable.

Are generalizations from these comparative studies possible? Could these generalizations be applied to the differences between bilateral and multilateral negotiations and (in a stricter sense) between plurilateral and multilateral negotiations? The SEA and the Uruguay Round negotiations exhibit both sharp differences and strong similarities. Differences concern size, the nature of preexisting institutional relationships, the purposes and constraints of actors, the nature of issues, the degree of symmetry/asymmetry of information, relative power imbalances, the involvement of constituencies, and the role of prenegotiations with regard to process. Agenda adjustment, the use of reservations, and declarations and compromises were prevalent in the SEA but not in the Uruguay Round negotiations, where strategies were more oriented toward fragmentation and confrontation. Except for this important factor, however, strategies (as influenced by congruence with goals and priorities) and tactics (as determined by opportunistic behavior) were not very different between and within coalitions. The practical limits of veto power were also somewhat similar, although veto threats were more effective in the Uruguay Round than in the SEA negotiations. The role of third

parties (and mediating groups of individuals) was also similar in both negotiations. Smaller, sometimes heterogeneous coalitions (such as the Cairns group) played a not insignificant role in the Uruguay Round negotiations, and they achieved a certain amount of effectiveness in exerting pressure of the main actors to convert the pyramidal structure of GATT-linked negotiations into a more diversified structure; however, this success did not extend to substantive as opposed to procedural outcomes. Time was in both cases an important variable, and the evidence was again that complex negotiations develop as a set of episodes in a cumulative process; successive phases have both similar and different functions: clarification, coordination, adjustment, counterproposals, compromises. Finally, postnegotiation issue resurgence can be observed in both cases.

This complex pattern of similarities and differences makes it difficult to draw generalizations; rather it shows the need for building up many more "experiences" of conference diplomacy. The emergence of coalitions, as well as veto power (together with the different nature of the negotiating relationship and of the organizational and time constraints), is no doubt an important criterion in differentiating bilateral negotiations from multinational negotiations. The differentiation between plurilateral versus multilateral negotiations is more difficult to depict. However, one could guess that size is more than a mere definitional variable. If there are n parties and n issues the situational variables are not added but multiplied. This simple, trivial observation has more important implications than would appear at first glance.

The previous chapters of the book have addressed some of these questions. This chapter has focused on coalitions from the perspective of how existing theories help us understand process and outcomes. The preliminary conclusion is that they shed light on observed developments, help delineate the relevant problems and issues, and offer typologies of interest. These theories seem to provide some relevant analytical/descriptive tools. Only further research advances—both theoretical and applied—can result in detailed and concrete prescriptive (and perhaps normative) propositions. But both cases convincingly show that parties in multilateral negotiations would be well advised to include the coalition dimensions in their prenegotiation and actual negotiation strategies.

Chapter 8

Leadership Theory
Rediscovering the Arts of Management

Arild Underdal (Norway)

In this chapter I argue that theories of leadership can offer important contributions to our understanding of multilateral negotiations. In order to substantiate this claim, I must demonstrate that leadership itself (the subject matter of the theory) is an important element of multilateral negotiations and that existing theories of leadership are capable of providing important nontrivial insights into the "logic" of leadership. Each proposition is a necessary premise for the main argument. Even an elegant and accurate theory of some peripheral aspect of negotiation can be of no more than marginal interest in predicting and explaining actor behavior or the outcomes. Conversely, a "poor" theory can easily be dismissed as being of little or no significance, no matter how important the phenomenon it attempts to grasp. These two propositions, then, set the agenda for this chapter.

Before addressing these issues, however, a brief discussion of the concept of leadership is necessary. *Leadership* can be defined as an asymmetrical relationship of influence in which one actor guides or directs the behavior of others toward a certain goal over a certain period of time.[1] Leadership clearly involves the exercise of influence and perhaps power, but only some relationships involving influence or power qualify as instances of leadership (compare Burns, 1978, p. 18). For one thing, a leader is supposed to exercise what might be called positive influence, guiding rather than vetoing collective action. Thus, leadership is associated with the collective pursuit of some common good or joint

I gratefully acknowledge comments to earlier versions from Dag Harald Claes, Morten Egeberg, Helge Hveem, Albert Weale, and I. W. Zartman.

purpose (see, for example, Burns, 1978, pp. 19–21; Lindberg and Scheingold, 1970, p. 128). According to this definition, being the first to defect from a joint undertaking would not qualify as leadership, however great and immediate the impact of that defection might be on the behavior of one's partners. Kindleberger (1981) even considers a particular "responsibility" of behavior to be a defining characteristic of leadership.[2] The notion of a joint purpose also implies that leadership cannot be based only on coercion, let alone brute force. There must be a platform of shared values, interests, and beliefs; successful leadership builds on and cultivates this platform. Finally, a particular instance of leadership may be confined to one single project, but as defined here it must at least be a fairly consistent pattern of interaction extending throughout a certain period of time. Once in a rare while having a bright idea accepted by some others is not sufficient to make you a leader.

Is Leadership an Important Aspect of Multilateral Negotiations?

Answering this question is clearly the easy part. The two case studies reported in this book speak well to the significance of leadership in multilateral negotiations. From Sjöstedt's account (Chapter Two) we may conclude that there would have been no Uruguay Round had not the United States, with varying degrees of support from other countries in the Organization for Economic Cooperation and Development (OECD), undertaken a strong campaign to put the new trading issues on the agenda of the General Agreement on Tariffs and Trade (GATT) (compare Winham, 1989). Lodge repeatedly refers to leadership as a key factor in determining the outcome of the SEA negotiations, in both the process taken as a whole and the work of specific committees and decision-making bodies. Similar conclusions are offered in many other case studies. Thus, in their analysis of the process leading the "1992 program" of the European Communities (EC), Sandholtz and Zysman (1989, p. 96) conclude that the process succeeded "because the institutions of the European Communities, especially the Commission, were able to exercise effective policy leadership."[3] In his account of "ozone diplomacy," Benedick (1991, p. 6) emphasizes that "the activities of a multilateral institution [U.N. Environmental Program] were critical to the success of the negotiations" and that "an individual nation's [the United States] policies and leadership made a major difference." Snidal (1990) argues that differences in the quality of American leadership explain why the United States has succeeded in exercising effective "hegemony" in some intergovernmental organizations but not in others.

Also, students working to develop general theories of international cooperation consider the quality of leadership to be an important determinant of success. To give a few examples: Lindberg and Scheingold (1970, p. 128) argue that "leadership is the very essence of a capacity for collective action." O. R. Young (1991, p. 302; compare Young, 1989, p. 23) suggests that the presence of leadership is a necessary, although not a sufficient, condition for reaching agreement on the terms of constitutional contracts.[4] In general, it seems that the more complex the negotiation setting (that is, the larger the number of actors and the

number and "intricacy" of issues), the more likely that some actors will emerge as leaders and others as followers (compare Berelson and Steiner, 1964, p. 358), and the more critical leadership becomes as a determinant of success.[5] A strong case can be made for concluding that students of multilateral negotiations would be well advised to invest a fair amount of their energy in efforts to understand how leadership emerges and how it is exercised. And this is where we would turn to existing theories of leadership for help.

The Study of Leadership: The State of the Art

Students of negotiations have generally considered influence and power to be key elements of bargaining, but only a small fraction of that interest has been geared toward the study of leadership in multilateral negotiations. Conversely, students of leadership have by and large paid little attention to the specifics of international negotiations. The dearth of research dealing specifically with leadership in the context of multilateral negotiations means that we shall to a large extent have to transpose findings and propositions from other settings, ranging from social life and business management to international politics in general. As indicated in Table 8.1, the setting to a large extent determines the kind of actors, the systemic context in which leadership is studied, the mode of leadership analyzed, and the set of independent variables examined. Transposing finding across these different settings is by no means a straightforward operation; clearly, there are important differences between leadership of a hierarchical organization (such as a firm) and leadership of a United Nations (UN) conference on strategies for controlling global environmental change.

Nonetheless, to understand the logic of leadership in multilateral negotiations, we shall have to try to integrate findings and propositions from these different perspectives. For example, although leadership in international negotiations obviously is exercised by individuals, these individuals act as representatives of states or organizations, and their roles as agents bring characteristics of the units they represent to bear on the negotiation process. Thus, a diplomat representing the present government of the Republic of Iraq, however strong his

Table 8.1. Main Themes in the Study of Leadership in Different Contexts.

	Domestic Politics, Business, Social Life	*International Politics*
Actors	Individuals	States, governments
Context (system)	Hierarchy, polyarchy, social group	Anarchy
Main Mode(s) of Leadership	Instrumental, charismatic	Unilateral action, coercion
Determinant	Supply side: behavior (strategy, tactics)	Supply side: capabilities, (interdependent) structures

or her personal standing might be, could hardly escape the fact that the status of the Iraqui government as an outcast in world politics significantly impairs the diplomat's prospects of exerting leadership in multilateral diplomacy. The relative significance of individual versus state capabilities may vary significantly from one setting to another, but available evidence seems in most circumstances to point in favor of state capabilities (see, for example, Cox and Jacobson, 1973, p. 394). Similarly, although leadership in an international conference may derive from the skill and effort displayed by a diplomat in the negotiation game itself (pointing toward what I shall call the instrumental mode), influence can also be derived from the position of the diplomat's country in the basic game (that is, the system of activities constituting the subject of negotiation). The basic game determines the capabilities for leadership through unilateral action or coercion. And, finally, to understand adequately the logic of leadership in multilateral conferences, we have to come to grips with the interplay of (state) capabilities and (individual) behavior.

Despite some obvious and important differences in focus and perspectives, there is much common ground as well. Thus, the study of leadership is generally concerned with identifying those actor capabilities and relationship structures that constitute the sources from which leadership can be derived, and with understanding the operation of the social mechanisms and behavioral strategies through which it is or can most effectively be exercised. More specifically, at least three main questions seem to constitute a common core of the field: Which are the primary sources from which (a position of) leadership can be derived? How (through which strategies and tactics) is leadership exercised or how can it be? What difference does it make? More specifically, how important is the quality of leadership to the overall outcome of different kinds of processes?

As defined above, leadership is a relationship between leader and followers. The strength of this relationship may be seen as a function of the supply of and the demand for leadership services. Some minimum supply is clearly a necessary condition for a leadership relation to emerge and be sustained. Positive demand on the part of prospective followers seems not to be strictly necessary in all modes of leadership, but it is generally an important determinant of the strength of leadership relations. Leadership will clearly be most effective when supply matches demand. Students of leadership have by and large paid more attention to the supply side than to the demand for leadership services. Some of the reasons for this "bias" are fairly obvious. For one thing, leaders tend to be more fascinating objects of study than followers. And those aiming at producing knowledge that can be of practical relevance will certainly find that the demand for insight into the "art" of leading by far outstrips the demand for manuals teaching how to follow. Nonetheless, we must insist that leadership is a relationship, shaped by the demand and responsiveness of the followers as much as by the supply offered by the leader(s) (compare Burns, 1978).

As indicated in Figure 8.1, the amount of leadership actually supplied by an actor can most simply be conceived of as a function of two major determinants: capabilities and structural positions, constituting sources of potential influence;

Figure 8.1. Potential and Actual Leadership.

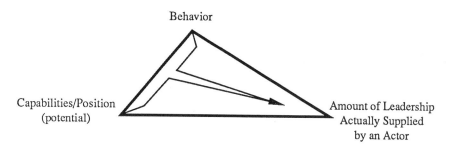

and behavior—which more or less effectively transforms potential into actual leadership. For all practical purposes, certain capabilities and a certain minimum of effort and (tactical) quality of behavior may be considered necessary conditions for being able to provide leadership in a negotiation process. As indicated by the roles played by the European Parliament and Italy in the SEA negotiations, enthusiasm and effort are not enough. However, much can be lost in the process of converting potential into actual influence, and effort and tactical ingenuity can to some extent compensate for a weak power base (see, for example, Bacharach and Lawler, 1981, pp. 96–98; Habeeb, 1988, p. 132). The fact that students of leadership often pay more attention to one of these determinants than to the other probably most often reflects different interests and perspectives of analysis rather than different assumptions about their relative significance in explaining outcomes. Thus, to provide inputs to praxis one would, for obvious reasons, concentrate on behavior—the only determinant that an actor alone can manipulate in the short term. Conversely, if one is engaged in macro studies of the rise and fall of hegemons, the focus would probably be on actor capabilities and (inter)dependence structures. But in either case the underlying model would almost certainly conceive of actual supply as a function of both capabilities and behavior.

The demand for or responsiveness to leadership can similarly be conceived of as a function of the characteristics of the followers themselves and of the negotiation problem they are faced with. Social psychologists have pointed to a set of personality characteristics that seem to imply a predisposition to subject oneself to and perhaps even demand leadership. The relevance of these findings to intergovernmental negotiations is not clear; presumably, individuals with a strong predisposition to subject themselves to the leadership of others would normally not aspire to the role of principal negotiator nor be considered strong candidates for such a position. Other actor characteristics—such as the level of subjective competence—may be more important than predisposition in this context. All things equal, we would expect negotiators with a low rating of their own competence in the subject matter itself or in procedural or communicative skills to be more inclined to accept for themselves a role as follower. Similarly, an actor who is close to indifferent with regard to alternative solutions is likely to accept (although not actively support) the leadership of others. Also, characteristics of the problem to be solved and of the negotiating situation are likely to have some

impact on the demand for leadership services. Thus, a short decision time, a strong element of potential surprise, and high complexity (number of actors multiplied by the number and intricacy of issues) are factors that can be expected to increase the demand for or at least the tolerance of leadership.[6]

A leader does not supply leadership in the abstract but provides a particular "product"—a particular set of services designed to achieve some particular purpose. Similarly, followers do not demand, and will not subject themselves to, any kind of leadership; they are prepared to let themselves be led only in a particular direction and perhaps only in a certain fashion. Only to the extent that supply matches demand will a transaction occur and a leader/follower relationship be forged.[7] Moreover, the consumers of leadership services may be approached by more than one supplier, perhaps offering different services. Facing two or more suppliers, a follower will presumably align with the one providing the most attractive product. And in making that choice followers can be expected to consider their "policy distance" to, as well as the negotiating effectiveness of, each of the candidates. At the macro level this line of reasoning suggests that the impact of leadership on negotiation outcomes depends not only on the amount and quality supplied but also on the "unidirectionality" of demand as well as supply.

Modes of Leadership

In order to examine the leader/follower relationship more closely, it may be useful to focus the analysis on different modes of leadership. Following the lead of Young (1989c, 1991), this is the path I propose to take. More specifically, I examine three basic modes of leadership: leadership through unilateral action, leadership by means of coercion, and instrumental leadership (including intellectual as well as political aspects). These modes can be distinguished, *inter alia*, by the mechanism(s) through which they work as well as by the kind of capabilities required to succeed. They also differ in their locus: leadership through unilateral action is exercised outside the negotiation framework, instrumental leadership within, while coercion can take place within as well as outside the negotiation game. In real life, however, different modes of leadership are often found in some kind of combination. For example, U.S. leadership in getting the Uruguay Round negotiations underway clearly rested on coercive as well as intellectual power. One relevant implication is that the empirical illustrations offered may well be "impure" cases, where more than one of the basic mechanisms are simultaneously at work. Nonetheless, the differences are so profound that different modes may be difficult to combine for any single leader; thus, open coercion does not go well with brokering or attempts at persuasion by means of a "good example."

Leadership Through Unilateral Action

This mode of leadership is exercised whenever one moves to solve a collective problem by one's own efforts, thereby setting the pace for others to follow.[8] As

indicated above, the actions in question are not moves in the negotiation game itself. Leadership by unilateral action is exercised through moves undertaken in the system of activities that constitutes the subject of negotiations (that is, in the basic game). However, leader/follower relations within the negotiation setting can sometimes be understood only in the context of leadership exercised outside that setting. For this reason I consider this mode of leadership relevant.

Unilateral action may provide leadership through at least two different mechanisms: one is the substantive impact it has on the options available to other actors; the other is social persuasion. Substantive impact occurs whenever actions undertaken by one party alter significantly the set of options available to others or the costs or benefits flowing from one or more of these options. This mechanism is operating when a "benevolent hegemon" provides collective goods to a "privileged group" at his or her own expense (see Olson, 1968; Kindleberger, 1981). The role played by the United States in providing military security for the North Atlantic area after World War II is, to a large extent, a case in point (Olson and Zeckhauser, 1966). So is also the unilateral supply control scheme previously implemented by the world's leading exporter of petroleum in support of oil prices. Note, though, that unilateral action to provide collective goods need not qualify as leadership as defined above. The hegemon certainly initiates and undertakes problem-solving efforts but does not thereby necessarily guide or control the behavior of others.[9] In fact, to the extent that prospective partners are allowed to be free riders, unilateral action by one actor may weaken rather than strengthen their incentives to contribute.

Unilateral action may change the set of options available to others or the consequences of one or more of these options in many other situations as well. Thus, the industries and governments of the small countries in the European Free Trade Association are likely to find that although formally free to choose whichever solutions they prefer, they have in fact little choice but to adopt many of the standards established by the EC for products and services within their own internal markets. The sheer size of the EC market and production of goods and services is such that its internal policy changes tend to alter the structure of opportunities facing other societies, whether this result is intended by EC decision makers or not.[10] Similarly, in the computer industry IBM has to a large extent, through the development, production, and marketing of its own products, set standards that smaller producers find it in their own best interest to adopt.

As indicated by the examples given above, leadership through unilateral action undertaken on its own substantive merits can be provided only by actors occupying a dominant or preponderant position within the basic game in question. Leaders need not be at the apex of the overall power structure of world politics but must have sufficient capabilities to accomplish alone significant results in a given system of activities and a position enabling them to secure (for themselves) a sufficient amount of the benefits produced to make unilateral efforts worthwhile. Put differently, the unilateral mode of leadership requires a considerable amount of control over events important to oneself (otherwise an actor would not go it alone) and—if it is to work through its impact on the set

of options available to others—also that prospective followers be highly sensitive to moves made by the leader (otherwise they will not follow).

Unilateral action may, however, provide leadership not only through its substantive impact on the set of opportunities facing others but also through social mechanisms, notably as a means of persuasion. Particularly in situations characterized by high problem similarity, unilateral action may be used for demonstrating that a certain cure is indeed feasible or does work, or to set a good example for others to follow. The power of demonstrating a cure can be found in some discussions about the feasibility of phasing out certain pollutants, such as chlorofluorcarbons (Benedick, 1991). The mechanism of setting an example is advocated by some groups of environmentalists who claim that by unilaterally imposing on one's own society strict standards of pollution control a government may help strengthen public demand in other countries for equally strict measures.[11] In fact, by imposing or threatening to impose unilateral environmental-protection measures, a government can strengthen demand within its own society for international regulations. Thus, in the case of stratospheric ozone depletion, the prospect of stringent national regulations seems to have been a major reason why several U.S. firms joined forces with environmental groups in calling for an international regime (Benedick, 1991; French, 1992). Moreover, in certain kinds of situations—for example, those corresponding to what is known as the "assurance game"—unilateral action by one party may help dispel doubts about its real commitment.[12] It can do so by providing what Jervis (1970) refers to as "indices" rather than mere "signals." Thus, a verified unilateral cutback in armaments by one state may help demonstrate that its bid for a peace treaty or an arms control agreement is indeed sincere. Osgood's (1962) well-known procedure for graduated reciprocation in tension reduction (GRIT) relies on a similar assumption about the reassuring effect of unilateral accommodative moves.

The persuasive impact of unilateral action depends primarily not on its actual impact but rather on the amount of uncertainty removed or on its moral force and symbolic significance. Even actions that by themselves make no substantial contribution toward solving the basic problem itself can indirectly make a significant difference by helping to persuade others to follow. Accordingly, although leadership through the substantive impact of unilateral action is a privilege of the strong, exercising influence through the persuasive impact of unilateral action is a role to which small and weak countries can also aspire. "Cheap" acts may not do, though: the moral significance of a move will often depend, *inter alia*, on the amount of sacrifice incurred by the actor—and so may the credibility of "indices" (Jervis, 1970, p. 28).

In the case studies reported in the book, leadership through unilateral action seems to be less salient than either of the other basic modes examined here. The traces of leadership through unilateral action in these accounts are largely confined to intracoalition relationships. Possibilities of multilateral action by a subgroup were considered at least in SEA negotiations. Thus, Lodge observes, "The United Kingdom was effectively seen as irrelevant because there was general acceptance that if the United Kingdom chose not to go along, the other members

would proceed anyway." According to Moravcsik (1991, p. 49), the threat of exclusion was a major reason why the United Kingdom accepted majority voting on internal market matters.

The less conspicuous role of the unilateral mode might, to some extent, be due to a methodological bias; as explained above, the kind of unilateral action at the core of this mode of leadership takes place within the basic game and may therefore attract less attention in studies focusing on the negotiation games themselves. Substantive explanations seem more plausible however. Recall that the official purpose of the SEA negotiations was to upgrade the EC constitution. This is a project that simply cannot be accomplished through unilateral action by any single actor. Nor does this particular project leave much scope for using unilateral action for purposes of moral suasion. In the Uruguay Round negotiations one major constraint was that unilateral adjustments by the United States (or, for that matter, any other major actor) would create significant competitive advantages for others. In world trade the United States was simply not a sufficiently predominant position to ignore free riders. Nor was this particular issue one where the United States could place much faith in the moral force of a good example. In such a situation a prospective leader must rely heavily on coercive or instrumental power (or both).

Coercive Leadership

Coercive leadership is a "sticks-and-carrots" approach to affect the incentives of others to accept one's own terms or at least make a concession. It is based on one actor's control over events important to others. One actor's (A) bilateral coercive potential vis-à-vis another (B) with regard to a specific set of issues (i) can be conceived of as a function of B's relative interest in i (U_{iB}) and A's share of control over i (K_{iA}) (formally, $U_{iB}K_{iA}$). Control over important events can be deliberately used as a device to reward those who join or comply or to punish anyone who refuses to go along or defects.[13] In the coercive mode of leadership such control is deliberately used to gain bargaining leverage.[14] Coercive leadership is thus exercised through tactical diplomacy, involving at least the communication of a promise or a threat and possibly also the fulfillment of that promise (if it succeeds) or the execution of the threat (if it fails). In tactical diplomacy an actor may promise or threaten to do things it would not contemplate except for the purpose of influencing the behavior of others. Such promises and threats often involve some kind of links to other issues, involving actors in an exchange of concessions across issues. If each actor pursues self-interest in a narrow sense, the exchange rate will be determined by the degree of asymmetry in their interdependence relationship. As defined above, coercive leadership is basically a relationship of distributive bargaining. This definition implies that, for this particular mode, bargaining theory may be as relevant to the study of leadership as leadership theory is to the study of multilateral negotiations.

In the era of complex interdependence, virtually every state is capable of exerting some coercion over some other state(s). But as coercion requires control

over events important to others, the prime candidate for this mode of leadership in any particular setting will be a state combining a predominant position within the system of activities in question with a high score on the overall power index. In the post-World War II period the United States has probably more often than any other state found itself in a position enabling it to exercise coercive leadership. Examples of the actual use of coercive techniques are not hard to find. In the period of reconstruction after World War II the U.S. government forged economic cooperation in Western Europe by making grants under the Marshall aid program contingent on a commitment to join the Organization for European Economic Cooperation and to accept a modest level of coordination of economic policies. In their efforts to work out a peace settlement between Israel and its Arab neighbors, the Nixon and the Carter administrations to some extent relied on arm-twisting as well as "bribery," promising economic assistance as a reward for cooperation and also hinting to Israeli leaders that future economic and military assistance might be jeopardized by further recalcitrance.

Also, in the GATT negotiations the United States is still, in the words of Winham and Kizer (1990, p. 6), "the driving force whose threat of unilateral action, an implicit reference to increased protection, is a formidable bargaining chip." In a similar vein, Sjöstedt concludes that "the wave of neoprotectionism" in the industrialized countries provided strong incentives to the reluctant members of GATT to agree to hold a ministerial meeting in 1982 to consider, *inter alia*, the new trade issues. Coercive elements of leadership seem to have been less prominent in the SEA negotiations, and the kinds of threats and promises mentioned by Lodge are all, it seems, internal to the negotiation game.[15]

As these examples indicate, exercising coercive leadership usually entails at least the risk of incurring costs.[16] Not only must a leader provide prospective partners with sufficient incentives to cooperate on the leader's terms or with disincentives to refuse to go along, but the more coercion that goes into forging acceptance of a certain solution, the more coercion is likely to be required to secure its implementation and maintenance. This relationship points to one of the basic assumptions behind the hegemonic stability hypothesis: the weaker the relative position of the hegemon, the higher the costs incurred in providing coercive leadership.[17] Consequently, a significant decline in the relative power of the leader may undermine the stability of an international regime or agreement established by means of coercion.

Instrumental Leadership

While coercion basically comes down to imposing one actor's preferences on some other(s) or preventing others from doing so to other actors, instrumental leadership is essentially a matter of finding means to achieve common ends. With instrumental leadership one actor's guidance is accepted by others either because they become convinced of the (substantive) merits of the specific diagnosis that actor offers or the cure he or she prescribes or because of a more or less diffuse faith in the actor's ability to "find the way."

Instrumental leadership pervades everyday life: when I heed the advice of my physician to subject myself to a certain cure, I do so not because I expect to be rewarded (for example, by a substantial discount in the bill) or because of fear that she will punish me if I refuse; I do so out of faith in her professional competence and personal integrity. Similarly, as a teacher I expect my students to heed my advice only if they consider it valid on its substantive merits or—when they find its substantive merits hard to determine—only to the extent that they have confidence in my competence and integrity. But the instrumental mode of leadership also seems to be more important in international negotiations than formal bargaining theory would lead us to expect. Actors quite often enter international negotiations with incomplete and imperfect information and also with tentative or vague preferences (Iklé, 1964, pp. 166). Whenever they do—and negotiations on some the new problems of environmental degradation, including that of global climate change, are evident cases in point—diagnosing the problem and discovering, inventing, and exploring possible solutions are likely to be important elements of the process (see, for example, Winham, 1977a; Haas, 1990). To the extent that negotiations involve searching, learning, and innovation, there is also scope for instrumental leadership.

This relationship is clearly demonstrated in both case studies reported in this book. In the Uruguay Round the United States, the OECD secretariat, and to some extent others (the EC, Canada) performed important functions of leadership in providing a more or less consensual base of knowledge on which the negotiations could build. Sjöstedt emphasizes that the GATT negotiations involved not only strict bargaining over the exchange of commitments but also a substantial amount of analytical groundwork. Similarly, in the SEA negotiations, key persons, informal groups, and actors in systemic roles (the Commission, Council presidents) played major roles in developing and "marketing" formulas that gave direction and impetus to the process. Sandholtz and Zysman (1989, p. 107) emphasize the role of "vision and leadership, an image of relationships that will respond to new tasks, and the skill to mobilize diverse groups to construct that future." In brief, the case accounts leave no doubt that instrumental leadership can indeed be considered an important factor in shaping the outcome of these negotiations.

In general, instrumental leadership seems to be based on three capabilities: skill, energy, and status. At least skill and energy may for all practical purposes be considered necessary conditions for success; Snidal (1990, p. 345), for example, talks about the need for a "conjunction of resources and initiative." The aggregate impact of the two seems to be largely "multiplicative" rather than "additive" (Sorrentino and Boutillier, 1975).

The *skills* relevant to instrumental leadership may be subsumed under two general headings: substantive and political. To qualify as good, a solution to a collective problem has to meet several substantive criteria. Consider, for example, a problem of environmental degradation. In evaluating policy measures actors would presumably ask, first, whether and to what extent each option can help achieve a certain state of environmental quality (for example, a sustainable pat-

tern of resource use). This question will often imply a concern also with technological feasibility. Second, they would probably prefer a solution prescribing or inducing behavior that yields an economically efficient allocation of resources. Third, it seems a safe assumption that actors would somehow be concerned with the distribution of costs and benefits, which would lead them to face the question of fairness. But they would also realize that if a joint solution is to be implemented, it has to meet an opportunistic criterion as well, that of political feasibility (see, for example, Underdal, 1992). Meeting each of these criteria calls for certain kinds of skills. But the skills required are different. This difference suggests that leadership roles may be differentiated within the instrumental mode itself; most likely one actor leads the way in developing substantive solutions (providing what O. R. Young, 1991, calls "intellectual leadership"), and another leads in the political engineering of consensus ("entrepreneurial leadership").[18]

This pattern is evident in both case studies. In the Uruguay Round the United States, the OECD secretariat, and some other actors (notably the EC and Canada) provided substantive, intellectual guidance. The role of brokering politically feasible compromises and packages was taken by delegates of other, smaller nations—including Colombia and Switzerland. Similarly, Lodge clearly draws a distinction between the proactive "champions" of European union and the "managers" or "brokers" in the SEA negotiations. The champion role was fulfilled by France ("the realist champion") and Italy (the "idealist") and by the Commission of the European Communities and the European Parliament—two Community institutions—while the mediative functions were to a large extent left in the hands of the Council presidents, even when the incumbent happened to be the representative of the smallest state (Lodge, Chapter One).

Skill may be a necessary condition for effective (instrumental) leadership, but it certainly is not sufficient.[19] Only if activated and brought to bear on the problem in question can skill make a difference. At this point *energy* or *effort* enters the equation. The more human energy geared to the task of solving a particular problem, the greater the achievement one can expect. In fact, experimental studies indicate that effort itself can to some extent serve as a basis for leadership, even in the absence of (superior) skills (Sorrentino and Boutillier, 1975).

The amount of energy an actor brings to bear on a problem can be conceived of as a function of available capacity, subjective political competence, and relative interest in the matter in question. Clearly, some countries—notably those that are large and rich—usually have a skilled staff available for diagnosing problems and developing solutions (Cox and Jacobson, 1973, pp. 393–396). From this perspective it is no accident that the United States led the drive for an extension of the GATT regime and that France assumed the mantle of leader in the SEA negotiations. Moreover, the more that is at stake for actors, the greater the efforts they will be prepared to make in order to shape the outcome. Note, though, that when it comes to the mediative aspects of political engineering, having a strong interest in the outcome is not necessarily an advantage. To the extent that prospective partners see the entrepreneur's own concerns as biased or in some

other way nonrepresentative, strong stakes may actually undermine the legiti-macy of the entrepreneur's leadership and impair confidence in the specific ideas that the entrepreneur develops or advocates.[20] In this perspective, inviting the OECD secretariat to produce further studies for the Uruguay Round negotiations may have been a good idea; although serving "the rich," the OECD secretariat was probably considered less biased than the U.S. administration. Sjöstedt's ob-servation that intellectual dominance by the proactive champion at one partic-ular stage of the GATT negotiations provoked substantial resentment among Third World countries is a nice illustration that aggressive efforts on behalf of one particular state may easily be counterproductive. Even a strong leader may be heavily dependent on the availability of "nonallies" to perform complemen-tary functions (compare the notion of a leadership complex introduced earlier).

The term *status* is used here to refer to an actor's formal role in an orga-nization as well as to the actor's position in an informal social order. In the context of international collaboration special authority is conferred on the in-cumbents of certain formal roles, including those of conference president, com-mittee chair, and secretary general. Informal status is partly a matter of personal reputation, seniority, and so on, but it also depends on the political orientation of and the prestige ascribed to the nation or government the person represents. The relative weight of these two components seems to vary depending on the institutional and political setting (see Keohane, 1966). Whatever its basis, status generally serves as a key to access (to decision makers, arenas, and issues) and as a source of legitimacy and respect: the higher the formal or informal status of actors, the more inclined others are to pay attention to those actors' contributions and to defer to their guidance. The relationship between formal authority and informal status is likely to be synergetic, in the sense that the combined effect will be larger than the sum of the parts.

As instrumental leadership is based partly on individual skills, status, and effort, it is a role to which representatives of small countries and international secretariats with constrained mandates can also aspire. In certain respects, notably when it comes to mediation, representatives of some small countries, particularly those in the middle position on an issue may even find themselves in an advan-tageous position compared with their great power colleagues. This proposition is supported by the fact that a Swiss-Colombian proposal and the brokering efforts of a group of middle powers built a bridge between the important camps in the Uruguay Round negotiations. Lodge makes a similar point in her case study by referring to "the more traditional honest-broker role of a small state holding the Council presidency." Lodge's account of the SEA negotiations shows that nongovernmental actors—in some cases even particularly prominent public figures, such as Paul Henri Spaak and Altiero Spinelli—can play significant roles. That being said, however, we should realize that effective instrumental leadership may require a substantial amount of human resources. The fact that it took large-scale research programs in Norway and Sweden and years of cam-paigning to convince other European countries to consider acid rain a serious problem illustrates the point. Therefore, the smaller and the poorer the country,

the more rarely it can (afford to) mobilize the amount of expertise and diplomatic activity needed to play a leading role, even in purely instrumental terms.

For obvious reasons, the case studies cannot provide detailed descriptions of the kind of strategies and tactics applied by instrumental leaders. Suffice it here to point out that in both cases procedural as well as substantive means of engineering were used by proactive champions as well as by brokers. In both cases coalition building—isolating the main opponents and undermining their status as pivotal actors—seems to have been the main path followed by the proactivists. Sjöstedt's analysis of the GATT negotiations reveals how the United States carefully moved by expanding step-by-step the group of partners from a small core of "allies." Both cases also illustrate how institutional devices, such as committees and working groups, can be used deliberately to expand the platform and to provide a seal of organizational legitimacy to a particular project. For the brokers, the calculated use of informal networks, as well as of compromise groups, was clearly an important strategy of consensus building in both cases. Moreover, both accounts illustrate the importance of timing. A mediator would most often like to get in on the act before a situation of stalemate is actually reached, but the premature introduction of compromise formulas and package deals may easily spoil the chances of having them accepted.

Conclusion

Now that we have examined these three modes of leadership one by one, what can we say about their relative significance in accounting for the outcomes of the two processes examined in this book and about their combined impact? Although the case studies provide no basis for determining explanatory power with great precision, some observations can be made. First, in both cases it seems abundantly clear that leadership was indeed exercised and that in its absence there would have been neither a Uruguay Round nor an SEA. More generally, leadership of one kind or another is an integral part of multilateral negotiations. A certain minimum of leadership—measured in amount, quality, and "unidirectionality"— also seems to come close to being a necessary, though by no means sufficient, condition for success (compare O. R. Young, 1991, p. 302).

Second, different modes of leadership are normally at play in the same conference. Moreover, one actor may be able to provide more than one mode of leadership in the same process, even though these modes are derived from different sources and are exercised through different behavioral strategies. From Sjöstedt's account we can see that coercive and intellectual leadership modes were at play in the GATT negotiations and that the United States to some extent was able to provide both. Arguably, this combination is precisely what gave the United States its political clout in the Uruguay Round. In the SEA negotiations, instrumental leadership was backed by the threat of subgroup action, and although leadership roles seem to have been more differentiated in this case than in the Uruguay Round, France was to some extent able to play both cards.

To see why some combination of leadership modes is so crucial to over-

coming the problems of multilateral negotiations, recall that each mode has a distinct function that cannot be fulfilled (equally well) by any of the others. For example, coercion is a means of altering the incentives of one's prospective partners, inducing them to accept one's own terms or breaking their will to resist. Instrumental leadership, by contrast, is basically a matter of inventing and clarifying options, integrating or balancing interests, and persuading others to adopt one's own views. It is easy to see that coercion can be largely irrelevant or even counterproductive when it comes to diagnosing problems, inventing effective cures, developing politically feasible solutions, or inspiring followers to contribute to a common cause. It is equally clear that instrumental leadership can be quite ineffective in breaking the informed resistance of others. This difference in functions has two important consequences.

First, there must be some optimal mix of leadership modes in multilateral negotiations. This optimal mix must include some version of instrumental leadership and (at least) one of the two power-based modes (coercion or unilateral action). They need not both (all) be provided by one particular actor or coalition of actors; in fact, roles must to some extent be differentiated (for example, coercive promotion and mediating do not go well together). The important thing is that they are both provided and in such a way that they do not undermine each other. Moreover, each mode seems to have its prime time—namely, one or more stages at which it is the critical element of leadership. Thus, Sjöstedt's account of the GATT negotiations suggests that coercion (the more or less implicit threat of protective measures) was critical in, *inter alia,* the agenda-setting stage but that once that stage was completed, the time was ripe for intellectual leadership to help diagnose the problem and clarify available options. At a later stage, negotiations were driven by a mix of coercion and brokering. The notion of the optimal mix may therefore be developed to include propositions about optimal role differentiation and optimal sequencing as well. And the two may be linked in the sense that the optimal mix requires one kind of leader to defer to another at a certain stage in the process. For example, overt and strong coercion during the stage of research is likely to impair it, even if the two modes of leadership are provided by different actors.

Second, because different modes of leadership to a large extent fulfill different functions, the relative importance of each mode in a particular negotiation process can be recast as a question of the relative salience of different functions in that process. I have already indicated that different functions are performed in different stages of the negotiation process. The salience of different functions is related also to issue characteristics, such as problem complexity and the configuration of interests: thus, the more complex the problem and the less incompatible the actors' interests, the greater the scope for instrumental leadership. Conversely, the more simple and clear-cut the issue, and the more competing the interests, the less the scope for intellectual leadership. The effectiveness of different kinds of leadership may also depend on the kind of decision to be made. Using Cox and Jacobson's (1973) terms, I would suggest that the power-based modes of leadership tend to be more salient with respect to programmatic, rule-creating,

and operational decisions than they are symbolic issues. And, everything else the same, they tend to be more critical in the implementation of international agreements than in the negotiation process itself. All this analysis suggests that in multilateral negotiations we may find not only a leader but perhaps a leadership complex consisting not only of the leader and its active supporters (recall Sjöstedt's "U.S.-led coalition") but also of "nonallies" performing complementary functions of leadership. Such a configuration can be seen most clearly in the GATT case. The United States was no doubt the principal champion of reform and the driving force in these negotiations, and the United States could by and large rely on the support of a number of allies. But other actors played complementary roles that also seem to have been critical in moving the process ahead. Among these actors were a set of brokers (including Switzerland and Colombia) and at least one international secretariat beyond GATT itself, that of the OECD.

To what extent, then, are existing theories of leadership capable of predicting and explaining who exercises what kind(s) of leadership in different settings of multilateral negotiation, with what (kinds of) effects on the outcome? On the basis of this analysis it seems fair to say that existing theories can specify rather well the capabilities required to provide different modes of leadership (and thus to identify the potential leaders), can identify the principal behavioral strategies available to these actors, and can provide important clues to how capabilities and behavior interact to affect outcomes. Determining effects on outcomes is, though, clearly the hardest part. Also, we do have rather elegant theories pertaining to the coercive mode, but instrumental leadership—particularly elements such as innovation and persuasion—seems to be less well understood. Arguably, it is also inherently less amenable to (formal) modeling. This drawback applies to negotiating theory more generally; our models of distributive bargaining are more "advanced" and conclusive than our models of the integrative mode.

To what extent can leadership theory, in an overall assessment, explain the outcomes, and the difference in outcomes, in these two cases? The prolonged stalemate in the GATT negotiations can be interpreted as a case in support of the hegemonic-decline hypothesis. The United States no longer commanded the mix of intellectual leadership and coercive bargaining power needed to add a new set of rules to the GATT regime, and no other state or coalition of states could yet aspire to fill that role. Many other countries probably saw themselves as being less dependent than previously on the United States. The growth in several other economies provided a material basis for more assertive policies than in the past on the part of important states, and the end of the Cold War circumscribed the opportunities of the United States to overcome the demand from major (European) allies for their own tariff protection. The problem was exacerbated by the fact that the governments of many industrialized countries had a rather weak (parliamentary) basis that made them highly vulnerable to parochial demands from domestic interest groups. Thus, the supply of leadership was rather weak on the domestic scene as well. In the EC negotiations a fortunate combination of formal and informal leadership, provided by multiple actors, made a decisive impact. The substantive driving roles were clearly played by a couple of major

member countries. But these governments were able to capitalize on the support of the Commission (particularly in ideology) and also to use the office of the Council presidency at critical points in the process. Instrumental leadership seems to have been important but so also was the fear on the part of the "laggards" that the majority might simply decide to go it alone. The EC case thus nicely illustrates the interplay of different modes of leadership and of formal and informal roles.

If we are to improve our understanding of how leadership works in multilateral negotiations, we shall have to look beyond conventional international relations theory for inputs. In the international relations literature, including the study of international cooperation, the power-based modes of leadership have so far attracted the most attention. A political realist may argue that this order of priorities simply reflects the relative significance of different modes of leadership in the realm of international politics. To drive home the point, the realist might add that if little attention has been paid to the persuasive impact of unilateral action, the explanation is simply that there is nothing out there to study; the category is virtually empty and hence irrelevant for all practical purposes.

As indicated above, this line of argument is based on an overly simplistic notion of the nature of international politics in general and international negotiations in particular. Admittedly, one can easily find instances where, in the end, power is paramount. But it is equally obvious that the instrumental mode of leadership serves purposes that power alone can never achieve. If we are to understand processes and outcomes of multilateral negotiations, we need to be able to grasp also the logic of intellectual and entrepreneurial leadership. The student of international negotiations must not only "rediscover the art of politics" (Sandholtz and Zysman, 1989, p. 107) but also be able to understand how politics work. This is no minor challenge because, arguably, the instrumental mode of leadership—like the integration mode of negotiation—is also the most complex of the three. In particular, processes of search, learning, innovation, and support building tend to be harder to grasp and model than the logic of incentive manipulation and rational choice.

Here the study of leadership seems particularly relevant. At least some traditions within the study of leadership are concerned primarily with the instrumental mode of leadership and more with strategies and tactics than with capabilities and structures. The intriguing challenge to the student of international negotiations becomes, then, to transpose and integrate findings and propositions from other settings and different traditions of research into a comprehensive framework for the analysis of multiparty conferences.

Notes

1. Admittedly, this is a rather crude definition, but it seems to capture the essence of those provided in, *inter alia*, *The Encyclopedia of Social Sciences* (vol. 9, p. 8), *The Handbook of Social Psychology* (compare Gibb, 1969, pp. 212-214), and Burns (1978, p. 18). It also corresponds reasonably well to *Webster's*

definition of a leader as, among other things, a "principle or guiding part in group action."

2. The argument is not that leaders are necessarily motivated by altruism. Leaders may act "responsibly" simply because they occupy a position (for example, as the dominant actor in a particular system) where their own self-interest, at least in some respects, corresponds well to that of the group as a whole.

3. For a somewhat different interpretation, emphasizing conventional statecraft and bargaining ("intergovernmental institutionalism"), see Moravcsik (1991).

4. This is, as O. R. Young himself points out (1991, p. 302), a "strong" hypothesis in the sense that one single observation of "success" without the presence of leadership is sufficient to falsify it. On closer examination, however, it seems that Young's definition of leadership reduces this proposition to a rather trivial statement: leadership, as conceived by Young (1991, p. 285), "refers to the actions of individuals who endeavor to solve or circumvent the collective action problems that plague the efforts of parties to reap joint gains in processes of institutional bargaining." If we insert this definition into the formulation of the hypothesis, the definition seems, in essence, to boil down to the statement that, without some action designed to solve or circumvent problems of collective action, agreement will not be reached. This hardly qualifies as a particularly bold statement. Nor is it as easy to test as it might appear; I strongly suspect that it would be hard to find instances of multilateral negotiations where no action of this kind has been undertaken. In conclusion, then, a stricter definition of leadership—and also an indication of some critical minimum—seems required to rescue Young's hypothesis from appearing as trivial or close to untestable.

5. Interestingly, we find in both case studies observations that indicate a large gap in levels of participation and influence. For example, Sjöstedt observes, "Approximately 70 percent of the formal participants were passive, or almost passive, in the negotiations following the Punta del Este meeting." Lodge points out in Chapter One, "It is axiomatic that no major initiative can proceed in the EC without the consent of France and Germany."

6. Compare findings in the study of crisis management—for example, Hermann (1972).

7. Here I am thinking not only of the matching of supply of and demand for specific services; even the more or less fortuitous matching of more diffuse moods may be relevant (compare the notion of "mood-matching" developed by Goodin, 1988).

8. The term *unilateral* is interpreted liberally to include not only actions undertaken by one single actor but also actions undertaken by a (small) subgroup of parties acting as a united coalition.

9. And "leadership without followers" would be a contradiction in terms.

10. In doing so, they may also affect the configuration of interests and the distribution of political influence within other societies—thereby, perhaps, reinforcing the adaptive response (see James and Lake, 1989, pp. 6-9).

11. If unilateral action produces positive externalities, there is, however,

a real risk that the persuasive impact of a good example will be offset by negative effects on partner incentives. Thus, if pollution control measures undertaken unilaterally by one country help protect the environment of its neighbors as well, the neighbors may very well find that their own optimal levels of abatement are now lower than they would otherwise have been. The general lesson may be stated as follows: before relying on the intrinsic persuasiveness of a good example to carry the day, check whether and to what extent unilateral action produces positive externalities as well.

12. The basic problem of the "assurance game" is that although both (all) actors prefer mutual cooperation to any other outcome, cooperation is not a dominant strategy for any of them. In fact, being the only one to contribute is the worst of all possible outcomes. In other words, whenever some amount of uncertainty pertains to the choice of one's prospective partner(s), an actor faces a dilemma.

13. Notice that the word *coercion* refers to the use of promises and rewards as well as threats and punishment. In the context of cooperative problem solving, positive instruments are, presumably, more frequently used than negative ones.

14. This formulation raises the question of what to make of moves that are coercive in effect but not in intent. The "wave of neoprotectionism" in industrialized countries mentioned by Sjöstedt may be one case in point; I suspect that at least some of these protectionist moves were undertaken for genuine rather than tactical reasons. Such moves may clearly be relevant to the exercise of leadership, but if we conceive of leadership behavior as a deliberate effort at guiding others, they will not be an integral part of that effort.

15. An internal threat is the threat not to accept a particular deal or to withdraw from the negotiations altogether and thus bring the other parties to their respective best alternative to a negotiated agreement. By contrast, an external threat is one referring to moves in the basic game or to some kind of linkage to external issues.

16. In this regard there is an important difference between positive and negative coercion. Promises entail costs if they succeed; threats are costly if they fail.

17. Another basic assumption is that regime preference is a function of a nation's relative power. More specifically, a decline in relative economic strength is assumed to weaken a hegemon's preferences for free trade and other liberal regimes (see, for example, Kindleberger, 1981; Gilpin, 1987; and Chapter Two in this book).

18. The concept of political engineering is elaborated in Underdal (1991).

19. In his study of the UN General Assembly, Keohane (1966, p. 37) argues that skill is more important for the representatives of small states than for those of large states: "Thus, the quality of a great power's delegation may determine the extent of its influence within certain limits, whereas the ambassador of a small state may determine whether or not his delegation's views are considered." The general proposition can also be found in Cox and Jacobson (1973, pp. 393–397).

20. Note that the combination of bias and strong stakes tends to worry other parties the most. As the role of the Norwegian delegation in the United Nations Conference on the Law of the Sea illustrates, having a strong stake in the outcome need not in itself disqualify a government from serving as a mediator—as long as its interests are seen by others as being fairly balanced.

PART THREE

EVALUATING
THE ANALYSES

Chapter 9

Lessons Drawn
from Practice
Open Covenants, Openly Arrived At

Winfried Lang (Austria)

Multilateral negotiations are different. They differ from bilateral negotiations, but they differ also from one another. The case studies in Chapter One and Chapter Two have to some extent demonstrated the broad variety of regional and global negotiations. The spectrum would have been even more complex if one of the negotiation processes in the United Nations context such as the Conference on the Law of the Sea or the negotiations on ozone depletion or climate change had been included. Yet another dimension of complexity would have been added by a description of the lengthy negotiations that have taken place in the framework of the Conference on Security and Cooperation in Europe (CSCE).

Multilateral negotiations are a tempting subject of analysis and research because they are much more accessible to the researcher than bilateral negotiations. This higher degree of transparency results mainly from the fact that multilateral negotiation material (summary records, documents on various national positions, and so on) is more easily available for public scrutiny than information on bilateral negotiations. To the extent that multilateral negotiations can be likened to parliamentary proceedings, they show a relatively high amount of transparency. Participants in such negotiations may even be tempted to use the media to influence other participants by building up public pressure or by mobilizing nongovernmental organizations. Thus multilateral negotiations reflect in some way the lofty goal of Woodrow Wilson: "Open covenants, openly arrived at."

This openness of multilateral negotiations is, however, only a relative one. Important deals are still struck in back chambers by a limited number of key players. The results of these nonpublic meetings are then transferred to the public

arena to be formalized and cast in legal rules. Thus, parties that had no part in the private proceedings are confronted with a sometimes difficult choice: either they swallow the result achieved without them or they resist. Their resistance, however, will work only if they dispose of some veto power. If they possess such power, either by means of existing rules (consensus) or by means of their sheer weight (economic, political), they should have been included from the outset in the nonpublic dealings. The transition from private bargaining to open decision making is certainly one of the most delicate moments in the multilateral negotiation process. At this juncture of the process it should be realized that in spite of their apparent transparency multilateral negotiations are not more "democratic" than bilateral negotiations. Although the impact of power may be somewhat mitigated by more or less stringent rules of procedure, power remains a dominant feature of multilateral negotiations.

Case Studies

The case study of the Single European Act (SEA) conveys comprehensive insight into the workings of the European Communities (EC), which by means of this important and new legal commitment made a major leap forward on the road toward full union. The most distinctive attribute of intra-EC negotiations is the plurality of types of actors. Not only do the various governments play their traditional roles and defend their national interests. They also have to compete with institutional actors such as the Commission and the European Parliament, which is closely linked to the parliaments in each member state. Coalition building is therefore much broader and also much more complex in EC negotiations than in other multilateral negotiations. Another specific feature of intra-EC negotiations is the presidency, which is assumed by a different governmental leader every six months. Each government assuming this function aims not only at performing as optimally as possible but also at achieving maximum results for the EC interest. As this interest may be at variance with the perceived national interest, dilemmas may arise for actors during their turn as president. Furthermore, as the negotiation on the SEA affected the future position of each actor in the newly organized EC, the intensity of negotiations sometimes went well beyond the average, when more mundane subjects such as foreign trade and the environment are on the agenda.

This study highlights also the importance of the power factor in any intra-EC negotiation; it identifies the big four (France, Germany, Italy, and the United Kingdom) as the key players and recognizes that the first two had to give their consent to any major initiative. Equally important is the statement that smaller states were likely to make the most of an opportunity for a statesmanlike diplomatic role such as the EC presidency. Tactics such as posturing, coalition formation, and the use of trade-offs were evident within and outside the EC, as were time pressure and agenda adjustment, through which issues without wide support were simply dropped from the agenda.

Contrary to some allegations that decision making in Brussels takes place

in an ivory tower, this study affirms the view that movement toward European union was kept alive by a steady media campaign. It also confirms that this negotiation would not have proceeded successfully if there had not been coalition makers or honest brokers such as Italy keeping the process on track. As in any other negotiation, the agenda was adjusted; as in any other negotiation, final decisions were postponed; as in any other negotiation, countries were persuaded to swap sides. One of the favorite tactics evidently was isolating the least communitarian actor (the United Kingdom): this isolation was achieved with some success by a close alliance between Italy and the European Parliament.

The Uruguay Round case study suffers from one drawback for analysis— namely, that the round has not yet ended and that no final conclusions can be drawn. But the long process and the difficulty in reaching results allow for certain lessons out of failure. The simple fact that 50 percent of this study is devoted to the prenegotiating phase stresses the importance of getting to the table (Stein, 1989). This period of continuous confrontation between the United States and certain developing countries (mainly Brazil and India), especially on the issue of including new times on the agenda (services, intellectual property), reflected a new phase of North-South relations: the more ideological confrontation of the 1970s, devoted to the "new international economic order," was replaced during the 1980s by a more subject-oriented and national-interest-related dispute. This new, more differentiated approach of the South to economic issues may have been a major reason why the so-called coalition of dissidents, opposed to the opening of the new round, faltered in the end and was unable to impede the start of substantive negotiations. Leadership and coalition theories are called on to explain these developments.

In many instances Sjöstedt highlights the role of mediators, this role being played in some cases by the director general of the General Agreement on Tariffs and Trade (GATT) and in other cases by the de la Paix group, an assembly of various medium and smaller powers. This middle-of-the-road group, as well as the Cairns group (agriculture), was able to cut through the traditional barriers between North and South and by its very existence contributed to fluidity, if not flexibility, in the negotiating situation.

Analytical and intellectual capacities are frequently referred to as another important element in this process. As the GATT secretariat, at least during the early phases of the process, was not authorized to do research and exploration because of the opposition of the dissident powers of the South, this work was done by the Organization for Economic Cooperation and Development (OECD), which the dissidents also resented. Here again emerges the issue of scientific certainty, of reliable and objective data, which may well affect not only respective national positions but also the overall outcome of a negotiation.

In his conclusion Sjöstedt attributes the difficulty of arriving at the end of the tunnel to two factors: the waning of leadership and the complexity of the endeavor as a whole. The first factor is certainly important; there need not be the proverbial hegemon (the United States), but at the very least a highly committed group of powerful states is needed to keep the process going and to lead it with

some adjustments to an outcome (it being understood that no outcome is final and that each and every negotiation may be reopened whenever circumstances and interests so demand). Complexity, however—the result of having many issues negotiated along various tracks (agriculture, services, and so on) and within different bodies—engenders the difficulty in agreeing on a compromise solution that cuts across these various processes and interests.

It should be noted, as Sjöstedt correctly mentions, that the final result of this round very much depends on an understanding being achieved between the chief players of the North (the United States and the EC) on agriculture and related subsidies (exports, internal support). Thus the initial North-South confrontation has turned into a North-North dispute. It remains to be seen whether sectoral interests or the survival of the international trading system as a whole will prevail. Indeed, the stakes are high.

Theories

Decision Theory

In multilateral negotiations, decisions have to be made not only at various points in time but also at different levels. These levels include the respective delegation, the interest group it is part of, and the full conference. These decisions are closely interconnected and depend not only on events at the conference table but also on developments back home.

Decision theory has been geared mainly to research and to explaining ex post the changes of preferences or the modification of positions on the way toward the final compromise (see the application of decision theory to the case studies in Chapter Three). But decision theory can also be helpful to practitioners. By applying the "what if" mode, they can learn how certain changes in their positions might facilitate or impede progress toward the conclusion of negotiations. This approach can also help practitioners in the prenegotiation phase to understand potential moves (alternatives) of counterparts and to react appropriately in due time. Scientific support and knowledge is likely to be available only to big power delegations. Delegates from smaller nations or developing countries may be at a disadvantage, unless some independent or impartial body is able to provide advice to those delegations that cannot afford it.

A problem not to be neglected in this context is the distinction between decisions on procedure and decisions on substance. Here it would be helpful to develop criteria that would assist the practitioner in making a meaningful distinction and in being fully aware of the respective consequences. As a matter of fact, some decisions on procedure, in spite of the benign neglect with which they are treated by some leading delegations, may have a major impact on the overall outcome of a negotiation.

Another area in which practitioners could benefit from theory is by gaining insight into the link between events at the conference table and decision making in the respective capitals. Most delegates would prefer to be closely as-

sociated with the domestic decision-making process. Some benefit could also be drawn from insights into the decisions (motivation, orientation, and so on) of nonnational actors such as chairpersons or leading representatives of international organizations in charge of the respective negotiation. This analysis would also produce a certain linkup with organization theory. Any lesson learned by negotiators with regard to improving transparency and with regard to reducing uncertainty facilitates decision making and is therefore conducive to progress.

Game Theory

Negotiations, bilateral or multilateral, are frequently considered games—note the term *key player*—although their outcome may be of the most serious nature. Game theory has attempted to apply its recipes of mathematical rationality to interactions, which at the top level (governments) may well be considered rational choices but which at the level of the individual negotiator could well be blurred by the so-called personality factor. Another factor that may erode the rationality of choices is the pressure of public opinion.

   Game theory, as presented in Chapter Four, gives some important insights to the practitioner, especially as regards the real-life impact of certain voting rules. It may well be that the drafters of these rules (being mostly lawyers) do not realize that qualified majority voting, which replaces the unanimity rule, increases the power of a decision-making body (such as an assembly or council) several hundred times or that marginal players may by the same token increase their voting power several times. Thus drafters of voting rules would be well advised to consult game theorists on such specific issues. Voting rules play a significant role not only in the EC context but also in global environmental treaties, especially as regards the use of force or the amendment of these treaties.

   At this juncture one caveat should be added. Most multilateral negotiations follow the so-called consensus rule, which excludes the possibility of variations of majorities on different issues. As consensus building has become the main feature of multilateral negotiations, national positions based on rational choices are exposed to sometimes highly effective social pressures, which emanate from participants that have already joined a different but mainstream opinion. A delegation may block such pressures only if it is among the key players or if it is able to rally a major interest group behind its position. Breaking the consensus is socially acceptable only if the delegation concerned can politically afford it. It would be most interesting if game theory could shed some light on this intricate web of pressures and counterpressures around the conference table and eventually predict the outcome of these "games."

Organization Theory

Most multilateral negotiations take place in the framework of an international organization. Among the few exceptions one may mention negotiations related to humanitarian law convened by the Swiss Federal Council or the negotiations

of the CSCE. Since the end of the Cold War, the CSCE has moved to an ever-increasing level of institutionalization, from which one may conclude that it now constitutes at least an international organization in the making.

Organization theories and whatever insights they are able to convey in respect to issues such as structure, decision making, culture, and conflict resolution are likely to benefit negotiators provided they are fully aware of the specifics of the organizational context within which they are acting. It goes without saying that rules and procedures valid within a certain organization affect negotiations conducted under the auspices of that organization.

Much can be learned from two case studies: differences in the respective strengths of secretariats, differences in the goals of participating governments, and so on, explain to a certain extent the different outcomes of the respective negotiations. This explanation does not mean that substance, the contest of political and economic interests, would not remain the dominating factor. The organizational features of a specific negotiation constitute, however, important background conditions, which are able to facilitate or to delay progress.

Organizations are not only settings for and players in multilateral negotiations, they may also be their stakes. This is particularly true in negotiations devoted to constitutional issues such as the SEA negotiations, which aimed at proceeding farther on the road toward full European union. Even the Uruguay Round has an organizational subgoal, namely, the establishment of a multilateral trade organization. In negotiations on global climate change and biodiversity, institutions were established to make the legal instruments operational. Exiting international organizations that convene a treat-making conference are as a rule interested either in obtaining for themselves new tasks or in creating new institutions. The existence of organizations and their vested interests in respect to a specific outcome may also explain some of the differences between negotiations on the depletion of the ozone layer and negotiations on global climate change. Whereas the ozone layer negotiations were managed largely by a well-established organization (UNEP) having its own interests in relation to institutional growth, the climate change negotiations were assisted and supported by an ad hoc secretariat that had not yet developed similar interests.

Organizations have an impact on multilateral negotiations even when their own future is not at stake. Beyond the technical servicing of a conference, they have to play important roles as advisers (because of their knowledge about previous practice, legal precedents, and so on) and as catalysts. The chief executive officers of these organizations can provide negotiators with compromise formulas that might not have been readily accepted if they had been submitted by one or more of the negotiators. Proposals coming from officials of the competent organization are most likely to be followed if they reflect credibility and impartiality.

It is certainly true that "negotiation is the organization in motion" (Chapter Five), especially if one considers highly formalized negotiating processes such as the codification conferences of the United Nations, which since 1961 have produced numerous conventions fixing to some extent the present state of inter-

national law. The complex interplay between the various organs of such conferences (plenary sessions, committee of the whole, drafting committee, and so on)
assimilate these conferences to parliamentary proceedings well known in most
Western democracies. But these organizational negotiations are in charge of producing international regulations as well as adapting them to changing circumstances (such as progress in science and technology and changes in economic
feasibility), as has been so ably demonstrated by environmental treaties such as
the Montreal Protocol on Substances That Deplete the Ozone Layer; because of
a high degree of built-in flexibility this treaty may be considered a "living
organism."

Multilateral negotiations take place in a certain organizational framework;
they are likely to produce new organizations or to endow existing ones with new
tasks; they are carried on within a more or less new context in order to meet the
evolving requirements of the international community. Thus organization theory
and negotiation theory are likely to enrich one another and to convey appropriate
insights to practitioners.

Small Group Theory

Small group theory, as developed by social psychology, may appear to have some
difficulty in proving its relevance to intergovernmental negotiations. First, there
is the argument based on size; how can we apply this type of theory to global
gatherings like the Rio Summit or even to GATT, which at first sight do not
appear to be small groups? Second, there is the argument that negotiators act not
on their own behalf but on behalf of a government; they are supposed to execute
instructions to the best of their abilities. Both arguments contain the proverbial
grain of truth but are not sufficiently strong for us to dismiss the relevance of
small group theory to multilateral intergovernmental negotiations.

As far as the problem of size is concerned, size has no major role to play
with regard to negotiations of the SEA type, but it has to be recognized that
conferences with a hundred or more participating governments could never
achieve meaningful results if there did not exist small negotiating bodies
("friends of the chair") in which representatives of certain interest groups (coalitions) and some key players meet in order to work out the most difficult solutions. Thus, most multilateral negotiations of the global type function as a two-
tier process: the full membership of a conference, divided into several interest
groups, "entrusts" the real bargaining to a smaller group of delegates; the outcome of these negotiations in smaller circles has to be approved within the respective interest group as well as by the plenary of the conference. Thus, it may
be reasonable to apply mechanisms developed by small group theory to multilateral negotiations, provided this two-step approach is followed.

As regards the problem of negotiators not acting as individuals but as
agents ("puppets on a string"), one should not neglect the personality factor.
Negotiators usually enjoy a certain freedom in carrying out their instructions, in
interpreting these instructions, in reporting back on intermediate results, and in

seeking new instructions in the light of evolutions at the conference table. Here negotiators may activate the various facets of their personality, their specific skills or energy, and so on, especially in smaller settings.

Thus, practitioners should not dismiss the insights conveyed to them by small group theory. The thesis that a specific sequence (generate fresh and interesting ideas, reach consensus on them) is likely to generate optimal results may take a different form in each case. However, insights such as those related to group cohesiveness are likely to have an overall bearing on the actual behavior of negotiators.

Coalition Theory

Coalitions are a distinctive feature of multilateral negotiations. They are indispensable for decision making because no meaningful bargaining can take place among some 100 or 150 participating governments. Coalitions of states are often called interest groups in global forums (GATT, United Nations). However, the notions of *coalition* and *group* are not necessarily identical. Coalition implies the formation and disbanding of associative relations; some governments cluster around a specific concern, while others move away and join another political or economic cluster. Thus coalition is a rather dynamic concept of the interactions in a multilateral framework. Interest groups reflect a somewhat higher degree of stability—for example, the Group of 77 in the North-South relationship or the Eastern (Communist) and Western groups in the Cold War. As regards the Cold War groups, the old structure of the CSCE had a middle group, called N+N (neutral and nonaligned states), which, because of its middle-of-the-road position, was in many instances instrumental in devising compromise formulas and building consensus around them.

More recent multilateral negotiations—for example, on global climate change—have demonstrated that permanent groups may not be a regular feature of negotiations conducted on a global scale: the group of industrialized states has been split in two (the United States versus the other OECD countries), especially as regards the fixing of target dates and concrete emission figures concerning certain greenhouse gases. The group of developing countries has been split in three: the oil-producing and oil-exporting countries, which are afraid that any move away from energy production from fossil fuels will destroy the basis of their wealth; the low-lying and island states, which are afraid of the possibility of rising ocean levels as a consequence of global warming; the remaining developing countries, which expect an increase of capital flows from North to South as a consequence of the transfer-of-technology obligations of industrialized states. Thus, at a certain juncture an "objective alliance" existed between the United States and those developing countries that were most strongly opposed to concrete measures mitigating the impact of global warming.

Coalition theories may have some bearing on the actual behavior of negotiators to the extent that these theories are able to convey a certain transparency as regards the behavior of coalitions in the past. Factors that contributed to the

formation of one coalition, its maintenance, and its impact on the outcome may again play a certain role in a different set of negotiations. Whereas the SEA negotiations involved a continuing confrontation between two relatively stable coalitions, the Uruguay Round was and still is characterized by associations of countries cutting across traditional boundaries (North versus South) and changing across a wide spectrum of issue areas (agriculture, services, market access). In both instances power, as a political and economic asset, determines the fate of coalitions. Developments (such as elections) within the respective countries may also influence their external behavior. Links of a nongovernmental nature but representing important economic or political interests may affect the life of coalitions, as do independent actors such as international or supranational institutions.

Leadership Theory

Multilateral negotiations are unthinkable without leadership. Any practitioner knows that leadership is a prerequisite for progress, be it within a delegation, within an interest group or coalition, or at the level of the conference as a whole. Modes of leadership (unilateral, coercive, or instrumental) may vary at the different levels or according to different issue areas. And it may well be that an optimal mix of these modes is likely to bring about a result acceptable to most participants.

Leadership theories, which originated in the context of smaller social groups or within a given national context, will have to be adapted to the specifics of multilateral negotiations in order to have an explanatory function with regard to this type of international and intergovernmental action. Leadership is not only a question of the skills, energy, and status of an individual. Leadership depends also on the respective position of the state or government this individual is representing. A person is unlikely to be elected to the presidency of a conference if the government he or she represents adopts partisan views not shared by the majority or certain key players. In multilateral negotiations leadership is therefore a composite factor. The leadership role rests not only on the qualifications of individuals but also on the political weight of certain countries, their degree of involvement, their interest in achieving a specific outcome, their willingness to contribute to this outcome by specific actions (concessions, trading of advantages against disadvantages, and so on)—in a word, on their chosen role.

Two caveats should be added. As multilateral negotiations usually evolve over a period of many years, it may well be that the leadership role will change (see the Uruguay Round) either as a consequence of the evolution of the negotiating situation itself or as a consequence of changes of national positions following domestic events. Furthermore, one should expect that leadership is not the prerogative of one single delegate or one single country; especially at the outset it may well be that a competition or even contest occurs for the leadership role. The outcome of these competing ambitions will be either the clear-cut victory of one participant or some kind of shared leadership, in which the dis-

tribution of tasks and roles in the various issue areas will again be subject to negotiations.

Practitioners could draw lessons from the application of leadership theories to specific case studies provided that similarities exist between the negotiating situations described in the case studies and the concrete negotiating situation the practitioner is involved in. Much of the impact of these lessons will also depend on the negotiator's inclination—either personal or national—to be a leader or a follower.

Lessons

Drawing lessons for practice amounts to the difficult task of bridging the gap between theory and real life. Although theories draw on real-life events, individuals acting in a real-life context are reluctant to use theories unless they contain lessons that can clearly explain and be applied to the situation.

What are the expectations of negotiators? They are most willing to learn because they have to accomplish a certain task; they are looking for advice; and they certainly would be grateful to learn, through the lens of a theory, why one specific negotiation has failed and why another negotiation has been successful. Negotiators usually are not able to familiarize themselves with all the intricacies of each of the above-mentioned theories. They would, however, benefit from a more general negotiation theory, which integrates the insights of the specific theories. Insights of theories are accepted by practitioners to the extent that the theories translate lessons of the past into recommendations valid for the present. The overall intellectual challenge to negotiators should not be underestimated; they have to decide whether the lessons of the past are really applicable to the negotiation situation they are confronted with.

What are the lessons negotiators are most likely to need in order to perform their task in a satisfactory manner?

- At a time when the actors in multilateral negotiations are not only governments but also economic-integration organizations and nongovernmental organizations, the negotiator would certainly appreciate information about the behavior of these new actors, their internal patterns of decision making, and their vulnerabilities.
- At a time when science (epistemic communities) and public opinion have a growing impact on negotiations, the negotiator would certainly welcome advice on how to handle these new factors in the negotiating situation.
- New issue areas such as the environment also require some specialized knowledge. Negotiators would certainly benefit from insights into substance. However, much more important for them is the ability to translate these insights into concrete negotiating positions.
- It would also be helpful to understand better which negotiating experiences acquired during the Cold War are useful today.
- As the growing size of many multilateral negotiations and the growing role

of the consensus rule (in spite of the continuing impact of power) constitute a serious challenge for everybody representing national interests, any advice on how to manage these problems would be welcome.

- As diplomats trained in negotiating techniques are gradually replaced by individuals (experts in other fields) less familiar with these techniques but better informed on questions of substance, advice on past negotiating experience and its applicability to present-day situations should be available.
- As negotiators do not act as "lonely riders" but are part of a larger team, advice should also be available on the internal behavior of delegations.

What lessons do the various theories offer to the practitioner?

- In the prenegotiation phase decision analysis allows negotiators to assess the size of the bargaining space and the distance that must be bridged among the parties (national interests, bargaining positions, and so on). During the negotiating process several adjustments are likely to be made; therefore, this type of analysis may also assist the negotiator in charting a later course of action.
- Game theory helps the negotiator to evaluate correctly the real-life impact of changing the rules of procedure (unanimity or consensus versus majority) and in distinguishing between the formal and informal roles played by different actors (such as veto power and preference for impasse).
- Organization theory is able to explain the context of multilateral negotiations and provide the negotiator with an understanding of the limits and direction offered by the structure, decision-making procedures, and conflict management approaches of the international organizational setting affected by the negotiation.
- Even in broad multilateral settings most important decisions are taken in smaller groups; therefore, negotiators acting in such settings and seeking to provide cohesiveness around innovation need to understand small group theory as it explains the effects on conformity and deviance.
- Coalition theory identifies different types of coalitions and the possibilities of their formation. Coalitions are the necessary stepping stones to consensus in multilateral negotiations, but they can also lead to blockage and stalemate, eventualities that coalition theory can explain and help negotiators attain or avoid.
- Leadership theory shows the need for appropriate mixes of unilateral, coercive, and instrumental leadership at prime times in the process of multilateral negotiation; it shows how drawing on skill, resource, status, and direction moves the proceedings creatively to a conclusion.

When comparing the list of lessons in demand with the list of lessons offered, one becomes aware that theory, whose objective is understanding complexity, cannot meet all the expectations of practice but that insights from theory may well be helpful tools for the practitioner, who is concerned mainly with managing complexity. It should also be stressed that the relevance of theory may

vary according to the various phases of the negotiating process. Probably no theory can provide lessons for all phases of this process. Thus, the above-mentioned theories should not be seen in isolation but as elements of a conglomerate negotiation theory that not only assists the negotiator in action but is also ready to draw on the negotiator's experience in an exercise of mutual learning and cross-fertilization.

Chapter 10

The Elephant
and the Holograph
Toward a Theoretical Synthesis
and a Paradigm

I. William Zartman (USA)

There is no winner to the contest; all approaches are winners. As might be anticipated, each approach in the preceding series of analyses has shown its merit in providing a compelling insight into the multilateral negotiation process. Each brings out a particular aspect of multilateral negotiation that is fundamentally different from bilateral bargaining and that contains an essential characteristic of a decision-making process with many parties, many issues, and many roles, and only the loosest of decision rules (consensus). In the process, each exposition has made some significant advances in its own field in carrying the approach further than usual. Together they have also shown a rather thorough coverage of the field. Additional approaches might be envisaged and might provide additional details that could be checked against the present analyses, but their absence has not left any glaring gaps.[1] Issues, parties, and roles have been analyzed from a number of overlapping but different angles and approaches to provide a complete picture of the multilateral negotiation process.

Before reviewing and synthesizing the results, I should note that the distinction between plurilateral and multilateral negotiations turned out to be unimportant, contrary to expectations. The reason for this lack of distinction is important, however: multilateral negotiations tend to take on a plurilateral structure by being reduced to a smaller number of leading parties—self-selected for various reasons—with others playing a lesser, defensive, or single-issue role. Multilateral encounters are pluralized as part of the process of making their multilateral complexity manageable (a point that foreshadows a crucial element to be

I am grateful for the research assistance of Anna Korula in preparing this chapter.

developed below). The two cases chosen had different outcomes and somewhat different dynamics but the differences are not a consequence of the number of parties.

Approaches

The decision approach using multiattribute utility analysis constructs preference tables of issue outcomes for each of the many parties and has already been used in this form to advise national delegations in negotiations. This static methodology can be turned dynamic, however, by using the preference figures to yield "weighted preference payoffs" and "deficiencies" for various outcomes and then to show how parties can unite to bring about outcomes that maximize their preferences and minimize their deficiencies. Multilateral negotiations are seen as a concession process from the main preferences of the principal parties. They result in a more or less satisfactory outcome—or an outcome at all—depending on the amount of each major preference "pile" the parties have to give away to equalize their payoffs. Decision analysis specifies the dynamics, amounts, and satisfactions in this multiconcession process.

The strategic approach used in game theory has been applied to n-person games to identify the coalitions that can occur and those that cannot. But it can be extended dynamically to define multilateral negotiation as the search for issue coalitions, trading off breadth of support for height of preference, until the different thresholds of nonagreement are reached and parties drop out one by one. The new extension of the methodology of noncooperative games is more useful for analyzing multilateral negotiations than that of cooperative games because the latter already assumes the existence of an agreement point that ensures all parties some value. Thus, noncooperative methodology is used to see whether such an agreement point exists at all, where it might be, and therefore how much movement is required of the parties for an agreement to be reached. By extension into the practical realm, noncooperative methodology also guides negotiators in getting to the agreement point, showing clearly the costs (in preferences) and the conditions (in partners) that the strategy implies. Practitioners, who seem to be put off by the very term *game theory,* would do well to learn from its simple logic and to make more explicit and precise their efforts to figure out individual party's preference and issue coalitions.

The organizational approach has been employed to identify formal and informal constraints operating on interactions between parties seen as organizational systems. But when parties are seen as dynamic entities seeking to move their organization through the modification of these constraints or rules, negotiation becomes a process of rectifying rules, limited by the same organizational rules under which the rectification process takes place, on one hand, and the nature of the parties themselves, on the other. Both payoffs and preferences are seen as rules because rules determine the payoffs. This approach not only fits the reality of most multilateral negotiations as rule-making encounters among organizational persons—bureaucrats, civil servants, and businesspeople—but also

identifies the key to the process: the procedural rules governing substantive outcomes.

The social psychological approach of small group theory has been the basis of the analysis of various effects channeling social behavior. The group is assumed to exist (a condition that cannot be assumed in the bilateral process), and maintaining that existence becomes the purpose or task of the group in order to accomplish other tasks. By extension, then, negotiation is the building of group consensus when confronted with innovation. The various effects that constrain small group behavior can be used to analyze that consensus-building or consensus-restoring process when consensus is disrupted by new issues. For practitioners, these effects can also be used directly. Negotiation becomes a system-maintenance process.

Coalition analysis has long been presented as one of the keys to multilateral negotiation but largely on the basis of issue preferences and therefore as a given. Combined with power analysis, however, it addresses the question of how coalitions are achieved and maintained. Because consensus is not unanimity but the construction of a coalition that agrees surrounded by a group that is willing to go along, power is the way in which consensual coalitions are created. Proximity of parties on issues and differentiation of coalitions among various types account for the types of power available and are applicable to building winning coalitions.

Finally, leadership theory is the other standard contender for the key explanation of multiparty agreement, based on some rules of conduct (O. R. Young, 1991). The analysis is usually conducted on the basis of leadership types. Leadership tied to parties' positions alone can produce nothing but deadlock; what is needed in multilateral situations is overarching leadership to provide a direction to the various parties' conflicting efforts. Leadership focuses on the competition between drivers and conductors to direct the efforts of the brokers, defenders, and cruisers, and so roles determine the outcome.

These approaches are presented as whole views of the subject and not seen as aspects or subsystems of it; they identify the essence of the subject in different terms and carry forward their analysis on that basis. Each approach defines the same process of multilateral negotiation differently and provides a different key to unlock that process. That key is not simply a disciplinary artifice; it corresponds to an identifying feature of the process as practiced and in turn yields important insights for the practitioner. Each chapter provides an improved tool for taking apart instances of multilateral negotiation and fixing them, and can profitably be used in the analysis of the many multilateral encounters that have marked the end of the twentieth century.

Each of these windows on the multilateral negotiating room has been opened wider by the preceding analyses, but in the process each has also opened further challenges to and opportunities for the particular approach. Each has shown some diffidence in claiming to hold the key to an explanation of the outcome rather than simply providing key insights into the process, however

penetrating the analysis. How can each approach be pushed further to strengthen its analysis?

The strategic approach could use a voting-type analysis because of the voting possibilities in the European Communities (EC), but these are usually not present in consensus proceedings and so all that is left is a ranking analysis in the General Agreement on Tariffs and Trade (GATT) talks. The strength of the approach lies in its ability to make outcomes understandable on the basis of preference structures; its weakness is its limitation to a two- (or at most three-) dimension matrix (Zagare, 1978). A computer analysis, however, could handle a larger number of dimensions—even the 150 involved in current international conferences. The graphic persuasiveness of a two-by-two matrix would be lost, but a tool of analysis would be gained that could show both the possibilities of building preference groups and of bargaining among reduced coalitions. But the approach still needs to be combined with some other methodology to explain change—in preferences, in N-levels, and in strengths. Similarly, decision analysis has been used less than it could because of its tedious data-coding requirements, but it has produced some rare and conclusive case studies (Friedheim, 1993). Additional studies are necessary to provide optimal or ideal-type portrayals that can be used as baselines for comparison with actual case behavior and to generate hypotheses to test whether deviation is the result of ignorance and lost opportunities or of other causes that need to be taken into account in a realistic model. Although it can show when the parties would move if they were to choose the best agreement point (as they sometimes do), the approach needs to be combined with some form of power analysis to show how parties make each other change values and move to other points.

The cybernetic loops enclosing the organizational analysis provide an unusually important dynamic framework for the analysis of institutionalized multilateral movement. As in other approaches, the most promising development would be simply to apply this framework systematically to cases. Such applications are rare (Moravcsik, 1991), and nothing thus far in the analysis of the Single European Act has prepared the audience for the ups and downs of the Maastricht intergovernmental conference and its aftermaths. Yet of all the approaches the organizational approach has the greatest potential value to practitioners as well as to analysts for such extended explanations; the theory needs developing.

Small group theory has concentrated on tactical interactions and needs development in the directions both of data and of theory. If gathering preference data is tedious, generating data on the social and personal dynamics of "who said what to whom and with what effect"—the essence of negotiation analysis—in a private group is intimidatingly difficult. Equally imposing is the need to develop a theory—rather than just insights—to handle such data and their process dynamics. Innovation and consensus are important dimensions, not tension-creating opposites of the same dimension, and they can overlap (consensus to create innovations, innovation to create consensus). The challenge of attaching a theoretical handle to these parameters is tantalizing.

Similarly, the need to sort out the conflicting meanings of power hangs

over all political (power) science and particularly over the political analysis of any type of negotiation (Habeeb, 1988). Relating roles (power positions) and coalitions (power aggregations) to power relations provides crosscutting variables that can generate typologies and propositions, as shown, but still leaves the basic concept unexplored. The explanatory variables have still not been identified in the search for the determinants of different-sized parties' effectiveness in creating (or destroying) coalitions. Coalition analysis in general is taking a rest after some decades of activity, awaiting discovery of new variables to carry it further.

Finally, leadership has long been a practitioner's rather than an analyst's concept. Studies that have gotten beyond the Book of Proverbs stage have focused on the typologies of the leader (Yukl, 1989) and less on matching those typologies with typologies of followers. Roles and strategies have been referred to above as a result of inductive analysis, but the three types of leadership need to be related to followership, preferences, and process to be complete. The question of how parties compete to give intended direction to multilateral encounters not only awaits an answer but stands in need of parameters along which an answer could be sought.

The Elephant

Yet the process is all, not each, of these. Each of these approaches has its own integrity—and sometimes its own discipline—yet at the same time there are overlaps and relations among them. Game theory and decision theory focus on preferences and the cost in priorities required to attain a winning consensus. Small group, coalition, and leadership theories all analyze the ways in which consensus, cohesion, or coalition is achieved, through behavior, power, or style, respectively. Small group theory and organization theory operate within an assumed entity characterized by cohesion or restraints; although, unlike any other approach, organization theory uses rules as its focus of analysis. Leadership roles are inherent in all but perhaps decision analysis, and power is implicit or at least can be read into each of them. However, these two concepts are explicit and central to only two of the approaches. Despite the differences in focus, the sense of a whole is found in the ways in which separate approaches handle the same concept from different angles.

These approaches can be joined together to present a whole picture of multilateral negotiations, each approach illuminating a different side of the object. They fit together, both in their overlap and in their complementarity, making a plated suit that contains the subject. But to make a composite whole out of them would destroy the analytical focus of each and, without a single overarching paradigm, would make the analysis, like the subject, unmanageably complex. Nor can it be said that they are sequentially rather than functionally linked; the effects they analyze are going on at the same time, sometimes even one within the other, or are the same effect conceived differently. Like the analysis of the famous elephant by an assortment of wise but blind scholars, each of these approaches latches onto a salient feature of the subject and presents it as the

whole. In the case of the elephant, the scholar who confronted the tail analyzed the elephant as a rope; the one who focused on the leg treated the elephant as a tree; the one who met the trunk found the elephant to be a type of hose; the one who found the ear, a tent; and so on. The wiser and sightful king who sent them out then proclaims that the elephant is all of these in its totality. Similarly, one can say that each of these approaches presents an important insight into the nature of multilateral negotiation, and all of these approaches combined present a whole that is at least the sum of the parts. But is the whole larger than the sum?

The Holograph

Independent of the different angles from which it can be viewed, there *is* an elephant, a single activity of multilateral negotiation, and its name is managing complexity. Each analytical approach is a particular answer to the essential question of multilateral analysis and practice alike: How is complexity to be managed? Although each is insightful as an analytical approach, none is exhaustive or comprehensive, and, as a window into reality, each misses large parts of the whole room that may be visible—but only partially—to other approaches. Yet there is a room—a subject, an activity—that has its own nature and integrity and that is larger and more coherent than the view any of the windows give of it.

Complexity is a subject of much inconclusive attention (Warsh, 1984, chap. 1), and management is only a small and even less developed portion of it (Casti, 1985; Checkland, 1989; Voge, 1985; von Glinow and Mohrman, 1990). Complexity is not chaos (which also has its own order, as we are beginning to discover); it is merely the existence of a large number of interacting variables with no dominant pattern or dimension (compare Casti, 1985; Klir, 1985). It is more than simply complicatedness and is a specific—if debated—analytical concept. The most striking characteristic of the subject is its diverse and inconclusive meanings—the complexity of "complexity" (Klir, 1985; Morin, 1985; Ploman, 1985)—most of which are relevant to multilateral negotiation only to the extent that they can serve as a helpful heuristic in thinking about the topic. Only limited aspects of their precise applications relate to subjects with the characteristics of multilateral negotiations. These subjects fall within the category of organized complexity (Weaver, 1948), which is not amenable to statistical analysis. "The fundamental difficulty with systems of organized complexity is that no general simplifying assumptions apply to them, that is, they do not possess any hidden simplicity under what is apparently complex" (Klir, 1985, p. 96). But they are also outside the areas amenable to soft systems management (Checkland, 1989) because the managers are many, play many roles, and are trying to manage within the system, not from outside; they themselves are part of the complexity. "A complex process is irreducible" (Casti, 1985, p. 150). The multiroled nature of the situation also puts it outside Simon's (1948) insight, that hierarchy is the key to a large category of complex systems; the sovereign equality of actors in multinational negotiations blurs if not eliminates hierarchy, and the variety of interests and roles tangles what is left of it. Although multilateral negotiations conferences

are systems, only in highly institutionalized instances—EC but not GATT—can they be analyzed as identity-preserving mechanisms (Gottinger, 1983, pp. 77) in addition to the dependent products of their participants. The problem of analyzing complexity in general has attracted much attention that has led to better understanding of the edges but that has left a central area, with characteristics that include multilateral negotiation, still unclear.

Complexity is the essential nature of multilateral negotiation, at many different—and hence complex—levels. The multiplicity of issues, actors, and roles and the variations possible in them over the course of the negotiations, already noted, determine the essential complexity of the process of reaching consensus. Complexity becomes overwhelming, and because it does not contain any single "hidden simplicity" on which analysis and practice can be based, the prime imperative of practitioner and analyst alike is thus to find rough ways of "decomplexifying" to the point where complexity becomes manageable, either for making something happen or for explaining what is going on. The only difference between the concerns of the practitioner and those of the analyst in this task relates to their position in regard to the outcome of the managed complexity: the practitioner seeks to produce a future outcome, the analyst seeks to explain a past one. Both use the same three methods to achieve their goal when confronted with characteristically daunting complexity: simplification, structuring, and direction. Although these three may relate in some minor way to bilateral negotiations, only in the complexity of multilateral negotiations do they have a key and necessary role in producing and analyzing results.

Complexity can be reduced and simplified in many ways. It is here that coalition, a basic effect in many approaches, comes in properly, not as the essential element in multilateral games but as one of the ways in which participants in many-partied encounters handle their own large numbers (Stenelo, 1972, p. 58). But coalition is not the only way to make large numbers manageable; role differentiation is another. There are a number of ways in which the large number of juridically equal parties can effectively be reduced through the assignment of different activities, functions, and strategies. These ways include among others:

- Mediation, which takes out some players as conductors or neutral go-betweens and turns multilateral negotiations into centralized bilateral negotiations
- Assignment of group (coalition) representatives, drafting groups, and executive committees, which relegate negotiations to a smaller (albeit still multilateral) number of parties, which then in subnegotiations presumably bring in the parties they represent
- Issue-role differentiation, using strategies such as drivers, defenders, and cruisers, as already indicated

Similarly, issue coalitions are ways of simplifying complexity. Game theory and decision theory focus on issue positions and indicate ways of packaging, linking, and trading; parties become vehicles for positions, a further reduction of complexity.

But simplification is not enough to deal with complexity in a constructive way to produce consensus on an agreement. Carried to its logical—if penultimate—conclusion, complexity reduction ends up in bipolarization, potentially the most obdurate obstacle to the desired conclusion of consensus. The multiple dimensions of complexity destroy any possibility of conducting or analyzing that process in simple bilateral terms. Whereas a two-party encounter limits roles and organizes issues, the presence of many parties imposes different roles and prevents issues either from being easily organized or from organizing the parties. Multilateral negotiation is not merely complexity reduction; it is the management of complexity, "a process of achieving organized action" (Checkland, 1989, p.78) that involves reduction (simplification) to make complexity comprehensible, structuring to make it manageable, and direction to produce a result.

Creative structuring is managing complexity whether carried out by the analyst or the practitioner (Bennett, Cropper, and Huxham, 1989, p. 308). Practitioners must find a way through the confusing complexity in order to produce a result that meets their states' needs and interests. A strategy must be worked out that will establish priorities for issues and parties and will create roles to fit that strategy. Strategies and priorities are structuring forms of simplification, an attempt to make some order out of the complex parties and issues. Similarly, analysts must provide some structure to the subject to turn data into knowledge. If hierarchy alone is inadequate as an ordering device for this subject, other simplifying mechanisms are needed.

Many of the mechanisms contained in the approaches mentioned above are clear steps to structuring. Organizations, coalitions, small groups, preference schedules and matrices, and typologies simplify and structure the complexities of the process for creative handling. Issue coalitions not only reduce the number of issues but combine them to produce interlocking agreements. Highly articulated sets of rules usually worked out among parties for fair and efficient operations, as identified by the organizational approach, produce a similar result. Chairs, committees, and secretariats help organize debates and establish decision procedures. Although these elements are usually treated as consequences or administrative details of multilateral negotiations, they are in reality parts of its essential characteristic—ways of managing party, issue, and role complexity by simplifying and structuring.

The best approach to understanding the process of simplifying and structuring multilateral complexity is through role analysis, for role complexity is not only a subject to be managed but also the means for managing the other elements of complexity as well. Roles have received some limited attention in the analysis of multilateral negotiations. The conceptual work that has been done focuses primarily on followers' roles—free riders, cooperators, clients (Olson, 1968, Krasner, 1983; and Oye, 1986; Ravenhill, 1984, respectively). Insightful case studies of multilateral negotiations tend to be structural, with some explicit attention to the roles that produce that structure and so produce the outcome (for example, Preeg, 1970; Ravenhill, 1984; Winham, 1986). "The structure of a system is generated by the interaction of its principle parts" (Waltz, 1979, p. 72), and those

interactions are the result of interrelating roles, directed in various ways at "trying to make something happen." The conduct of these interactions to cut through complexity by providing structure can best be characterized as direction, understood to include the many ways that the leader, the manager, and the follower roles in this relation can be played. These roles—which are cloaks to be donned and shed, not necessarily fixed labels synonymous with parties—take on their meaning in relation to the leadership function as it is played, resisted, followed, exploited, circumvented, ignored, and so on.

Direction and its surrounding roles provide the dynamics to multilateral negotiations, understood to comprise both issues and parties. In his comprehensive analysis of a complex multilateral negotiation, Winham (1986, p. 386) concludes that "leadership was clearly in evidence during the Tokyo Round, but it was exercised by two parties" so that the structure "that would best describe the Tokyo Round was a harmonious bi*polar* system" (emphasis added). As this analysis suggests as well, leadership or direction was necessary to move from a mere recognition of coalitions to an understanding of the mechanism that gave them dynamics and direction and of the relations of the various roles within and between the two coalitions.

Other analyses of multilateral negotiation also show how leadership was used to manage complexity by structuring issue and party relations. Leadership's uses of deduction (formula/detail) versus induction (concession/convergence) to construct an agreement (Winham, 1986; Sebenius, 1984, chap. 3; Friedheim, 1993; Bunn, 1992), of centralizing orchestration (for example, through a single negotiating text) (Raiffa, 1982, pp. 211–217), of multiple bilateralism (trial-and-error construction of multiparty agreements with dyadic blocks) (Preeg, 1970, pp. 130–134, 184–188), or of two-tiered problem solving (Malmgren, 1973, p. 228) show how different strategies of guided interaction are the essence of both the practice and the analysis of managing complexity in multilateral negotiation.

Similarly, decision theory and game theory are tools or decision support systems (Flood and Carson, 1988; Spector, 1993c) for leaders to use to manage the complexity of their issues, although the parties will use the aggregating and ordering possibilities in different ways according to the particular role chosen. Thus, this type of analysis for managing issue complexity needs to be combined with other means of managing party and role complexity. Roles are further analyzed on the basis of power position as they are used to manage complexity through coalitions—making them, joining them, playing them off, breaking them up. On the other side, organization theory and small group theory provide analyses of the means of reducing party and role complexity and focus largely on procedural aspects, leaving the complexity of nonprocedural issues to be reduced by being subsumed under parties and roles. The advice presented under the small group approach is in the form of maxims for direction, and the cybernetic (etymologically, "steering") loops that underlie the organizational analysis diagram the ways in which leadership can direct the consideration of procedural issues so as to benefit from and reform the contextual institutional constraints.

Managing complexity, as presented, is a paradigm, not a theory (Morin,

1985, p. 65). It is the context for theorizing but more basically a way of thinking about multilateral negotiations in order to achieve a better comprehension of the full process. If the basic analytical question for any negotiation analysis is How to explain outcomes?, the question is answered for multilateral negotiations in the form of another question: How did/do the parties manage the characteristic complexity of their encounter in order to produce outcomes? Analysts and practitioners give a conceptual scan of the complexity, followed by a cognitive model of interrelated categories of simplification, structuring, and direction (Wolkomer, 1993, p. 58). The model has not been presented with hypotheses (although many of the approaches presented do not have hypotheses of their own either). It is the setting for the generation of hypotheses, however, that focus on correlations between strategies and outcomes. When the overarching "name of the game" is recognized and used to inform the analysis, then the different analytical approaches can be seen to explain the important components of the whole.

Note

   1. Notably, an attempt at an "economic analysis" was tried but resulted in a duplication of coalition analysis by a somewhat different methodology (see Bennett, 1987, and other chapters in Humber, 1987). Negotiation analysis has also been suggested, but, for all of its usefulness in complementing other approaches used here, it does not have a single analytical focus of its own (see P. Young, 1991).

References

Activities of OECD in 1981. Paris: Organization for Economic Cooperation and Development, 1982.

Activities of OECD in 1982. Paris: Organization for Economic Cooperation and Development, 1983.

Activities of OECD in 1985. Paris: Organization for Economic Cooperation and Development, 1986.

Activities of OECD in 1986. Paris: Organization for Economic Cooperation and Development, 1987.

Ad Hoc Committee for Institutional Affairs. *Report to the European Council*. Brussels: Ad Hoc Committee for Institutional Affairs, Mar. 1988.

Adams, J. S. "The Structure and Dynamics of Behavior in Organizational Boundary Roles." In M. D. Dunnette (ed.), *Handbook of Industrial and Organizational Psychology*. Skokie, Ill.: McNally, 1976.

Aggarwal, V., Keohane, R., and Yoffie, D. "The Dynamics of Negotiated Protectionism." *American Political Science Review*, June 1987, *81*(2), 345–366.

Aida, S., and others (eds.). *Science and Praxis of Complexity*. Tokyo: UN University, 1985.

Albregts, A.H.M., and van de Gevel, A.J.W. "Negotiating Techniques and Issues in the Kennedy Round." In F. A. van Geusau (ed.), *Economic Relations after the Kennedy Round*. Amsterdam: Sijthoff, 1969.

Antrim, L. *Multilateral Negotiations: Practices and Bibliography*. Washington, D.C.: American Academy of Diplomacy, 1992.

Asch, S. E. "Opinions and Social Pressure." *Scientific American*, Nov. 1952.

Astley, G. T., and Van de Ven, A. H. "Central Perspectives and Debates in Organizations Theory." *Administrative Science Quarterley*, June 1983, 224–241.

Attali, J. *Analyse économique de la vie politique*. Paris: Presses Universitaires de France, 1972.

Bacharach, S. B., and Lawler, E. J. *Power and Politics in Organizations: The Social Psychology of Conflict, Coalitions, and Bargaining*. San Francisco: Jossey-Bass, 1980.

Bacharach, S. B., and Lawler, E. J. *Bargaining: Power, Tactics, and Outcomes*. San Francisco: Jossey-Bass, 1981.

Baldridge, B. "GATT Ministerial Sets Stage for Uruguay Round." *Business America*, 1986, *9*, 21.

Baldwin, R. *Non-Tariff Distortions of International Trade.* Washington, D.C.: Brookings Institution, 1970.

Baldwin, R. *The New Protectionism: A Response to Shifts in National Economic Power.* Cambridge, Mass.: National Bureau of Economic Research, 1986.

Bales, R. F. *Interaction Process Analysis: A Method for the Study of Small Groups.* Reading, Mass.: Addison-Wesley, 1950.

Banzhaf, J. F., III. "Weighted Voting Doesn't Work: A Mathematical Analysis." *Rutgers Law Review,* 1965, *19*(2), 317–343.

Barclay, S., and Peterson, C. *Multiattribute Utility Models for Negotiations.* Technical Report 76-1. McLean, Va.: Decision and Designs, 1976.

Belous, R. S., and Hartley, R. S. (eds.). *The Growth of Regional Trading Blocs in the Global Economy.* Washington, D.C.: National Planning Association, 1990.

Benedick, R. E. *Ozone Diplomacy: New Directions in Safeguarding the Planet.* Cambridge, Mass.: Harvard University Press, 1991.

Bennett, P. "Nash Bargaining Solutions of Multiparty Bargaining Problems." In M. J. Humber (ed.), *The Logic of Multiparty Systems.* Dordrecht, The Netherlands: Martinus Nijhoff, 1987.

Bennett, P., Cropper, S., and Huxham, C. "Modelling Interactive Decisions." In J. Rosenhead (ed.), *Rational Analysis for a Problematic World.* New York: Wiley, 1989.

Bentsen, L. "Don't Jump the Fast Track." *New York Times,* Apr. 25, 1991, p. A25.

Berelson, B., and Steiner, G. A. *Human Behavior.* Orlando, Fla.: Harcourt Brace Jovanovich, 1964.

Bhagwati, J. *Protectionism.* Cambridge, Mass.: MIT Press, 1988.

Bhagwati, J. "Jumpstarting GATT." *Foreign Policy,* 1991, *83* (Summer), 107–118.

Bhagwati, J., and Patrick, H. T. (eds.). *Aggressive Unilateralism: America's 301 Trade Policy and the World Trading System.* Ann Arbor: University of Michigan Press, 1990.

Bieber, R., and Schwarze, J. *Verfassungsentwicklung in der Europäischen Gemeinschaft.* Baden-Baden: Nomes, 1984.

"A Big Win-Win on Trade" (editorial). *New York Times,* Feb. 24, 1991, p. A16.

Blau, P. M. *The Dynamics of Bureaucracy.* Chicago: University of Chicago Press, 1955.

Bonham, G. M. "Cognitive Mapping as a Technique for Supporting International Negotiation." *Theory and Decision,* 1993, *34*(3), 214–232.

Bradley, J. "Intellectual Property Rights, Investments and Trade in Services: Laying the Foundations." *Stanford Journal of International Law,* 1987, *23*, 1.

Bradsher, K. "Chip Pact Set by U.S. and Japan." *New York Times,* June 4, 1991, pp. D1, D7.

Brams, S. J. *Game Theory and Politics.* New York: Free Press, 1975.

Brams, S. J. *Superior Beings: If They Exist, How Would We Know? Game-*

Theoretic Implications of Omniscience, Omnipotence, Immortality, and Incomprehensibility. New York: Springer-Verlag, 1983.

Brams, S. J. *Rational Politics: Decisions, Games, and Strategy.* Washington, D.C.: Congressional Quarterly Press, 1985; San Diego, Calif.: Academic Press, 1989.

Brams, S. J. *Negotiation Games: Applying Game Theory to Bargaining and Arbitration.* New York: Routledge & Kegan Paul, 1990.

Brams, S. J. "Comment on Fritz W. Scharpf, 'Games Real Actors Could Play.'" *Rationality and Society,* 1991, *3*(2), 252–257.

Brams, S. J. *Theory of Moves.* Cambridge, England: Cambridge University Press, 1993.

Brams, S. J., and Affuso, P. J. "Power and Size: A New Paradox." *Theory and Decision,* 1976, 7(1/2), 29–56.

Brams, S. J., and Affuso, P. J. "Addendum to: New Paradoxes of Voting Power on the EC Council of Ministers." *Electoral Studies,* 1985a, *4*(3), 290.

Brams, S. J., and Affuso, P. J. "New Paradoxes of Voting Power on the EC Council of Ministers." *Electoral Studies,* 1985b, *4*(2), 135–139.

Brams, S. J., Affuso, P. J., and Kilgour, D. M. "Presidential Power: A Game-Theoretic Analysis." In P. Brace, C. Harrington, and G. King (eds.), *The Presidency in American Politics.* New York: New York University Press, 1989.

Brams, S. J., and Doherty, A. E. "Intransigence in Negotiations: The Dynamics of Disagreement." Preprint. New York: Politics Department, New York University, 1992.

Bressand, A., and Calypso, N. (eds.). *Strategic Trends in Services: An Enquiry into the International Service Economy.* New York: HarperCollins, 1989.

Brockner, J., and Rubin, J. Z. *Entrapment in Escalating Conflicts.* New York: Springer-Verlag, 1985.

Bronisz, P., Krus, L., and Lopuch, B. *MCBARG: A System Supporting Multicriteria Bargaining.* WP-88-115. Laxenburg, Austria: International Institute for Applied Systems Analysis, 1988.

Budd, S. *The EEC: A Guide to the Maze.* London: Kogan Page, 1987.

Bunn, G. *Arms Control by Committee.* Stanford, Calif.: Stanford University Press, 1992.

Burns, J. M. *Leadership.* New York: HarperCollins, 1978.

Butler, M. *Europe: More Than a Continent.* London: Heinemann, 1987.

Cameron, D. R. "The 1992 Initiative: Causes and Consequences." In A. M. Sbragia (ed.), *Europolitics: Institutions and Policymaking in the "New" European Community.* Washington, D.C.: Brookings Institution, 1992.

Caplow, T. A. "A Theory of Coalitions in a Triad." *Sociological Review,* 1956, *21*, 489–493.

Caplow, T. A. *Two against One.* Englewood Cliffs, N.J.: Prentice-Hall, 1968.

Cardozo, R., and Corbett, R. "The Crocodile Initiative." In J. Lodge (ed.), *European Union: The European Community in Search of a Future.* London: Macmillan, 1986.

Cartwright, D., and Zander, A. *Group Dynamics.* (2nd ed.) New York: Harper-Collins, 1960.

Casti, J. *On System Complexity.* WP-85-22. Laxenburg, Austria: International Institute for Applied Systems Analysis, 1985.

Checkland, P. *Systemic Thinking, Systemic Practice.* New York: Wiley, 1981.

Checkland, P. "Soft Systems Methodology." In J. Rosenhead (ed.), *Rational Analysis for a Problematic World.* New York: Wiley, 1989.

Chertkoff, J. M. "Sociopsychological Theories and Research on Coalition Formation." In S. Groenmings, E. W. Kelly, and M. Leierson (eds.), *The Study of Coalition Behavior.* New York: Holt, Rinehart & Winston, 1970.

Church, C., and Keogh, D. *The Single European Act: A Transactional Study.* London: UACES, 1991.

Cline, W., Kawanabe, N., Kronsjö, I., and Williams, T. *Trade Negotiations in the Tokyo Round.* Washington, D.C.: Brookings Institution, 1978.

Coleman, J. S. "Control of Collectivities and the Power of a Collectivity to Act." In B. Lieberman (ed.), *Social Choice.* New York: Gordon and Breach, 1971.

Coleman, J. S. *The Mathematics of Collective Action.* London: Heinemann, 1973.

Commission of the EC. *Working Document COM(88)134.* Brussels: European Communities, 1988.

Corbett, R. *The Intergovernmental Conference.* Hull, England: European Community Research Unit, Hull University, 1986.

Corbett, R., and Lodge, J. "Progress and Prospects." In J. Lodge (ed.), *European Union: The European Community in Search of a Future.* London: Macmillan, 1986.

Cox, R. W., and Jacobson, H. K. *The Anatomy of Influence.* New Haven, Conn.: Yale University Press, 1973.

Crozier, M. *The Bureaucratic Phenomenon.* Chicago: University of Chicago Press, 1964.

Cyert, R. M., and March, J. G. *A Behavioral Theory of the Firm.* Englewood Cliffs, N.J.: Prentice-Hall, 1963.

Dalton, G. *Organizational Change and Development.* Homewood, Ill.: R. D. Irwin, 1959.

Dam, K. *The GATT: Law and International Economic Organization.* Chicago: Chicago University Press, 1970.

Das, B. "The GATT Ministerial Meeting 1982: An Interpretive Note." *Journal of World Trade Law,* 1984, *18,* 1.

Davis, M. *Game Theory.* New York: Basic Books, 1970.

Druckman, D. (ed.). *Negotiations.* Newbury Park, Calif.: Sage, 1977.

Druckman, D. "The Social Psychology of Arms Control and Reciprocation." *Political Psychology,* 1990, *11,* 553–581.

Eccles, R. "Negotiations in the Organizational Environment: A Framework for Discussion." In M. H. Bazerman and R. J. Lewicki (eds.), *Negotiating in Organizations.* Newbury Park, Calif.: Sage, 1983.

Emery, F. E., and Trist, E. L. "The Causal Texture of Organizational Environments." *Journal of Human Relations,* 1965, *18*(1), 21–32.

Etzioni, A. *Modern Organizations.* Englewood Cliffs, N.J.: Prentice-Hall, 1964.

European Parliament. *Report on the Substance of the Preliminary Draft Treaty Establishing the European Union.* Working Document 1-575/83C. Strasbourg, France: European Parliament, 1983.

European Parliament. *Draft Treaty Establishing the European Union.* Strasbourg, France: European Parliament, 1984.

European Parliament. *Report on the Institutional Costs of Non-Europe.* Working Document A2-39/88. Strasbourg, France: European Parliament, 1988.

Farnsworth, C. H. "Trade Talks Will Continue in Informal Settings." *New York Times,* Dec. 14, 1990, p. D2.

Faure, G.-O. "Mediator as a Third Negotiator." In F. Mautner-Markhof (ed.), *Processes of International Negotiations.* Boulder, Colo.: Westview Press, 1989.

Faure, G.-O. "Culture and Negotiation Behavior: A Survey among EEC Negotiators." *Negotiation Magazine,* 1990, *2,* 4.

Faure, G.-O., and Rubin, J. Z. *Culture and Negotiation.* Newbury Park, Calif.: Sage, 1993.

Feketekuty, G. "International Trade in Services: An Overview and Blueprint for Negotiations." *American Enterprise Institute.* New York: Ballinger, 1988.

Fiedler, F. E. *A Theory of Leadership Effectiveness.* New York: McGraw-Hill, 1967.

Finger, M., and Oleschowski, A. (eds.). *The Uruguay Round: A Handbook for the Multilateral Trade Negotiations.* Washington, D.C.: World Bank, 1987.

Fishburn, P. C. "Lexicographic Orders, Utilities and Decision Rules: A Survey." *Management Science,* 1974, *20*(11), 1142–1471.

Fisher, R., Ury, W. L., and Patton, B. *Getting to YES: Negotiating Agreement without Giving In.* (Rev. ed.) Boston: Houghton Mifflin, 1991.

Flood, R., and Carson, E. *Dealing with Complexity.* New York: Plenum, 1988.

Fraser, N., and Hipel, K. *Conflict Analysis.* Amsterdam: Elsevier, 1984.

"Free Trade Loses a Round." *Newsweek,* Dec. 17, 1990, p. 44.

Freedman, J. L., and Fraser, S. C. "Compliance without Pressure: The Foot-in-the-Door Technique." *Journal of Personality and Social Psychology,* 1966, *4,* 195–202.

Freil, R. "The Example of the Single European Act." In C. Church and D. Keogh (eds.), *The Single European Act: A Transnational Study.* London: UACES, 1991.

French, H. F. *After the Earth Summit: The Future of Environmental Governance.* Worldwatch Paper 107. Washington, D.C.: Worldwatch Institute, 1992.

Friedheim, R. L. "North-South Bargaining on Ocean Issues." In I. W. Zartman (ed.), *Positive Sum: Improving North-South Negotiations.* New Brunswick, N.J.: Rutgers University Press, Transaction, 1987.

Friedheim, R. L. "Modeling Parliamentary Diplomacy." Unpublished paper, School of International Relations, University of Southern California, 1991.

Friedheim, R. L. *Negotiating the New Ocean Regime.* Columbia: University of South Carolina Press, 1993.

Friedman, R. "The Culture of Mediation: Private Understanding in the Context of Public Conflict." In D. M. Kolb and J. M. Bartunek (eds.), *Hidden Conflict in Organizations: Uncovering Behind the Scenes Disputes.* Newbury Park, Calif.: Sage, 1992.

Galbraith, J. *Designing Complex Organizations.* Reading, Mass.: Addison-Wesley, 1973.

Galtung, J. "Small Group Theory and the Theory of International Relations: A Study of Isomorphism." In M. A. Kaplan (ed.), *New Approaches to International Relations.* New York: St. Martin's Press, 1968.

Gamson, W. A. "An Experimental Test of a Theory of Coalition Formation." *American Sociological Review,* 1961a, *26,* 565–573.

Gamson, W. A. "A Theory of Coalition Formation." *American Sociological Review,* 1961b, *26,* 373–382.

Garrett, G. "International Cooperation and Institutional Choice: The European Community's Internal Market." *World Politics,* 1992, *46*(2), 533–560.

"GATT inför Uruguay-rundans slutförhandling." In *UD informerar.* Stockholm: Utrikesdepartementet, 1992.

Gibb, C. A. "Leadership." In G. Lindzey and E. Aronson (eds.), *The Handbook of Social Psychology.* Vol. 4. Reading, Mass.: Addison-Wesley, 1969.

Gilpin, R. *The Political Economy of International Relations.* Princeton, N.J.: Princeton University Press, 1987.

Glick, L. A. *Multilateral Trade Negotiations: World Trade after the Tokyo Round.* Totowa, N.J.: Rowman & Allanheld, 1984.

Goffman, E. *The Presentation of Self in Everyday Life.* New York: Doubleday, Anchor, 1959.

Golt, S. *The GATT Negotiations 1973–1979: A Guide to the Issues.* London: British–North American Committee, 1978.

Goodin, R. E. "Mood Matching and Arms Control." *International Studies Quarterly,* 1988, *32,* 473–481.

Gottinger, H. W. *Coping with Complexity.* Dordrecht, The Netherlands, and Boston: Riedel, 1983.

Gouldner, A. *Patterns of Industrial Bureaucracy.* New York: HarperCollins, 1954.

Granovetter, M. "The Strength of Weak Ties." *American Journal of Sociology,* 1973, *78*(6), 1360–1380.

Greenhouse, S. "GATT Chief Sees Break in Farm Trade Impasse." *New York Times,* Jan. 16, 1991, p. D2.

Haas, M. (ed.). *International Systems.* New York: Chandler, 1974.

Haas, P. *Saving the Mediterranean.* New York: Columbia University Press, 1990.

Habeeb, W. M. *Power and Tactics in International Negotiation.* Baltimore, Md.: Johns Hopkins University Press, 1988.

Hamilton, C., and Whalley, J. "Coalitions in the Uruguay Round." *Weltwirtschaftliches Archiv, Review of World Economics,* 1989, *125,* 3.

Hampson, F. *Multilateral Negotiation: Lessons from Arms Control, Trade and Environment.* Baltimore, Md.: Johns Hopkins University Press, 1994.

"Hedging." *Economist,* Oct. 13, 1990, p. 74.

Hermann, C. F. *International Crises: Insights from Behavioral Research.* New York: Free Press, 1972.

Higgott, R. A., and Cooper, A. F. "Middle Power Leadership and Coalition Building: Australia, the Cairns Group, and the Uruguay Round of Trade Negotiations." *International Organization,* 1990, *44*(4), 589–632.

Hillinger, C. "Voting on Issues and On Platforms." *Behavioral Science,* 1971, *16*(6), 564–566.

Hofstede, G. *Culture's Consequences.* Newbury Park, Calif.: Sage, 1984.

Homans, C. *Social Behavior.* San Diego, Calif.: Harcourt, Brace Jovanovich College Division, 1961.

Hufbauer, G., and Schott, J. *Trading for Growth: The Next Round of Trade Negotiations.* Washington, D.C.: Institute for International Economics, 1985.

Humber, M. J. (ed.). *The Logic of Multiparty Systems.* Dordrecht, The Netherlands: Martinus Nijhoff, 1987.

Iklé, F. C. *How Nations Negotiate.* New York: HarperCollins, 1964.

Jackson, J. "GATT and Recent International Trade Problems." *Maryland Journal of International Law and Trade,* 1987, *11,* 1.

Jacobs, F., and Corbett, R. *The European Parliament.* Harlow, England: Longmans, 1991.

Jacque, J. P. "The European Union Treaty and the Community Treaties." *Crocodile,* 1985, *11.*

James, S. C., and Lake, D. A. "The Second Face of Hegemony: Britain's Repeal of the Corn Laws and the American Walker Tariff of 1846." *International Organization,* 1989, *41,* 1–29.

Janis, I. L. *Groupthink.* (2nd ed.) Boston: Houghton Mifflin, 1982.

Jervis, R. *The Logic of Images in International Relations.* Princeton, N.J.: Princeton University Press, 1970.

Jervis, R. "From Balance to Concert," *World Politics, 38,* 58–79.

Johnston, R. J. "On the Measurement of Power: Some Reactions to Laver." *Environment and Planning,* 1978, *A10*(8), 907–914.

Kadane, J. B. "On Division of the Question." *Public Choice,* 1972, *13* (Fall), 47–54.

Kahneman, D., and Tversky, A. "Choices, Values, and Frames." In H. Arkes and K. Hammond (eds.), *Judgment and Decision Making: An Interdisciplinary Reader.* New York: Cambridge University Press, 1986.

Kanter, R. M. *Men and Women of the Corporation.* New York: Basic Books, 1977.

Kanter, R. M. *The Change Masters: Corporate Entrepreneurship at Work.* New York: Simon & Schuster; London: Allen & Unwin, 1983.

Kaufmann, J. *Conference Diplomacy.* (2nd ed.) The Hague: Nijhoff, 1989a.

Kaufmann, J. (ed.). *Effective Negotiation.* The Hague: Nijhoff, 1989b.

Keatinge, P., and Murphy, A. "The Single European Act." In R. Pryce (ed.), *The Dynamics of European Union.* London: Croom Helm, 1990.

Keohane, R. O. "Political Influence in the General Assembly." *International Conciliation*, 1966, *557*, 5-64.

Kindleberger, C. P. "Dominance and Leadership in the International Economy." *International Studies Quarterly*, 1981, *25*, 242-254.

Klir, G. J. "The Many Faces of Complexity." In S. Aida and others (eds.), *Science and Praxis of Complexity*. Tokyo: UN University Press, 1985.

Kolb, D. M. "Roles Mediators Play in Different Contexts." In K. Kressel and D. Pruitt (eds.), *The Mediation of Disputes: Empirical Studies in the Resolution of Social Conflict*. San Francisco: Jossey-Bass, 1989.

Kolb, D. M., and Bartunek, J. M. (eds.). *Hidden Conflict in Organizations: Uncovering Behind the Scenes Disputes*. Newbury Park, Calif.: Sage, 1992.

Komorita, S. S. "A Weighted Probability Model of Coalition Formation." *Psychological Review*, 1974, *81*, 242-256.

Komorita, S. S., and Chertkoff, J. M. "A Bargaining Theory of Coalition Formation." *Psychological Review*, 1973, *80*, 149-162.

Krasner, S. (ed.). *International Regimes*. Ithaca, N.Y.: Cornell University Press, 1983.

Kremenyuk, V. (ed.). *International Negotiation: Analysis, Approaches, Issues*. San Francisco: Jossey-Bass, 1991.

Kunda, G. *Engineering Culture: Culture and Control in a High-Tech Organization*. Philadelphia: Temple University Press, 1991.

Lang, W. "A Professional's View." In G. O. Faure and J. Z. Rubin (eds.), *Culture and Negotiation*. Newbury Park, Calif.: Sage, 1993.

Lawler, E. J., and Young, G. A. "Coalition Formation: An Integrative Model." *Sociometry*, 1975, *38*(1), 1-17.

Lawrence, P. R., and Lorsch, J. W. *Organization and Environment*. Cambridge, Mass.: Harvard University Press, 1967.

Lax, D., and Sebenius, J. "Thinking Coalitionally." In P. Young (ed.), *Negotiation Analysis*. Ann Arbor: University of Michigan Press, 1991.

Lewin, K., Lippitt, R., and White, R. K. "Patterns of Aggressive Behavior in Experimentally Created 'Social Climate.'" *Journal of Social Psychology*, 1939, *10*, 271-299.

Lindberg, L. N., and Scheingold, S. A. *Europe's Would-Be Polity*. Englewood Cliffs, N.J.: Prentice-Hall, 1970.

Lodge, J. (ed.). *Direct Elections to the European Parliament 1984*. London: Macmillan, 1986a.

Lodge, J. (ed.). *European Union: The European Community in Search of the Future*. London: Macmillan, 1986b.

Lodge, J. (ed.). "European Union and the First Elected Parliament: The Spinelli Initiative." *Journal of Common Market Studies*, 1986c, *29*, 352-377.

Lodge, J. "The Single European Act: Towards a New Euro-Dynamism?" *Journal of Common Market Studies*, 1986d, *3*, 203-233.

Lodge, J. "The Single European Act and the New Legislative Cooperation Procedure: A Critical Analysis." *Journal of European Integration*, 1987, *1*, 5-28.

Lodge, J. "EC Policymaking: Institutional Considerations" and "The European

Parliament—From 'Assembly' to Co-Legislature: Changing the Institutional Dynamics." In J. Lodge (ed.), *The European Community and the Challenge of the Future.* London: Pinter, 1989.

Lodge, J. (ed.). *The 1989 Election of the European Parliament.* London: Macmillan, 1990.

Lodge, J. "Plurilateralism and the Single European Act." Preprint. European Community Research Unit, Hull University, Hull, England, 1991.

Louis, J. V. (ed.). *L'Union Européenne: Le Projet de traite du Parlement Européen aprè Fountainebleau.* Brussels: University Libre de Belgique, 1985.

Lukmann, N. "Complexity and Meaning." In S. Aida and others (eds.), *Science and Praxis of Complexity.* Tokyo: UN University Press, 1985.

McDonald, J. W. "Managing Complexity through Small Group Dynamics." In J. Burton and F. Dukes (eds.), *Conflict: Readings in Management and Resolution.* New York: St. Martin's Press, 1990.

Mahon, J. F., and Bigelow, B. "Coalitions: The Strategic Bridge within and across Organizations." Working Papers 90-68. Unpublished paper, Boston University, 1990.

Malmgren, H. *International Economic Peacekeeping in Phase II.* New York: Quadrangle, 1973.

March, J. G., and Olsen, J. P. *Ambiguity and Choice in Organizations.* Bergen, Norway: Universitetforlaget, 1976.

March, J. G., and Simon, H. A. *Organizations.* New York: Wiley, 1958.

Marcus, M. J. "Theory of Complexity." In *65th Proceedings of the IEEE.* Washington, D.C.: Institute of Electrical and Electronics Engineers, 1977.

Mathijsen, P.S.R.F. *A Guide to European Community Law.* (3rd ed.) London: Sweet & Maxwell, 1980.

Mautner-Markhof, F. *Processes of International Negotiations.* Boulder, Colo.: Westview, 1989.

Midgaard, K., and Underdal, A. "Multiparty Conferences." In D. Druckman (ed.), *Negotiations.* Newbury Park, Calif.: Sage, 1977.

Milner, H. "A Three Bloc Trading System?" In T. Laidi (ed.), *The Collapse of the World Order.* London: Berg, 1993.

Mintzberg, H. *The Structuring Organizations.* Englewood Cliffs, N.J.: Prentice-Hall, 1979.

Mintzberg, H. *Power in and around Organizations.* Englewood Cliffs, N.J.: Prentice-Hall, 1983.

Moravcsik, A. "Negotiating the Single European Act: National Interests and Conventional Statecraft in the European Community." *International Organization,* 1991, *45*(1), 19–56.

Morgan, G. *Images in Organization.* Newbury Park, Calif.: Sage, 1986.

Morin, E. "On the Definition of Complexity." In S. Aida and others (eds.), *Science and Praxis of Complexity.* Tokyo: UN University Press, 1985.

Mortimer, R. A. *The Third World Coalition in International Politics.* Boulder, Colo.: Westview Press, 1984.

Mouzelis, N. P. *Organization and Bureaucracy: An Analysis of Modern Theories.* Hawthorne, N.Y.: Aldine, 1967.

Murnigham, J. K. "Models of Coalition Behavior: Game Theoretic, Social Psychological, and Political Perspectives." *Psychological Bulletin,* 1978, *85,* 1130–1153.

Nash, J. "The Bargaining Problem." *Econometrica,* 1950, *18*(1), 155–162.

Nicolis, G., and Prigogine, I. *Exploring Complexity.* New York: W. H. Freeman, 1989.

Odell, J. "Constraints on International Economic Bargaining: Theorizing via Game Models and Beyond." Paper presented at the American Political Science Association annual meeting, 1987.

Olson, M. *The Logic of Collective Action.* Cambridge, Mass.: Harvard University Press, 1965; New York: Schocken Books, 1968.

Olson, M. *The Logic of Collective Action.* Cambridge, Mass.: Harvard University Press, 1971.

Olson, M., and Zeckhauser, R. "An Economic Theory of Alliances." *Review of Economics and Statistics,* 1966, *47,* 266–279.

Orwell, G. *1984.* Orlando, Fla.: Harcourt Brace Jovanovich, 1949.

Osgood, C. E. *An Alternative to War and Surrender.* Urbana, Ill.: University of Illinois Press, 1962.

Oxley, A. *The Challenge of Free Trade.* London: Harvester Wheatsheaf, 1990.

Oye, K. "The Sterling-Dollar-Franc Triangle," *World Politics,* 1985, *38*(1), 173–200.

Oye, K. *Cooperation under Anarchy.* Princeton, N.J.: Princeton University Press, 1986.

Passel, P. "Adding Up the World Trade Talks: Fail Now, Pay Later." *New York Times,* Dec. 16, 1990, p. E3.

Passel, P. "Second Thoughts on Mexico Trade." *New York Times,* May 15, 1991, p. D2.

Perrow, C. "The Analysis of Goals in Complex Organizations." *American Sociological Review,* Dec. 1961, *26,* 6.

Perrow, C. "A Framework for the Comparative Analysis of Organizations." *American Sociological Review,* 1967, *32,* 2.

Pettigrew, A. *The Politics of Organizational Decision-Making.* London: Tavistock, 1973.

Pfeffer, J. *Organizations and Organization Theory.* Boston: Pitman, 1982.

Pfeffer, J., and Salancik, G. R. *The External Control of Organizations: A Resource Dependence Perspective.* New York: HarperCollins, 1978.

Pippinger, N. "Théorie de la Complexité." *Pour la Science,* 1978, *1,* 86–95.

Ploman, E. "Introduction." In S. Aida and others (eds.), *Science and Praxis of Complexity.* Tokyo: UN University Press, 1985.

Ponssard, J. P. *Logique de la négociation et théorie des jeux.* Paris: Les Editions d'organisation, 1977.

Preeg, E. *Traders and Diplomats.* Washington, D.C.: Brookings Institution, 1970.

Prestowitz, C. V., Jr. "Life after GATT: More Trade Is Better Than Free Trade." *Technology Review*, 1991, *94*(3), 21–27.

Prestowitz, C. V., Jr., Tonelson, A., and Jerome, R. W. "The Last Gasp of GATTism." *Harvard Business Review*, Mar.-Apr. 1991, pp. 130–138.

Pruitt, D. G. *Negotiation Behavior*. San Diego, Calif.: Academic Press, 1981.

Pugh, D. S., Hickson, D. J., Hinings, C. R., and Turner, C. "Dimensions of Organizational Structure." *Administrative Science Quarterly*, 1968, *13*(1), 65–105.

Raiffa, H. *The Art and Science of Negotiation*. Cambridge, Mass.: Harvard University Press, 1982.

Rapoport, A. "Conflict Resolution in the Light of Game Theory and Beyond." In Paul Swingle (ed.), *The Structure of Conflict*. San Diego, Calif.: Academic Press, 1970a.

Rapoport, A. *N-Person Game Theory*. Ann Arbor: University of Michigan Press, 1970b.

Ravenhill, J. *Collective Clientelism*. New York: Columbia University Press, 1984.

Riker, W. H. *The Theory of Political Coalitions*. New Haven, Conn.: Yale University Press, 1962.

Rosenhead, J. (ed.). *Rational Analysis for a Problematic World*. New York: Wiley, 1989.

Rothstein, R. *Global Bargaining*. Princeton, N.J.: Princeton University Press, 1979.

Rubin, J. Z. (ed.). *Dynamics of Third Party Intervention*. New York: Praeger, 1981.

Rubin, J. Z., and Zartman, I. W. *Power and International Negotiation*. Laxenburg, Austria: International Institute for Applied Systems Analysis, 1994.

Rummel, R. *Zusammengesetzte Aussenpolitik*. Kehlem Rhein: N. P. Engel, 1982.

Rusk, D. "Parliamentary Diplomacy: Debate vs. Negotiation." *World Affairs Interpreter*, 1955, *26*(2), 121–138.

Russell, C. *Collective Decision Making*. Baltimore, Md.: Johns Hopkins University Press, 1979.

Samuels, M. "The Decline of Multilateralism: Can We Prevent It?" *World Today*, 1990, *40*, 3.

Sandholtz, W., and Zysman, J. "1992: Recasting the European Bargain." *World Politics*, 1989, *42*, 95–128.

Sanger, D. "U.S. Companies in Japan Say Things Aren't So Bad." *New York Times*, June 12, 1991, pp. A1, D6.

Schein, E. H. *Organizational Culture and Leadership: A Dynamic View*. San Francisco: Jossey-Bass, 1985.

Scherer, F. M., and Ross, D. *Industrial Market Structures and Economic Performance*. Boston: Houghton Mifflin, 1990.

Sebenius, J. K. *Negotiating the Law of the Sea*. Cambridge, Mass.: Harvard University Press, 1984.

Sebenius, J. K. "Negotiation Analysis." In V. A. Kremenyuk (ed.), *International Negotiation: Analysis, Approaches, Issues*. San Francisco: Jossey-Bass, 1991.

Shapley, L. S. "A Value for N-Person Games." *Annals of Mathematical Studies,* 1953, *28,* 307–317.

Shapley, L. S., and Shubik, M. "A Method of Evaluating the Distribution of Power in a Committee System." *American Political Science Review,* 1954, *48*(3), 787–792.

Sherif, M., and Sherif, C. W. *Groups in Harmony and Tension.* New York: HarperCollins, 1953.

Siebe, W. "Game Theory." In V. A. Kremenyuk (ed.), *International Negotiation: Analysis, Approaches, Issues.* San Francisco: Jossey-Bass, 1991.

Silk, L. "A Better Feeling on Trade Talks." *New York Times,* June 7, 1991a, p. D2.

Silk, L. "Trade Bloc War? Concern Grows." *New York Times,* Apr. 26, 1991b, p. D2.

Silverman, D. *The Theory of Organizations: A Sociological Framework.* New York: Basic Books, 1971.

Simon, H. "Architecture of Complexity." In H. Simon, *The Sciences of the Artificial.* Cambridge, Mass.: MIT Press, 1948.

Sjöstedt, G. "Multilateral Negotiations: The Story of the Uruguay Round." Preprint, Swedish Institute of International Affairs, Stockholm, 1990.

Sjöstedt, G. (ed.). *International Environmental Negotiations.* Newbury Park, Calif.: Sage, 1993.

Slovic, P., Fischhoff, B., and Lichtenstein, S. "Behavioral Decision Theory." *Annual Review of Psychology,* 1977, *28*(1), 1–39.

Snidal, D. C. "The Limits of Hegemonic Stability Theory." *International Organization,* 1985, *39,* 579–614.

Snidal, D. C. "The Game Theory of International Politics," *World Politics,* 1985, *38*(1), 25–58.

Snidal, D. C. "IGOs, Regimes, and Cooperation: Challenges for International Relations Theory." In M. P. Karns and K. A. Mingst (eds.), *The United States and Multilateral Institutions.* Boston: Unwin Hyman, 1990.

Sorrentino, R. M., and Boutillier, R. G. "The Effect of Quantity and Quality of Verbal Interaction on Ratings of Leadership Ability." *Journal of Experimental Social Psychology,* 1975, *11,* 403–411.

Spector, B. "A Social Psychological Model of Position Modification: Aswan." In I. W. Zartman (ed.), *The 50% Solution.* New Haven, Conn.: Yale University Press, 1983.

Spector, B. "Decision Analysis for Practical Negotiation Application." *Theory and Decision,* 1993a, *34,* 2.

Spector, B. (ed.). "International Negotiation: Theory, Methods, and Support Systems." *Theory and Decision,* Mar. 1993b (special issue), *2,* 177–181.

Spector, B. "Preference Adjustment and Opportunities for Agreement: Decision Modeling to Assess Negotiating Flexibility at UNCED." *Group Decision and Negotiation,* 1993c.

Spinelli, A. "Die parlamentarische Initiative zur Europäischen Union." *Europea Archiv,* 1983, *38,* 739–746.

Stein, J. (ed.). *Getting to the Table.* Baltimore, Md.: Johns Hopkins University Press, 1989.

Stenelo, L. *Mediation in International Negotiations.* Lund, Malmö, Sweden: Studentlitteratur, 1972.

Stevenson, W. B., Pearce, J. L., and Porter, L. W. "The Concept of Coalition in Organization Theory and Research." *Academy of Management Review,* 1985, *10*(2), 256–268.

Strange, S. "GATT and the Outlook for North-South Trade." *Australian Outlook,* 1984, *38*(2).

Strauss, A. *Negotiations: Varieties, Contexts, Processes, and Social Order.* San Francisco: Jossey-Bass, 1978.

Strauss, A., and others. "The Hospital and Its Negotiated Order." In E. Friedson (ed.), *The Hospital in Modern Society.* New York: Macmillan, 1963.

Sullivan, J. D. "International Alliance." In M. Haas (ed.), *International Systems.* New York: Chandler, 1974.

Swap, W. C. (ed.). *Group Decision Making.* Newbury Park, Calif.: Sage, 1984.

Taylor, P. "The New Dynamics of EC Integration in the 1980s." In J. Lodge (ed.), *The European Community and the Challenge of the Future.* London: Pinter, 1989.

Thompson, J. D. *Organizations in Action.* New York: McGraw-Hill, 1967.

Tolbert, P. "Institutional Environments and Resource Dependence: Sources of Administrative Structure in Institutions of Higher Education." *Administrative Science Quarterly,* Mar. 1985, *30.*

Tolbert, P., and Arthur, J. "Institutionalization and Negotiations in Organizations." In B. Sheppard, M. Bazerman, and R. Lewicki (eds.), *Research on Negotiations in Organizations.* Vol. 2. Greenwich, Conn.: JAI Press, 1988.

Touval, S. "Multilateral Negotiation." *Negotiation Journal,* 1989, *5*(2), 159–173.

Touval, S., and Rubin, J. Z. "Analysis of Multilateral Negotiation." Working Paper 87-5. Unpublished paper, Harvard University Program on Negotiations, 1987.

"Trade Representatives Meet." *New York Times,* Apr. 26, 1991, p. D6.

Uchitelle, L. "Blocs Seen Replacing Free Trade." *New York Times,* Aug. 26, 1991, pp. D1, D4.

Ulvila, J. "Turning Points: An Analysis." In J. McDonald, Jr., and D. Bendahmane (eds.), *U.S. Bases Overseas.* Boulder, Colo.: Westview Press, 1990.

Ulvila, J., and Brown, R. "Decision Analysis Comes of Age." *Harvard Business Review,* 1982, *60*(5), 130–141.

Ulvila, J., and Snider, W. "Negotiation of International Oil Tanker Standards: An Application of Multiattribute Value Theory." *Operations Research,* 1980, *28,* 81–96.

Underdal, A. "International Cooperation and Political Engineering." In S. S. Nagel (ed.), *Global Policy Studies.* London: Macmillan, 1991.

Underdal, A. "Designing Politically Feasible Solutions." In R. Malnes and A. Underdal (eds.), *Rationality and Institutions.* Oslo: Scandinavian University Press, 1992.

Ungerer, W. "Europäische Perspektiven nach Fountainebleau." *Aussenpolitik,* 1984, *35*,(4), 394–408.

United Nations Conference on Trade and Development. *Assessment of the Tokyo Round of Multilateral Trade Negotiations.* New York: United Nations, 1982.

The Uruguay Round: Freeing World Trade in Manufacturing, Agriculture, Services, and Investments. Conference Report. London: Wilton Park Papers, 1988.

Van Maanen, J., and Barley, S. R. "Cultural Organization: Fragments of a Theory." In P. J. Frost and others (eds.), *Organizational Culture.* Newbury Park, Calif.: Sage, 1985.

Viravan, A. "Crisis in the GATT System of International Trade." In *Trade Routes to Sustained Economic Growth.* New York: Trade Policy Research Centre, United Nations, 1987.

Voge, J. "Management of Complexity." In S. Aida and others (eds.), *Science and Praxis of Complexity.* Tokyo: UN University Press, 1985.

von Glinow, M. A., and Mohrman, S. (eds.). *Managing Complexity in High Technology Organizations.* Oxford, England: Oxford University Press, 1990.

Walton, R., and McKersie, R. *A Behavioral Theory of Labor Negotiations.* New York: McGraw-Hill, 1965.

Waltz, K. *The Theory of International Politics.* Reading, Mass.: Addison-Wesley, 1979.

Warsh, D. *The Idea of Economic Complexity.* London: Viking, 1984.

Weaver, W. "Science and Complexity." *American Scientist,* 1948, *36*(3), 536–548.

Weick, K. *The Social Psychology of Organizing.* (2nd ed.) Reading, Mass.: Addison-Wesley, 1979.

Weiler, J. "The Genscher-Colombo Draft European Act." *Journal of European Integration,* 1983, *6,* 129–154.

William, B., and Rubin, J. Z. (eds.). *Negotiation Theory and Practice.* Cambridge, Mass.: Harvard University Program on Negotiation, 1991.

Williamson, O. E. *Markets and Hierarchies: Analysis and Antitrust Implications.* New York: Free Press, 1975.

Williamson, R. "U.S. Multilateral Diplomacy at the United Nations." *Washington Quarterly,* 1986, *9*(1), 3–18.

Winham, G. R. "Complexity in International Negotiation." In D. Druckman (ed.), *Negotiations.* Newbury Park, Calif.: Sage, 1977a.

Winham, G. R. "Negotiation as a Management Process." *World Politics,* 1977b, *30,* 87–114.

Winham, G. R. *Multilateral Economic Negotiation.* New York: International Peace Academy, 1982.

Winham, G. R. *International Trade and the Tokyo Round Negotiations.* Princeton, N.J.: Princeton University Press, 1986.

Winham, G. R. "The Prenegotiation Phase of the Uruguay Round." *International Journal,* 1989, *44*(2), 280–303.

Winham, G. R. "The Prenegotiation Phase of the Uruguay Round." In J. Stein (ed.), *Getting to the Table.* Baltimore, Md.: Johns Hopkins University Press, 1989.

Winham, G., and Kizer, K. *The Uruguay Round: A Midterm Review, 1988–1989.* Case 20. Washington, D.C.: Foreign Policy Institute, Johns Hopkins University School of Advanced International Studies, 1993.

Wolkomer, R. "An Architect Who Takes Stairways One Step at a Time." *Smithsonian,* 1993, *24*(3), 55–63.

Yarbrough, B. V., and Yarbrough, R. M. *Cooperation and Governance in International Trade: The Strategic Organizational Approach.* Princeton, N.J.: Princeton University Press, 1992.

Young, O. R. "Bargaining, Entrepreneurship, and International Politics." Paper presented at the 30th annual convention of International Studies Association, London, Mar. 28–Apr. 1, 1989a.

Young, O. R. *International Cooperation.* Ithaca, N.Y.: Cornell University Press, 1989b.

Young, O. R. "The Politics of International Regime Formation." *International Organization,* 1989c, *43* (Summer), 349–376.

Young, O. R. "Political Leadership and Regime Formation: On the Development of Institutions in International Society." *International Organization,* 1991, *45*, 281–308.

Young, P. (ed.). *Negotiation Analysis.* Ann Arbor: University of Michigan Press, 1991.

Yukl, G. *Leadership in Organizations.* Englewood Cliffs, N.J.: Prentice-Hall, 1989.

Zagare, F. "Game Theoretic Analysis of the Vietnam Negotiations." In I. W. Zartman (ed.), *The Negotiation Process: Theories and Applications.* Newbury Park, Calif.: Sage, 1978.

Zartman, I. W. *The Politics of Trade Negotiations between Africa and the EEC.* Princeton, N.J.: Princeton University Press, 1971.

Zartman, I. W. (ed.). *The Negotiation Process: Theories and Applications.* Newbury Park, Calif.: Sage, 1978.

Zartman, I. W. (ed.). *Positive Sum: Improving North-South Negotiations.* New Brunswick, N.J.: Rutgers University Press, Transaction, 1987.

Zartman, I. W. "Lessons for Analysis and Practice." In G. Sjöstedt (ed.), *International Environmental Negotiation.* Newbury Park, Calif.: Sage, 1993.

Zartman, I. W., and Berman, M. *The Practical Negotiator.* New Haven, Conn.: Yale University Press, 1982.

Zucker, L. G. "The Role of Institutionalization in Cultural Persistence." *American Sociological Review,* Oct. 1977, *42*(5), 726–742.

Index